POPEYE

SECOND EDITION

POPEYE

An Illustrated Cultural History

FRED M. GRANDINETTI

SECOND EDITION

McFarland & Company, Inc., Publishers
Jefferson, North Carolina, and London

ACKNOWLEDGMENTS

I am grateful to the following people for their help in making
this book possible: Frank Caruso, Ita Golzman, and
Mark Johnson of King Features Syndicate; Bill Maling, Craig Davison,
Tim Hollis, Jackson Beck, Gordon Sheehan, Leonard Kohl,
Mike and Debbie Brooks of the International Popeye Fanclub;
Jerry Beck, Steve Bierly, Donnie Pitchford, and Barry I. Grauman.
Special thanks go to my family and friends for all their support.

All opinions in this book are those of the author and
do not represent the opinions of anyone else
who has been connected with the Popeye character over the years.

Popeye cartoons and images are reprinted throughout this book
by permission of King Features Syndicate.
The cover drawing is by the author.

LIBRARY OF CONGRESS CATALOGUING-IN-PUBLICATION DATA

Grandinetti, Fred M.
Popeye : an illustrated cultural history / Fred M. Grandinetti.—2nd ed.
p.   cm.
Includes index.

ISBN 0-7864-1605-X (softcover : 50# alkaline paper) ∞

1. Popeye (Fictitious character) in mass media.   I. Title.
P96.P65G73   2004   741.5'0973—dc22   2003027765

British Library cataloguing data are available

Manufactured in the United States of America

*McFarland & Company, Inc., Publishers
Box 611, Jefferson, North Carolina 28640
www.mcfarlandpub.com*

CONTENTS

INTRODUCTION

Having written a number of articles on the career of Popeye the Sailor and being co-founder of "The International Popeye Fanclub" (also known as the "Official Popeye Fanclub") for more than two decades, I'm often asked why the sailor has endured for 75 years. I had notions, but the answer came into focus after I had mailed a Popeye doll to "The Children's Room," a hospice for the terminally ill located in Waltham, Massachusetts, in 1993. Though the doll was in great shape, I didn't think much of it because I had found another with Popeye's pipe intact.

Several weeks later I received a call from the woman who ran the hospice, and she told me that the children were going up to the Popeye doll and hugging it for strength. I was surprised that the doll was providing such comfort, but then I recalled moments in the newspaper comic strip and the animated cartoons where Popeye would often assist people in trying times or offer words of comfort without asking for a reward. I realized, throughout Popeye's career in all types of media, he has not only entertained millions through his humorous adventures but also inspired many with his values and beliefs. In fact, "The Popeye Club Creed" from the 1930s stated that to join, you must be a good citizen to your city, state and country, obey your parents and teachers, lend a hand to young and old when they need help and tell the truth even when it hurts.

I believe Popeye has endured because of his values and the inner strength he provides. This book discusses Popeye's career in various media and the people who helped bring him and his crew to life.

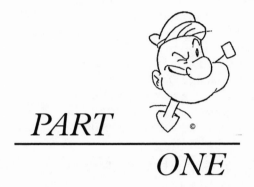

PART
ONE

Popeye in Print

Though most people know Popeye from his adventures in animated films, the spinach-eating sailor actually made his debut in newspaper comic strips. Popeye was created by cartoonist and writer E.C. (Elzie Crisler) Segar. Segar was born and raised in the Mississippi River town of Chester, Illinois. He began his varied apprenticeship in the entertainment industry at the age of 12, working in the Chester Opera House, which featured both movies and live performances. He drew advertisements for slide projection and posters and also played the drum to accompany the movies. After completing an 18-month W.L. Evans correspondence course in cartooning, Segar was certified as a cartoonist. He then took off for Chicago, where he found a job on the *Chicago Herald*.

On March 12, 1916, his first comic strip work appeared in the Sunday funnies when he took over the comic strip antics of Charlie Chaplin in "Charlie Chaplin's Comic Capers." In 1917 he started a strip called "Barry the Boob," fea-

Segar's "Thimble Theatre" featured stories filled with narrative and humor. Despite his early passing he left behind creations that are now legend.

Though today Popeye is often thought of as a children's character, Segar's Thimble Theatre strip was written for the adult audience as indicated by this exchange between Olive Oyl and Wimpy.

turing a nutty soldier in the European War. Later Segar began drawing for the *Chicago American*. On June 1, 1918, he began drawing "Looping the Loop," a strip that made comic commentary on movies, plays, exhibitions and other doings in downtown Chicago.

In late 1919 Segar was sent to Hearst's *New York Journal* and began work on "The Thimble Theatre." Initially this strip starred Olive Oyl and her family: Castor Oyl, her pint-sized brother; Cole Oyl, her father; and Olive's boyfriend, pickle-nosed Ham Gravy. Castor and Ham got involved with all sorts of crazy misadventures. On January 17, 1929, Castor was looking for a sailor to run his ship when he ran across an odd-looking, fat-forearmed, pipe-smoking sailor. Castor hailed him: "Hey there, are you a sailor?" The sailor's reply: "'Ja think I'm a cowboy?" With that simple remark, Popeye was born.

Olive was based on Chester, Illinois, resident, Dora Paskel. Ms. Paskel was

Two early "Braccio Di Ferro" magazines from the 1930s featuring Segar's comic strips in Italian. Popeye continues to be a popular attraction in Italy.

the proprietor of the general store in town. Her physical description certainly matched Olive Oyl! She was tall, lanky and wore her hair rolled tightly in a bun. She also dressed like Miss Oyl, complete with the button-up shoes of the period.

The lore of Chester, Illinois, holds that the character of Popeye was inspired by town resident Frank "Rocky" Fiegel. Lee Huffstutler, herself a Chester local, makes and well supports this argument. According to Huffstutler, Rocky Fiegel was of Polish descent and lived with his mother in a house near the Evergreen Cemetery. Mrs. Huffstutler describes him as "tall, strong, always ready for a fight and always a winner." She once mentioned five local boys who decided to gang up on Rocky and, with all of them involved, win in a fight with him. However, it was not to be. The fight started, five against one, and in short order it was over. Rocky had whipped three of the boys, and the other two couldn't be found anywhere. Once again, Rocky (or Popeye) was the winner even without spinach.

Rocky worked part-time at George Gozney's saloon. When he finished his work and had consumed a couple of beers, he would take a chair outside, seat himself, tilt the chair back, and, with pipe in his mouth, proceed to take a nap in the sunshine. Of course, the sleeping Rocky became an amusing target for the school children who came by. They would creep near, yell loudly, and run. Rocky would awaken with a start and jump out of his chair, arms flailing, ready for a fight. But alas, there would be no opponent. The children would be a block away by that time.

In the March 28, 1947, issue of the *Chester Herald Tribune*, there is an obituary of Mr. Fiegel, who died at his home in Chester on March 24, 1947. Born January 27, 1868, he was 79 years of age at the time of his death.

The editor wrote that Frank "Rocky" Fiegel was a familiar character in Chester and was credited for being the inspiration of Elzie Segar's "Popeye." The article reads: "In his younger days he performed amazing feats of strength. Because of his hardened physique he was affectionately known as "Rocky." His angular jaw and familiar corn-cob pipe apparently impressed the young Segar.

Elzie Crisler Segar, creator of Popeye.

On September 7, 1996, due to the membership of "The International Popeye Fan Club," Fiegel's unmarked grave was given a headstone. The marker was inscripted with the 1929 version of Segar's Popeye. It is the original design of the sailor, which most resembles his real life counterpart.

Segar's "Popeye" in turn impressed the newspaper-reading public with his crude but direct approach to solving a problem, and the sailor became an overnight hit. By 1931 the strip was retitled, "Thimble Theatre ... Starring Popeye." Popeye would often perform feats of strength to assist people but never wanted any reward in return. As time passed Segar revealed that spinach was the source of Popeye's strength, but months would pass before Popeye would be seen eating the vegetable. (This was unlike the animated cartoons, where spinach would play a vital part.) Over the next few years Segar introduced several memorable characters to the strip, including J. Wellington Wimpy, the hamburger moocher whose phrase, "I will gladly pay you Tuesday for a hamburger today," is known worldwide; Swee'pea, Popeye's adopted son; Oscar, Popeye's big-nosed, buck-toothed buddy; the Sea Hag, Popeye's first real enemy and the last true witch on earth; Poopdeck Pappy, Popeye's tough-as-nails father; Bluto, whom Popeye first battled in 1932; Alice the Goon, a hairy, hulking monster who later became the family babysitter; Toar, a monstrous brute; and Rough House, the belligerent cafe owner.

The creation of Alice the Goon was so frightening that parents told their misbehaving children that if they didn't watch out, "the Goon will get you." Eugene the Jeep, another Segar creation, was a magical animal from the 4th dimension. If you look in most dictionaries, you will read that the words "goon" and "jeep" are credited to Segar.

Of these popular characters, we can trace the inspiration for only one.

"Got Any More Wood W'ich Need Splittin'?"

A page by Segar from a 1930s Popeye Big Little Book. Early collectibles drawn by Segar are worth thousands of dollars today.

Townspeople of Chester largely agree that J. Wellington Wimpy was based on William "Windy Bill" Schuchert, the manager of the Chester Opera House where Segar held his first job. Schuchert was known about town for his pleasant, friendly manner, his fondness for telling tall tales, and, yes, his love of hamburgers. Evidently, even though Segar's "Wimpy" was a bit of a scoundrel, the cartoonist managed to imbue him with some of the characteristics that had made "Windy Bill" a beloved figure in Chester, for Wimpy was always a well-loved member of the Popeye cast.

With remarkable characters like Popeye and Wimpy, it is no wonder that under Segar's pen, "Thimble Theatre" eventually appeared in over 600 newspapers and spawned a Popeye radio show. Popeye and his pals were soon appearing on all kinds of merchandise. Even this early in the history of "Popeye," Segar's memorable creations were beginning what would be a decades-long expansion into every conceivable medium, the better to delight generations of "Popeye" fans.

Successors to Segar

In 1937, E.C. Segar was diagnosed with leukemia. During his remaining year of life, the "Thimble Theatre" strip was often ghosted by both Joe Musial and Doc Winner. (Winner's tenure was longer during Segar's life.) When Segar died in late 1938, Winner continued both the daily and Sunday strip. In the years to follow, Bela Zaboly, Tom Sims, Ralph Stein, Bud Sagendorf, Bobby London and Hy Eisman would continue the adventures of Popeye in strip form. Because each new "Popeye" author or illustrator influenced the strip in his own way, a closer look at these Segar successors makes for a short course in the evolution of the comic strip Popeye.

A "Thimble Theatre" comic strip by Segar during the height of Popeye's popularity.

Doc Winner

Charles "Doc" Winner, who ghosted the "Thimble Theatre" comic strip for periods in 1938, 1939 and the Sunday pages during the 1940s, was an American artist born on December 18, 1885, in Perryville, Pennsylvania. He was barely able to walk on two legs when he took paper and pencil and copied a portrait of a dog, which was woven into a rug, near the family fireplace. His zealous grandmother gave him a nickel for the doodle. Doc later recalled, "I spent the nickel as soon as I could get to the corner candy store, but it influenced my life tremendously. I reasoned that if one could get money for drawing pictures, why work? This wasn't Dad's idea of how to spend my time, but he later was very proud of the cartoons appearing in the papers delivered to his doorstep." Winner began a position with the *Pittsburgh Post*, where he attracted national attention for his editorial cartoons. In 1914, he left the paper to dabble in animation and drew a series of women's cartoons.

A "Thimble Theatre" strip by Doc Winner, who took over the strip when Segar fell
ill in 1937 and continued producing the strip for a time after Segar's death.

In 1918 Winner was offered a job with the comics art department of the Hearst Corporation (also known as King Features Syndicate), where he would remain for 38 years. Winner was the most active of all the bullpen artists and ghosted many strips as well as handling his own for King Features Syndicate. Other bullpen artists working alongside Winner were Paul Fung, Sr., Joe Musial, Bob Naylor, Vern Greene (who produced "Bringing Up Father" for a time), Bela "Bill" Zaboly and Bud Sagendorf.

Doc Winner was assigned Segar's "Thimble Theatre" during the last year of Segar's life and did a reasonably good job of matching Segar's style (except when it came to drawing Eugene the Jeep, whom Winner apparently had a hard time grasping). Winner also began his own strip, "Elmer," inherited from A.C. Fera, under whom it had been titled "Just Boy."

"Elmer" was a quiet strip but popular enough to last for two generations. King Features had wanted Winner to continue on "Thimble Theatre," but producing "Elmer" as well as filling in for other cartoonists kept him from stepping into Segar's footsteps on a more permanent basis. Instead the task went to Tom Sims and Bela Zaboly in 1939.

Winner later took over "The Katzenjammer Kids" and worked on the strip for King Features Syndicate until his passing in 1956.

Tom Sims

Tom Sims was born on May 26, 1898, in Cave Springs, Georgia. His father was a farmer. Sims had early ambitions to become a writer. He migrated to Birmingham and then to Nashville, gathering work experience along the way. Finally, he landed a job as a cub reporter for the *Nashville Tennessean*. After a stint in the Marines, he returned home with a Purple Heart and continued his career at the *Tennessean*. Eventually, he landed a job as a humor-columnist. Sims had at last found his destined vocation. Sims was hired by King Features Syndicate in 1926 as a comic strip continuity writer and idea man. He left King Features in 1929 to work for Kay Features. Kay Features collapsed during the great depression. The very day that Kay folded, Sims won a $1500 prize from *Life* magazine's "Best Story of the Year" contest. Sims joined *Life* magazine as a staff writer and later as a gag writer for "Amos and Andy." Sims returned to King Features in 1937 and began writing "Thimble Theatre" while Doc Winner was handling the art in 1939.

Sims was later paired with artist, Bela "Bill" Zaboly. Sims' scripts continued Segar's tradition with continuity during the week and occasionally with the Sunday pages. Together with Zaboly, Sims created "Gran'ma Peg" (Poopdeck Pappy's mother), "Aunt Jones" and Popeye's mother. Oscar became Swee'pea's buck-toothed buddy and was given a more prominent role to play in the Sunday pages throughout the 1950s. In 1955, Ralph Stein replaced Sims on the daily strip, though Sims continued to write the Sunday pages, which began to read more like a situation comedy. Though Sims passed on several years ago, Popeye scholars continue to seek out his work on "Thimble Theatre."

Joe Musial's artwork graced many products featuring Segar's characters from the 1930s to the 1960s. He was a talented "ghost-artist."

Joe Musial

Joe Musial apparently did at least some work on "Thimble Theatre" during the period when Doc Winner was officially handling the strip. It is certain, at any rate, that he drew the covers for the "King Comics" featuring Popeye and friends and was involved in compiling those reprint collections of Popeye strips. For whatever reason, Musial was billed as "the man who draws Popeye" in the *Popeye's How to Draw Book*, which Musial wrote for King Features in the late 1930s.

Joe Musial was born in Yonkers, New York, and studied at the Pratt Institute. Associated with King Features from the 1930s onward, he assisted cartoonist Billy DeBeck and later became a member of the syndicate's bullpen staff. He ghosted many strips, but usually for just a short period of time.

In 1936 Musial became actively involved with the production of the comic books which featured reprints of King's comic strips, including "Popeye," "Blondie," "The Phantom" and "The Lone Ranger" ... to name a few. He also produced his own strips for the comic books. For "Ace Comics" he produced "Teddy and His Sitting Bull," about a child and his dog, and for "Magic Comics" there was "Jan and Aloysius," about a girl and her parrot. Later Musial ghosted the popular comic strip "Barney Google and Snuffy Smith." In none of the strips he ghosted did he sign his name, though the initials J.M. appeared.

In 1956, following the death of Doc Winner, Musial was given the strip "The Katzenjammer Kids" to write and draw. "The Katzenjammer Kids" was the oldest comic strip still currently being syndicated. Musial remained with that strip, while also assisting Bud Sagendorf with the production of Popeye toys, until his passing in 1977.

Bela "Bill" Zaboly

In mid–1939, King Features Syndicate gave the drawing chores for "Thimble Theatre" to Bela Zaboly (also known as "Bill"). Zaboly signed his work with

Popeye's mother was created by Tom Sims and Bela Zaboly for a 1951 "Thimble Theatre" strip. She is a long forgotten creation.

An historic moment in the "Thimble Theatre" strip from 1957, Swee'pea wears pants that reveal his legs. He will wear this outfit in the strip until the latter part of 1959 though it will continue to be seen on products during the 1960s.

a bumblebee (Segar, punning on his own name, had signed his with a cigar). He was born in Cleveland, Ohio, and attended high school there while drawing for the school paper. Upon graduation he went to the art department of NEA Syndicate, which was located in his hometown. Zaboly started as an office boy and worked his way up to a staff position as a cartoonist.

Zaboly began assisting Roy Crane on his strip "Wash Tubbs." Zaboly helped to draw the lead characters and a bevy of pretty ladies. It was at this time he started a strip of his own, "Otto Honk," featuring a blond, moon-faced young boy who wasn't too bright. This Sunday strip followed the lad through some humorous antics in different occupations including football player, movie stuntman and private eye. Zaboly retired the strip in 1936. After the creator of "Our Boarding House" (featuring Major Hoople) left the cartoon panel, Zaboly was chosen to continue Hoople's misadventures.

Zaboly was hired away by King Features Syndicate as the artist for "Thimble Theatre." Zaboly would only draw the strip; Tom Sims was hired to write the stories. (He was replaced in 1955 on the daily strip by Ralph Stein.)

Zaboly did an excellent job matching Segar's style, but made some changes. Under Zaboly's pen, Swee'pea stopped wearing his nightgown and adopted a little sailor's uniform. With his legs now defined, the lad also began walking. Most Popeye strip fans prefer the "walking Swee'pea" Zaboly created.

Zaboly also produced much of the artwork for a series of Popeye coloring books during the late 1950s through the early 1960s. His rendition of the Popeye cast also appeared on numerous Popeye collectibles which appeared on the market after the original Popeye theatre cartoons debuted on television. Many of these collectibles feature "the walking Swee'pea," which marks them as Zaboly's artwork.

Zaboly (along with Tom Sims) also continued Segar's strip "Sappo" for several years, into the late 1940s. Much of Zaboly's work was reprinted in King Features' "Ace," "Magic" and "King Comics" reprint collections.

Although Bud Sagendorf has stated that he took over the comic strip in 1958, the work of Zaboly, Sims and Stein continued to appear in 1958 through the summer of 1959. An artistic change was in the air as Zaboly's rendition of Popeye began looking more and more like Sagendorf's design in both the daily and Sunday comic strips. Zaboly's art appeared for the final time on August 8, 1959, in the daily "Thimble Theatre," though his Sunday art would continue to be published for a few months longer. King Features replaced Zaboly, Sims and Stein as it was more economical to have one person do both the writing and illustrating. Many Popeye products during the late 1950s and throughout the 1960s often combined Zaboly's art with Bud Sagendorf's. For example, Kenner Toys' "Popeye's Presto Paints" (1961) featured both Zaboly and Sagendorf art. After his long tenure on "Thimble Theatre," Zaboly returned to Cleveland and again worked with NEA. He attempted to begin his own syndicate but did not have success. He passed away in 1985. As with Tom Sims, Zaboly's work on "Thimble Theatre" is sought after by Popeye collectors.

Ralph Stein

Ralph Stein was born in New York City on November 13, 1909. In his early years, Stein was promotional art director for *The New York World Telegram*, illustrating everything from promotional ads to major news and feature stories. He later became a freelance artist and photographer, selling his artwork to major general-interest publications such as *Collier's* and *Look*.

After serving in the army in World War II, he revived his career as illustrator and photographer. He wrote feature stories for publications in New York City. From 1955 to 1958, Stein was assigned the writing for the daily "Thimble Theatre" strip. Popeye went on globe trotting adventures with a Stein creation, "Sir Pomeroy" ("Pommy" to his pals) who was a monocled, chubby British big game hunter. Stein's scripts took the adventuring pair all over the world and on a trip to outer space! Popeye encountered natives, monsters and an old foe from Segar's period on the strip: "Bluto!"

Bluto was now portrayed as a pirate on a quest for treasure and he and his gang had action-packed encounters with Popeye and Sir Pomeroy. Bluto's twin brother, "Burlo" appeared toward the end of Stein's tenure on the strip. Bela Zaboly, now signing his work as "Bill" Zaboly illustrated Stein's scripts.

Stein was also the author of books on various topics, including antique autos, and was instrumental in founding *Yank*, a magazine published in World War II for servicemen. He passed on November 27, 1994. Though Stein's stint on "Thimble Theatre" was a short one, it is memorable for his creation of "Sir Pomeroy,"

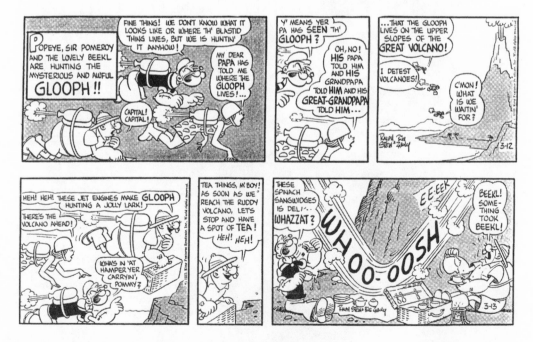

Ralph Stein's scripts for the daily "Thimble Theatre" strip often took Popeye and Sir Pomeroy on exciting adventures.

who continued to appear on Popeye collectibles during the late 1950s and early 1960s (this character was later revived by Bobby London for the daily strip), and for bringing back "Bluto" during the period where there was a copyright dispute over the origin of the brute's name.

Bud Sagendorf

Bud Sagendorf was born in Wenatchee, Washington, and grew up in Southern California. One day he happened to walk into a stationery store where Segar bought his art supplies. Sagendorf's sister introduced him to Segar, who invited the lad to his house to discuss cartooning. Some time later, Segar had to take a trip and asked Sagendorf to help out on "Thimble Theatre" for three weeks. This assignment soon became full-time. The pair often came up with gags for the strip while hunting or fishing.

After Segar's passing, King Features Syndicate gave Sagendorf a job working in the bullpen but felt he was too young to assume the "Thimble Theatre" strip. Instead, Doc Winner and then Bela Zaboly took over the strip. Sagendorf did fill in on the strip every once in awhile during Zaboly's tenure and also helped produce the top piece.

Above: Professor O.G. Wotta-Snozzle was featured in "Sappo," Segar's companion strip to "Thimble Theatre." WottaSnozzle was a crazy inventor who lived with John Sappo. *Left:* WottaSnozzle appeared as shown in the Popeye TV cartoons of 1960–61, wearing a graduation cap.

Bud Sagendorf chose to change the facial features of the "Thimble Theatre" cast. Sagendorf was instructed by King Features to give Popeye a sailor's hat to match his TV animated counterpart but the sailor's huge chin, Olive's pickle-shaped nose that moved from the bottom of her face to the middle, were Sagendorf's creations.

In 1946, Sagendorf became the artist/writer for the "Popeye" comic books and was allowed to sign them. These comic books are highly prized collectibles today. He also drew a few fillers for early funny books. In 1958 Sagendorf was handed the task of both the daily and Sunday "Thimble Theatre," though his work was not published until 1959.

Sagendorf's storytelling is like Segar's but without his mentor's touches of genius and ability to blend suspense and comedy in just the right manner. His early artwork on "Popeye" implies the Segar style, but as Sagendorf progressed he began drawing the characters his own way, straying not only from Zaboly's versions but from Segar's also when he expanded the size of Popeye's chin, replaced his captain's hat with a sailor's hat, gave Olive's nose a lift from the bottom of her face to the middle and made it look like a pickle and changed the Sea Hag's face to a female version of Popeye's. This change in character design became somewhat confusing during the 1960s as some of Zaboly's art was still being used on Popeye collectibles and the animated versions of the Popeye cast populated the television screen.

Sagendorf was also responsible for the creation of many Popeye collectibles and children's books including *Popeye, Popeye Goes on a Picnic, Popeye's Big Surprise* and *The House That Popeye Built* for Wonder Books from 1955 to the 1960s. He also wrote *Popeye: The First Fifty Years*, a look at the comic strip that puts the animated cartoons in the background. (The work of Segar's other successors is also touched upon only slightly.) Sagendorf created his own characters for the strip including "Dufus," "Granny" (Poopdeck Pappy's mother) and a wild assortment of criminals and relatives. Taking his cue from the success of the animated cartoons on television, Sagendorf revived "Bluto" as "Brutus" for the strip and comic books.

In 1986, Sagendorf retired from the daily strip to spend more time with his family. (Oddly enough, his last daily strip did not feature Popeye as was the same with Segar's.) He continued on the Sunday page until his passing in 1994. Sagendorf's renditions of the cast influenced a great many cartoonists drawing Popeye for products.

Bobby London

Bobby London is a native of New York City and attended Adelphi University. He began his cartooning career selling his work to counterculture and underground comic books during the late 1960s. He sold "Dirty Duck" to the *Los Angeles Free Press* in 1971. He later produced "Dirty Duck" for *Playboy* and continued to do so until 1987. While producing the "Duck" for *Playboy*, London contributed to underground comic books, and his work showed up in such publications as "Dopin' Dan" and "Merton of the Movement." He also drew "Air Pirates Funnies," which used the character of Mickey Mouse, prompting legal action from Walt Disney Studios. London has stated that much of his style is influenced by early cartoonists including Billy DeBeck ("Barney Google and Snuffy Smith"), Bud Fisher ("Mutt and Jeff"), Al Capp ("Li'l Abner"), Walt Kelly ("Pogo") and E.C. Segar. He also became quite good at imitating George Herriman's style ("Krazy Kat") so much so that one publication intending to show an example of Herriman's work actually published a piece of London's art instead.

King Features Syndicate, noticing London's style matched that of Segar, chose him as successor to Bud Sagendorf on the daily "Popeye" comic strip, which by then was appearing in a relatively small number of newspapers in the United States (although syndicated more widely in Europe). London decided to have Popeye and his gang face current problems and took them out of their previous gag-a-day mode. London also brought back continuity—something thought long banished from the daily strip—and revived Segar's original "Thimble Theatre" star, Castor Oyl. London's "Popeye" had the sailor man dealing with gambling, real estate takeovers, anorexia, muggers, street fighting, pop idols, Middle East menaces and any topical subject matter. This "topical subject" matter caused conflict with King Features Syndicate in the summer of 1992. London had produced a series of strips titled "Witch Hunt" in which Olive has received, in error, a baby "Bluto" doll. Popeye and Olive discuss taking it back but are overheard by a priest, who thinks Olive is expecting. Olive's "right to choose" is then discussed in the strip.

King Features Syndicate, already annoyed with a strip sequence London had done poking fun at its licensing department, fired London over the "Baby

Bobby London wrote a "Popeye" plot line that poked fun at King Features Syndicate's sales and licensing divisions. London's topical storylines led to his dismissal in July of 1992. His departure caused a furor of media coverage, awakening the public to the fact that a "Popeye" comic strip still exists, although it appears in only a small number of papers.

Bluto" storyline, deeming it not suitable for a "family strip" like "Popeye." When asked why London thought he was dismissed, he stated, "I can recall that in actuality, my copy was coming back totally uncorrected for six months. I couldn't understand why this was happening. I think it was because nobody was reading my copy. Nobody cared. But I took it as sort of a green light that I was doing OK. And I kept writing stuff that I really wanted to do." London's comments have roots to the daily strips, which featured "Bluto" in the late 1950s, written by Ralph Stein. Stein's use of the name "Bluto" apparently went unnoticed by King Features Syndicate, but that name wasn't allowed to be used in the "Popeye" comic books by Bud Sagendorf during the exact same period of time. King Features' cartoon editor, Jay Kennedy, called London and fired him. When newspaper editors asked London why he was dismissed, he stated it had to do with his *Roe vs. Wade* storyline in "Popeye." A swirl of media frenzy circled London as the story was covered by the major networks and publications. The firing of London is regrettable as his scripts were riots. One storyline titled, "The Return of Bluto" featured every version of Popeye's bearded foe since Bluto's debut in 1932 battling the one-eyed sailor. Though adding a contemporary feel to the strip, London retained a good deal of Segar's storytelling and revived long forgotten characters including Olive Oyl's brother, Castor Oyl.

Hy Eisman

Hy Eisman, who took over the Sunday "Popeye" strip in 1994, developed a reputation as a talented "ghost artist." Eisman works in the style of the original creator of a particular strip. This talent has served him well over the years for he has written and drawn, "Nancy," "Bringing Up Father," "Blondie," "Archie," "Mutt and Jeff" and "Tom and Jerry." He was awarded the prestigious Reuben award from the National Cartoonist Society in 1984 and drew the "Little Iodine" strip for 17 years. When "Little Iodine" folded, Eisman said, "You're working with a character who becomes real to you. When I lost Iodine, I really felt a member of the family had died. But that's the whole cartooning business. You're constantly starting over. I like the physical act of drawing pictures. It gives you the chance to poke fun at the human condition." Eisman, born on March 27, 1927, in Paterson, New Jersey, had wanted to draw cartoons since he was five years old. "If I got a dime," Eisman said, "instead of spending it on a movie or a malted, I would buy the *New York American* because of the comics. They were all my favorites. I drew everyone."

Eisman shares honors with the late Charles Schultz of "Peanuts" fame, as being recognized in *The Guinness Book of World Records* for writing and drawing "The Katzenjammer Kids," the oldest, continuously published (since 1887) comic strip. Eisman stated, "The kids have been wearing the same clothes for 103 years; I hope they at least changed their underwear."

Eisman has brought Popeye and his crew into the 21st century. (He's gotten

Opposite page: **Hy Eisman's Sunday strips have featured Popeye and his crew encountering contemporary situations.**

Olive hooked on the Home Shopping Network. Brutus is involved with computer dating. Popeye uses a cell phone and Swee'pea has his own computer.) While attending a cartoon festival in Lucca, Italy, Eisman and a friend visited Rome. Eisman had given his friend a "Popeye" pin to wear, which she wore as they toured the Sistine chapel. Their guide asked where she got the pin. "He draws 'Popeye,'" the friend said, pointing to Eisman. The guide then begged Eisman to sketch the lovable sailor for her. Popeye is extremely popular in Italy. "There I was drawing Popeye in the Sistine Chapel," Eisman said. "I had upstaged Michaelangelo!"

The "Popeye" daily strip still exists as reprints of Bud Sagendorf's earlier work while Eisman continues to produce a new Sunday page. While the Sunday has wider circulation than the daily, the reason "Popeye" is not published as widely as it once was is that today's editors think of the sailor as a television character forgetting his comic strip roots. The decline in circulation has been gradual; no one cartoonist or writer can be blamed. The Popeye comic strip can be viewed on King Features Syndicate's website at www.kingfeatures.com/features/comics/popeye/about.htm.

Popeye in Comic Books

Original "Popeye" comic books began production in 1948 by Dell Comics. Prior to that the sailor appeared in a series of reprints of the "Thimble Theatre" comic strip in King Features Syndicate's "King Comics" and "Magic Comics" (later "Ace Comics"). The reprints were either by Segar (making the comic books very collectible) or the team of Sims and Zaboly. "Popeye" also appeared in a series of comic books published by Dell under the title of "Four Color." "Popeye" was later picked up by Gold Key Comics, then King Comics, Charlton Comics, back to Gold Key and concluded its run with Whitman Comics. Bud Sagendorf, Segar's assistant on "Thimble Theatre" who took over the comic strip in 1958, handled both the writing and art for the comic book series until Charlton Comics picked up the series in 1969. The Charlton series was produced by George Wildman (art) and Joe Gill and Bill Pearson (writers).

Donnie Pitchford, writer for "The International Popeye Fan Club" got to know George Wildman very well and provides this background information on the artist: Wildman was born on July 31, 1927, and loved to flop the Sunday paper on the floor and copy his favorite comic strip characters, "Popeye," "Alley Oop" and "Smokey Stover." Wildman majored in advertising and spent twenty years in the field before becoming involved with comics. When King Features closed down their comic book business, Charlton Comics picked up their line and Wildman was offered either "Blondie" or "Popeye" to draw. He chose the one-eyed sailor and his first work appeared in an issue dated, February 1969, Issue 94. His enthusiasm, creativity and business skills led Wildman to become the managing editor of Charlton Comics in 1971. Wildman later oversaw the production of several educational "Popeye" comic books, used to guide children through career endeavors. Wildman brought joy to countless children who were hospitalized, doodling "Thimble Theatre" especially for them. Joe Gill wrote the "Popeye" comic books while the series was published by Charlton, but in 1976, they dropped their King Features line. Bill Pearson became the new writer when Gold Key picked up the "Popeye" comic book series in 1979. Pearson and Wildman produced many book-length adventures while working at Gold Key, including an issue celebrating Popeye's 50th birthday!

Gold Key later became known as Western Comics, but when sales fell off on all their titles, the "Popeye" series came to an end in the early 1980s. Wildman was presented with the "Best Comic Book Humor Cartoonist Award" in 1982. In 1983, he presented a hand-painted Easter Egg to the White House, featuring Popeye, which now resides in the Smithsonian Institution. Wildman also illustrated two best-selling "Popeye" books for Random House, a pop-up book and a flip-it book. Wildman continues to draw for many companies but Popeye remains close to his heart. Harvey Comics published seven issues of a Popeye comic book reprinting stories from the Charlton era in 1993–1994.

Ocean Comics published two Popeye specials in the late 1980s. They featured a more adult version of the characters and Popeye was drawn less cartoonishly (if you can believe that can be done!). The first issue dealt with the origin of the sailor and his adventures while serving in the Navy. The second (and last) issue dealt with a trip to Australia and a duel with Brutus' twin brother, "Bluto." Brutus was the good brother in this tale.

In 1999, Popeye celebrated his 70th birthday, but unfortunately there was little, if any, media celebrating this occasion, other than an article spotlighting my Popeye collection in *The National Enquirer* toward the end of the year.

The media circus following Popeye

"Popeye," No. 108, June 1971 featured George Wildman's rendition of the 1929 version of Popeye (note the misspelling of Segar's middle name in the text). Also featured in this issue was a self-portrait of the cartoonist.

Eugene the Jeep predicts "The Wedding of Popeye and Olive" (Ocean Comics, 1999), a one shot comic book adventure that received a lot of press to the dismay of King Features Syndicate and fans of the sailor.

had to do with Ocean Comics' "The Wedding of Popeye & Olive" special comic book, released in February of 1999. The 32-page color comic was illustrated by Dave Garcia, inks by Sam de la Rosa and letters by Grass Green. The editor of the comic, Bob Palin, stated to the press that he thought it would be fitting for Popeye to get married on the occasion of his 70th birthday, and he was trying to get publicity to sell some books. Mr. Palin, apparently to the dismay of King Features Syndicate, who asked him at the last minute to change the ending of the story so the couple would not wed, was bombarded with publicity. The comic book release was reported on all the major news networks and cable outlets. The announcement was featured in *Newsweek*, *Time* and various newspapers across the country.

The story itself was an entertaining one with the return of Olive's original boyfriend, Ham Gravy, setting off the chain of events which lead Popeye to the altar. The artwork, as in Ocean Comics' other two issues, was neither the comic strip or animated versions of the cast, but more of a realistic design. Since the artwork was so far removed from the well-known designs of the "Thimble Theatre" cast, it's safe to say that this story took place in an alternate universe.

Popeye comic books have also been published outside of the United States. In Italy, where he is called "Braccio Di Ferro" (Iron-Arm), Popeye books and magazines continue to flourish. Some of the Italian books are reprints of Segar stories dubbed in Italian.

Comic books and magazines using Segar, Sims/Zaboly and Sagendorf stories have appeared in various languages over the years. In Britain, a "Popeye Annual" has been published for many years. These annuals have featured original material as well as reprints from the United States.

Popeye Reincarnate: Other Comic Book
Characters with That Popeye Punch

There is no doubt that Popeye has had an influence on the creators of other comic book characters. Though it may come as a surprise to some, the best-known of these characters is the Man of Steel, the mighty Superman. Jerry Siegel, one of Superman's creators (along with Joe Shuster), readily admits that the animated Popeye cartoons were a primary influence. He envisioned similar fast-paced action turning on the hero's superhuman strength, but played straight instead of for laughs. With the addition of a few other influential types, notably Tarzan, very popular at the time, Superman was the inevitable result. (Oddly enough, the connection between Popeye and Superman would continue through coincidence. It was the Fleischer Studios who brought "Superman" to the world of animated cartoons as they did Popeye. And Jackson Beck, who was the voice of Bluto in the majority of the Famous Studios films and Brutus in the King Features TV cartoons, later provided the narration and voices for "The New Adventures of Superman" television cartoons for CBS Saturday mornings in the late 1960s.)

Then there was "Captain Strong," a direct tribute to Popeye by the writers of Action Comics (issue number 421). Captain Strong was a one-eyed sailor who swallowed an alien seaweed called "Sauncha." This alien greenery gave Strong super-strength, and an overdose caused the sailor to lose his self-control. In a sequel to this story, which occurred in Action Comics number 566, we also meet Strong's "sweet Patootie," Olivia who looks a lot like Olive Oyl. Also appearing in this tale were J. Wellington Jones (in Popeye cartoons, Wimpy always told people he was one of the "Jones" boys to get out of trouble), Strong's "Pappy," and a sea-witch.

Captain Strong looked, acted, and sounded a lot like Popeye. Consider the following scene from issue 566, in which the Captain prepares to fight a Superman clone who is under the control of the sea-witch. Captain Strong speaks:

> Yer Super-Spirit don't scare me none, Haggy! He may got super power but I got my Sauncha Power! Course even if I didn't have me sauncha-power I'd still win this li'l scuffle cause this phony super-swab is fightin' on the side of evil! I'm fightin' for good! And as me friend, the real Superman would say in a scrap between good and bad, the good always comes out on top!

Captain Strong then floors the super-clone with an army of punches.

Olivia closes the adventure with a remark to Lois Lane regarding Superman, Clark Kent, and Captain Strong: "They are what they are."

Another Popeye clone of sorts was the cartoon character "Sinbad Jr.," who appeared in a series of TV cartoons in the 1960s and a few comic books published by Dell. Sinbad wore a short-sleeved white T-shirt and a captain's hat. Sinbad's source of super-strength was his magic belt. When he pulled on the belt, strength would surge through his arms, inflating his muscles. Sinbad's sidekick was a parrot named "Salty."

Other animated cartoon characters would take after Popeye and have their own power sources. "Underdog" had his super-energy pill, Felix the Cat had his magic bag of tricks which helped get him out of all sorts of scrapes, Fearless Fly wore glasses which increased his strength, and the Mighty Hercules wore a ring which gave him his strength while staying on earth. Apparently Popeye started a popular trend which was picked up by other cartoon characters.

Popeye Goes Mad

Mad magazine has often poked fun at established cartoon and comic strip characters, and Popeye has received his fair share of ribbing over the years. Many Popeye spoofs have included mock signatures of Segar, Tom Sims, Bill Zaboly and Bud Sagendorf (often misspelled on purpose), though of course the cartoons are actually the work of *Mad*'s talented staff of writers and artists.

The first spoof on Popeye was titled "Poopeye" and first appeared in the early 1950s. All the characters looked the same as those in the real strip, but Olive Oyl was called "Mazola Oil," Swee'pea was known as "Swee'back," and Wimpy was seen chasing after animals or humans with a pair of hamburger buns in his hands. One panel had the moocher chasing after a woman, saying, "Girl-Burger." The plot of the story has Swee'back hiring characters from other comic strips to beat up Poopeye. With the aid of his spinach (which he finds in the oddest places) Poopeye beats up the likes of "Mammy Jokeum," "Melvin of the Apes," and "Superduperman." Poopeye finally manages to beat up Swee'back, who is actually the mad Broccoli King! Poopeye's punch turns Swee'back to dust, which Wimpy sweeps up, saying, "Swee'back Burger."

One of *Mad*'s best Popeye spoofs was titled "Future Educational Pamphlets" and had John Kennedy (then president) introducing Popeye as the spokesperson for Navy recruitment. The cartoon shows a typical Popeye day: Brutus smashes Popeye into the ground with a club, Olive gives Popeye spinach, Popeye punches Brutus, and Olive kisses Popeye. Then Popeye advises readers to join the U.S. Army! "*I* joined the U.S. *Navy*," the sailor

"Don't swallow it, sailor! It's no good for you!"

From *Mad*'s spoof "If Comic Strip Artists Drew Editorial Cartoons." Note the tough-in-cheek credits: "Tim Soms & Bull Zabbly." ©1958 by E.C. Publications, Inc.

From *Mad*'s education pamphlets spoof featuring the TV cartoon version of Brutus. Illustrated by Wallace Wood. ©1963 by E.C. Publications, Inc.

POPEYE

A very old Popeye, Brutus, Wimpy and Swee'pea from *Mad*'s "If Comic Strip Characters Were as Old as Their Strips." Note the mock signature of "Bub DorpenSag" in the second panel; in the final panel, a tired cigar (for E.C. Segar) emits a bored "BZ" (for Bill Zaboly). ©1962 by E.C. Publications, Inc.

spouts, "and *look* at me! I gets into silly fights all the time, I talks lousy Englich, I eats nuttin' but (UGH!) spinich, an' I goes out wit' skinny, ugly broads!"

Another interesting takeoff on Popeye was included in a spoof called "If Comic Strip Characters Were as Old as Their Strips." In this piece, Popeye and Brutus are old men fighting (as much as they can with canes) over who will bring flowers to Olive Oyl. The old men decide it's a draw and then fight over who will plant their flowers first at Olive's grave. Popeye fans with an eye for detail will note that this spoof includes subtle tributes: a cigar (for Segar), the letters "BZ" (for Bill Zaboly) in the cigar's smoke, and, in an earlier panel, the "signature" of "Bub DorpenSag" (Bud Sagendorf). King Features Syndicate was usually referred to with names like "Fang Features Syndicate" or "United Creatures Sin."

The artwork on spoofs of Popeye and his crew was often based solely on the comic strip designs of the characters rather than on the animated films. Brutus was sometimes illustrated in the 1960-61 TV version, sometimes in Bud Sagendorf strip design. One spoof featuring the Sagendorf version of Brutus was titled "If This 'Nudity' Trend in Movies Ever Spreads to the Comics." Popeye is skinny-dipping, and Brutus (called "Pluto" in this spoof) takes his clothes. Popeye shouts, "Avast there, Pluto, don't take me clothes, I got nuttin' on!" "Pluto" replies, "I wooden wantchya to catch cold ol' buddy ... wear dis ... ha, ha, ha!" The brute throws a bucket over Popeye's head. The sailor, bucket still on his head, tries to find some clothes, but Olive Oyl comes across him in his search. Olive scolds Popeye, and the sailor asks how she was able to recognize him. Olive glances at his butt, which is shaped exactly like his famous chin, and says, "It was easy!" Seeing this as a child, I was a little shocked not so much at seeing Popeye's rear end, but at the writers of this strip calling Brutus "Pluto."

Recently *Mad* did an excellent parody of the live-action movie *Popeye*, wittily pointing out many of its flaws. Other magazines, *Crazy*, for example, have likewise poked fun at Popeye.

All the parodies and Popeye imitators serve to remind us of one old saying: Imitation is the sincerest form of flattery. Over the years, many cartoonists have sought to pay tribute to the squint-eyed sailor whose influence is prominent in their work and in the popular culture. In honoring Popeye, they favor his fans with still more fun.

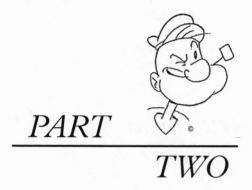

PART
TWO

Popeye on Film: Cartoons of Fleischer and Famous Studios

"Between 1933 and 1957, Max Fleischer's (USA) "Popeye the Sailor Man" had 233 one-reelers and a single two-reeler, "Popeye the Sailor Meets Sindbad the Sailor" (USA, 1936). An additional 220 Popeye cartoons were produced for TV by King Features from 1960 to 1962, followed by 192 all new Popeye cartoons made for the CBS network from 1978 to 1983. The series was first aired on TV in September 1956, making it the longest running syndicated cartoon series."

Though some information is incorrect, the above was taken from the 2002 edition of *The Guinness Book of World Records*. I had tried for many years to get Popeye's film career honored and at last it was.

Fleischer Studios (1933–1942)

Segar's "Thimble Theatre" comic strip had long been a favorite of Max Fleischer, the man whose Fleischer Studios produced the animated antics of "Ko-Ko the Clown" and "Bimbo" and the highly popular "Betty Boop" cartoons for Paramount Pictures. Max thought to make a cartoon featuring Popeye. Arrangements were made with Popeye's copyright owner, King Features Syndicate, and soon a financial agreement was worked out. Fleischer decided to test audience reaction to the squint-eyed sailor by featuring him, Olive Oyl and Bluto (who was the villain in Segar's "Thimble Theatre" strip at the time) in one of the "Betty Boop" films. This 1933 cartoon, called "Popeye the Sailor," features a newspaper headline blaring, "Popeye a movie star ... the sailor with a sock accepts movie contract." The camera zooms in on a photo of Popeye, which comes alive. Popeye begins to sing his now-famous theme song, which was written by Sammy Lerner. While Popeye strolls along the deck of a ship, singing his song, Olive Oyl is on the dock awaiting the arrival of her boyfriend. The hulking Bluto comes along and makes an attempt to grab her. Popeye steps between the two and shoves Bluto to one side. Popeye and Olive then go to a carnival, unaware that Bluto has followed them. At the carnival, Bluto tries to outdo Popeye at different games of skill but fails. Later Popeye joins hula dancer Betty Boop on stage until he sees Bluto running off with Olive. Bluto ties Olive to the railroad tracks and begins pounding on Popeye. As the train fast approaches Olive, Bluto stomps on the sailor, who then casually opens a can of spinach and eats it. With two swings of his fists, he knocks Bluto into a tree (which conveniently becomes a coffin). With another smashing punch, he turns the oncoming train into scrap, then sings, "I'm Popeye the Sailor Man (*toot, toot*)."

Many tend to believe that the majority of the Popeye cartoons feature Popeye and Bluto battling over Olive Oyl. However, this was far from the truth while Fleischer Studios produced the series. Just when you thought you knew what was going to occur in the cartoon, the Fleischers often threw a curve. For instance, in the film "I Likes Babies and Infinks" (1937), Olive calls upon both Popeye and Bluto to stop baby Swee'pea from crying. They both fail, and Bluto winds up beating on Popeye. The camera zooms in on Popeye's hand reaching for a can of spinach on Olive's kitchen cabinet. We hear the spinach theme music start up;

The Fleischer Popeye cartoons from 1933's "I Yam What I Yam" to 1938's "Cops Is Always Right" featured the pictured ship door opening. Not all of the Fleischer Popeye cartoons featured the sliding doors.

then Popeye grabs a can of onions by mistake. Bluto breaks open the can of onions with his fist, and soon the bearded bully, Olive and Popeye are all crying. This scene delights Swee'pea, who begins laughing at the bawling trio.

"The Adventures of Popeye" (1935) features live scenes of a little boy, reading a Popeye book, being bullied. Popeye jumps out of the book and acts out scenes from his earlier adventures and then jumps back into the book. The boy, eating what looks like burnt leaves from an oversized can of spinach, finds the bully and smacks him through a window and sings, "I'm strong to the finish cause I eats me spinach like Popeye the Sailor Man! Woo, Woo!"

The 1939 cartoon "Wotta Nitemare" is a surreal fantasy where Popeye dreams he's living in the clouds in pursuit of Olive Oyl, the Angel. Bluto, whose body is dressed in fur, is the thorn in the sailor's side. Everything that Popeye touches, which he thinks is real, is fake or something entirely different. When the sailor is about to be run over by a stream roller, it turns to butterflies as the machine touches his body. Popeye, in the dream, stuffs his mouth with spinach while his sleeping self ends up eating stuffing from his mattress! This cartoon was certainly a far cry from the traditional "Popeye" story.

"Puttin' on the Act" (1940s) was a salute to the days of vaudeville as Popeye

Bluto stomps on Popeye in a scene from the sailor's first animated cartoon appearance, "Popeye the Sailor" (1933), which was a "Betty Boop" film. The song that introduced this film and the first official Popeye film, "I Yam What I Yam" (1933), was a tune called "Strike Up the Band."

and Olive think they have a chance to perform "their old act again." Popeye entertains us with his impersonations of Groucho Marx and, by literally stretching his face into shape, Stan Laurel of "Laurel and Hardy."

Despite the fact that Segar rarely showed Popeye eating spinach in the comic strip, Paramount Pictures insisted that it be worked into the majority of the animated cartoons. It became such a staple that soon all the characters, as well as the audience, were quite well aware of what happened when Popeye consumed spinach. In the 1936 cartoon "A Clean Shaven Man," Bluto is dragging Popeye across the ground. Popeye pulls out a can of spinach, but Bluto sees it and tosses it away, declaring, "Hey, none of that stuff!"

Other characters soon began to eat the spinach. In the cartoon "Hospitaliky" (1937), Bluto and Popeye try to injure themselves to land in the hospital under the care of Nurse Olive. In this cartoon, Bluto feels the effects of eating spinach when Popeye feeds it to him so that he'll beat Popeye to a pulp and send him to the hospital. Olive, too, ate the spinach (only once while the Fleischers produced the series, though she would do so again in later cartoons). In "Never Kick a Woman" (1936), Olive is beaten up by a Mae West-type gym instructor. She crawls over to the can of spinach sticking out of Popeye's pocket, devours its contents, and beats up the teacher, who's been making a play for Popeye. In "Lost and Foundry" (1937), baby Swee'pea saves the day after he eats Popeye's spinach and saves both Popeye and Olive from being squashed by a giant press.

In one of the later Fleischer-produced cartoons, "Pip-eye-Pup-eye-Poop-eye and Peep-eye" (1942), Popeye's nephews are forced to eat spinach after their uncle spanks them. The nephews promptly beat the tar out of Popeye and then head off to go fishing.

In 1941, the Fleischers started a theme that would often repeat itself in Popeye cartoons. "Flies Ain't Human" features Popeye attempting to take a nap but being bothered by a pesky fly. Popeye sucks the fly into his pipe and flings it into a can of spinach. The fly eats the spinach and trounces Popeye, even though it was the fly who started the trou-

In "Pleased to Meet-Cha" (1935) Popeye pulls a huge can of spinach from his shirt pocket. As a child watching this I never thought of this as a shirt pocket. I always believed Popeye had a shelf nailed to his chest where the spinach cans rested until he needed one. Popeye was known more for his spinach consumption in the Fleischer cartoons than Segar's strip.

ble. This theme of an animal battling Popeye would often be repeated, with the sailor usually on the losing end.

Besides Bluto and Olive, the Fleischers featured many other characters from Segar's strips. Poopdeck Pappy, Popeye's father, appeared in "Goonland" (1938, also featuring Segar's "Goons"), "My Pop My Pop" (1940), "With Poopdeck Pappy" (1940), "Problem Pappy" (1941), "Quiet Pleeze" (1941), "Child Psykolo-jiky" (1941) and "Pest Pilot" (1941). Eugene, the magical Jeep from the fourth dimension, made his animation debut in "The Jeep" (1938). Baby Swee'pea appeared in "Little Swee'pea" (1936), "Lost and Foundry" (1937), "I Likes Babies and Infinks" (1937), "The Football Toucher Downer" (1937) and "The Jeep" (1938). Swee'pea also appeared in "Never Sock a Baby" (1939). In this cartoon, Swee'pea runs away and Popeye goes after him. The pair end up cling-ing for dear life on a cliff. Popeye goes to pull out a can of spinach only to dis-cover (despite the spinach music playing in the background) that the can is empty ... another twist the Fleischers threw at the audience. In "Nurse Mates" (1940) Bluto and Popeye make a shambles of trying to care for Swee'pea. In "Doing Impossikible Stunts" (1940), Swee'pea became a stuntman after showing a movie director his heroic scene from his earlier appearance in "Lost and Foundry." "Puttin' on the Act" (1940), "Child Psykolojiky" (1941) and "Baby Wants a Bot-tleship" (1942) rounded out Swee'pea's appearances in the Fleischer-produced Popeye films. (Many people believe that the 1934 cartoon "Sock-a-Bye-Baby" was Swee'pea's first animated appearance, but the baby in that cartoon was Betty Boop's little brother, Billy Boop.)

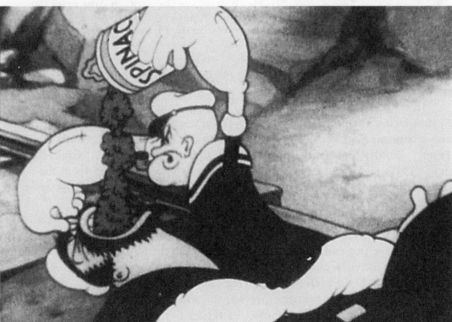

In "Hospitaliky" (1937), Popeye feeds Bluto his spinach so the bearded bully will lose control of his strength and beat him up, sending Popeye to the hospital so he can be near Nurse Olive Oyl. As Popeye feeds the spinach to Bluto, he mutters under his breath, "C'mon, open wide ... yer gonna eat the spinach dis time." This plot device of the two swabs trying to get injured to be near Olive was later used in the 1945 Famous Studios film "For Better or Nurse" and the 1960 King Features TV cartoon "I Bin Sculped" (produced by Gerald Ray).

J. Wellington Wimpy, the hamburger moocher, was featured in many Fleischer-produced Popeye cartoons. He was always on the lookout for food. His first animated appearance was in the first official Popeye cartoon, "I Yam What I Yam," where we see him taking live fish out of the ocean and sticking them in his mouth for lunch. But perhaps Wimpy's most memorable appearance was in "What ... No Spinach?" (1936). In this cartoon, Wimpy works in Bluto's diner and attempts to con Popeye out of his meal. The film ends with Popeye and Bluto in a

Olive is not very happy that her plumbing is going haywire in "Plumbing Is a Pipe" (1938). Her plumbing would go crazy again in Famous Studios' "Floor Flusher" (1954), "Plumber's Pipe Dream" (Jack Kinney, 1960) and "Popeye the Plumber" (Hanna Barbera, 1978).

brawl and Wimpy emerging from the safe where Bluto keeps his food, with a full tummy and a contented smile.

Besides being the first to introduce many now-familiar characters to the animated screen, the Fleischers began many of the traditions that have become so familiar to Popeye watchers over the years. Popeye first pulled out his can of spinach in his first appearance in animated form in the Betty Boop cartoon "Popeye the Sailor" (1933). "Seasin's Greetinks" (1933) was the first holiday-themed Popeye cartoon and also the first cartoon where any type of fanfare was heard when Popeye pulled out his can of spinach. "Shoein' Hosses" (1934) was the first cartoon where Popeye and Bluto competed against each other for work. This job competition theme would often occur during the run of the Popeye film series. "Adventures of Popeye" (1935) was the first cartoon where footage from previously produced cartoons was used. Fleischer Studios would go to the trouble of re-recording the soundtracks to the old footage to match the new scenes. "A Clean Shaven Man" (1936) was the first cartoon where Bluto acknowledges what will happen to him if Popeye eats his spinach, but it wasn't till "The Twisker Pitcher" (1937) that Bluto got smart and ate Popeye's spinach himself. "Lost and Foundry" (1937) features the first time baby Swee'pea eats Popeye's spinach and saves his elders a theme that would often be repeated. "Fightin' Pals" (1940) features Popeye and Bluto as friends for the first time, and they did work together as buddies in a few later cartoons produced by other studios. "Flies Ain't Human" (1940) is the first cartoon where Popeye battles some kind of "pest" other than human ... and ends up the loser. "Pip-eye–Pup-eye–Poop-eye and Peep-eye" (1942) first featured four Popeye look-alike children as his nephews, though they did appear previously in "Wimmin Is a Myskery" (1940) as Olive Oyl's children in a dream sequence.

Top: Olive is confused by a Popeye double, actually Wimpy, in a scene from "Hello, How Am I" (1939). *Bottom:* Pictured are Olive's children from a dream she was having in the 1940 cartoon "Wimmin Is a Myskery." These four lads later became known as Popeye's nephews, Pipeye, Pupeye, Poopeye and Peepeye.

Popeye watches Olive Oyl being carried off by a giant bird in the 1936 two-reeler, "Popeye the Sailor Meets Sindbad the Sailor." This cartoon would be nominated for an Academy Award but then lose to a Disney short. Popeye would have his revenge by besting Disney's "Mickey Mouse" in popularity polls with theatres across the country.

Fans of early Popeye films also regard the sailor's World War II related adventures as an important part of his cartoon history. Those topical adventures began with the Fleischers' 1941 cartoon "The Mighty Navy." In this cartoon, the sailor first donned his white Navy uniform and was aboard a battleship. The film shows him training to be a sailor (though he always felt he was a sailor!). Popeye messes up his training until an enemy ship comes along and, with the aid of his spinach, the one-eyed swab saves his battleship from danger. At the conclusion of the cartoon he is informed that his picture (oddly, in his original comic strip uniform) will be the symbol for the Navy's fighter squadron. "Fleets of Stren'th" came along in 1942 and was similar to "The Mighty Navy," with Popeye creating more confusion aboard ship. He has to do battle in the air and sea as a spy plane shoots at him from above and two missiles stream towards him in the sea. While in the ocean, Popeye has a tough time opening his spinach can, and the missiles collide, blowing Popeye skyward. As the plane's bullets head towards Popeye, he raises his spinach can to deflect them. The bullets rip open the top of the can, and Pop-

A model sheet used for animators drawing "Olive as the Princess" from the 1939 two-reeler, "Aladdin and His Wonderful Lamp" (1939).

eye eats its contents. The sailor then dives into action against the enemy. "Blunder Below" (1942) had the sailor causing further headaches for his general, but once again, thanks to his spinach, Popeye saves the ship and gets many medals pinned on his chest by cartoon's end.

From the very beginning, the Popeye series was a success, and in many key markets the Popeye cartoons were more popular than Disney's short subjects. In 1936, Popeye was featured in color for the first time in the two-reeler film "Popeye the Sailor Meets Sindbad the Sailor." The film's great visual delights were all the more enhanced by the 3D background process invented by Max Fleischer. This process, which had also been used in earlier Fleischer cartoons including some of the one-reel Popeyes, was used in several "Sindbad" scenes to give realistic depth to the backgrounds. A Paramount handout described the setup for the process:

> Ordinarily cartoons today are drawn and the drawings are photographed. With the method which Fleischer has introduced for Popeye the cartoon studio looks like a duplicate in miniature of a regular Hollywood production camp. Sets are built and scaled down so that they will fit on a revolving turntable. This "set" is within six feet of a special lens and camera. The machinery

entailed in the new process weighs some three tons. It has trusses, movable tables, cranks, steel framework, gears and gadgets enough to make a mechanical engineer dizzy.

This device provided dimensional backgrounds and foregrounds, and with the cels containing the animated characters photographed in the middle a remarkable effect of depth and perspective was obtained.

"Sindbad" was followed by another two-reeler, "Popeye Meets Ali Baba's Forty Thieves" (1937). Inside Ali Baba's cave, wonderful three-dimensional backgrounds of treasure chests, gems, and golden items highlighted this cartoon.

The last of three two-reel Popeye films was "Aladdin and His Wonderful Lamp" (1939). In this film, Olive is a scriptwriter for "Surprise Pictures" and writes a picture featuring herself as a princess and Popeye as Aladdin. No three-dimensional effects were used in this cartoon, but it is still an entertaining picture.

In many of the Popeye cartoons of the 1930s, the black-and-white backgrounds contrasted strongly with the gritty old stone pavements and worn-down building sets used in the films. These features have become a hallmark of the 1930s Popeye cartoons. In 1938, Fleischer Studios moved to Miami, Florida, and the Popeye series took on a different look. The animation became more relaxed, and the gritty stone backgrounds vanished in favor of a "lighter" feel, apparently influenced by the Miami look.

The Production of Popeye

The care and attention evident in the backgrounds; the liquid motion of the characters; the startling three-dimensional work in the two-reelers; these are some of the aspects of the Popeye cartoons that point to a staggering amount of work behind each of the original films.

In 1938, the magazine *Foto* published "Life Cycle of Popeye," an article describing the process of creating a Popeye cartoon. Information in the article is corroborated by a press release of about the same date from Fleischer Studios. According to these sources, the process ran as follows.

First, in the story conference, director Dave Fleischer, story chief William Turner, and the chief animators (of whom there were either six, according to *Foto*, or 14, according to the press release) planned the basic storyline and action. Each animator was then assigned one part of the story, which he usually embellished with gags and details of his own invention. Theirs were the basic drawings that laid out the action, but for continuous, smooth motion, the films required thousands of "in-between" drawings; as many as 24 were needed to move Popeye from one basic pose to the next. These drawings were the work of "in-betweeners," a group of some 30 (*Foto*) to 60 (press release). In the large, darkened room where the in-betweeners worked, the press release describes the atmosphere as casual but "absorbed," stating that "everyone was hard at work and obviously enjoying it." The artists, mostly men and a few women, worked at light tables, placing the drawing just completed on the lighted surface and covering

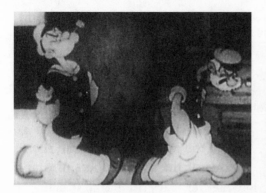 

Left: Popeye walks his father back home after saving the old sailor from a brawl in "With Poopdeck Pappy" (1940). Poopdeck Pappy was featured in several of the cartoons Fleischer produced in their Miami studio. *Right:* A pencil animation test drawing used in the production of the film "Females Is Fickle" (1940). The animation in the cartoons produced after Fleischer Studios moved to Miami, Florida, took on a brighter look.

that drawing with a new sheet of 8 × 10 paper. The light from below made the lines of the first drawing shine through the new paper, so that the artist could trace the basic lines of the previous drawing while making small changes in the position of an arm or leg whatever was supposed to be moving. In all, from 8,000 to 10,000 drawings were needed for a six-minute cartoon.

After approval by Nelly Sanborn, whom *Foto* describes as a 20-year veteran of the animation business and the head of Fleischer's "timing and general check-up department," the paper drawings moved on to the inking department, where they were traced onto 8 × 10 celluloid sheets with India ink. From there, the drawings (now called "cels," for "celluloids") went to the coloring room, where some 50 workers used watercolors to paint the cels in black, white, and various shades of gray. (Coloring was apparently a foot-in-the-door job for young artists. The press release states that coloring "does not require the skill and attention of the original drawings" and describes the workers as younger than the in-betweeners, adding that "a larger proportion are girls." The same may have been true of the inking department; the *Foto* article names an 18-year-old girl as one of the 30 members of that group.)

Meanwhile, another department worked on background shots, which were clearly never neglected or relegated to secondary status in the Fleischer cartoons. The *Foto* article describes a process in which a cameraman, Charles Schettler, "pulls down the glass plate of a flat background camera and automatically records a shot; 12,000 shots make a complete cartoon." These were just the flat backgrounds; the article goes on to mention Max Fleischer's three-dimensional camera and how miniature, revolving sets were constructed to make the most of that device.

When the animation cels were complete in every way, the whole lot were sent to the filming room, where each was individually photographed, as the press release describes:

A animator's model sheet of Poopdeck Pappy from the early 1940s.

The camera is a regular motion camera, and the film is wound exactly as in a regular movie except that the camera is overhead and photographs the drawings placed beneath. The process, however, is much slower when filming a cartoon than when photographing live people. The camera has to be geared so that you can film one drawing at a time. After one is filmed, by pushing a lever, it always takes a little while to arrange the next drawing to be filmed. When making a regular movie, 90 feet of film run through the camera every minute; in making an animated cartoon, it takes three days to cover 90 feet. So, in spite of the fact that Popeye and the rest of the cartoon characters are not in the least temperamental before the camera and always do as they're told, the process is pretty slow. And often there are times when certain sections must be done over if they don't fit in the finished picture.

The product of this laborious process was lovely to look at, but silent. The completed film moved on to the synchronization department at Paramount News Laboratories, where the musicians and sound-effects men, already well rehearsed, watched the film and played along, following a cue sheet for music and sounds arranged by Sam Timberg. (*Foto* states that Timberg "directs the crew of musicians," while the press release refers to Emanuel Baer as "the conductor"; it is conceivable that each conducted on different occasions, or that Timberg's duties as director did not include conducting the orchestra.)

Finally, performers such as William "Billie" Costello (Popeye in the earliest cartoons), Jack Mercer (Popeye in later cartoons), and Mae Questel (Olive Oyl) added the voices for dialogue and songs. The press release describes Costello as "a short, stocky man of about 28, whom Max Fleischer ... discovered while Billie was imitating the voice of a frog." Of Questel, the release notes that she gave voice to many other cartoon characters, including Betty Boop, under whose name "she even made personal appearances."

Clearly, a lot of creative thinking, planning and hard work went into the production of the original Fleischer (and later Famous Studios) Popeye films. Later, when the TV cartoons were produced, many short cuts would be taken to avoid the rising cost of producing animated films.

Apparently Paramount Pictures was not happy with the success of just the Popeye films and wanted other successful series from Fleischer Studios. However, their later series did not have the same success as the Popeye cartoons, and their two attempts at feature-length cartoons, "Gulliver's Travels" (1939) and "Mr. Bug Goes to Town" (1941) didn't generate much excitement either. In 1942 Paramount Pictures took control of Fleischer Studios. They removed the Fleischer brothers, Max and Dave, and moved the studio from Miami back to New York. The exact cause of Paramount's decision to take control of the studio has never been fully revealed. Whatever the cause, this decision left the spinach-eating sailor in the hands of Famous Studios (named after Paramount Pictures' Famous Music Corporation).

Other Work by Fleischer Studios

The complete history of the Fleischer Studios begins with the birth of Max Fleischer in Vienna, Austria, in 1884. Max was taken to the United States when he was four years of age. He studied at the New York Evening High School, the Mechanic's and Tradesman's School, the Arts Students League and the Cooper Union and finally got a job as a photo engraver on the *Brooklyn Eagle*. In 1915 Max began doing research in the field of animation. He and his brother Dave began turning out the "Ko-Ko the Clown" cartoon series in 1915. Max and his brothers (who were involved with the productions of the silent cartoons) often used "rotoscoping" for the cartoons. Rotoscoping, developed by Max Fleischer, is the process of taking a live character's movements and adapting them to animation.

Max and Dave began working for pioneer animator J.R. Bray before forming their own partnership in 1921 called Out-of-the-Inkwell Films, Inc. During the 1920s, the Fleischers turned out many animated films. Besides Ko-Ko cartoons, they produced "Screen Song" films, using the follow-the-bouncing-ball treatment to present song lyrics. The Fleischers' first successful cartoon character actually debuted in the 1930 film "Dizzy Dishes," though she is hard to recognize in this early persona: a sexy, Mae West-type dog. By 1932 and the cartoon "Any Rags," she had become Betty Boop, a very human female.

Betty Boop was the first female cartoon star, and she flaunted her sexuality. Remember that these cartoons weren't aimed at children, but shown prior to or after a big screen movie production, with adults the target audience. (In fact, in the film "Betty Boop's Rise to Fame" [1934], Betty is changing costumes and her breast is briefly revealed in front of the camera.) She was always being approached by characters who wanted to take her "Boop-Boop-a-Doop" away. Ko-Ko the Clown and Bimbo, a moon-faced dog, shared in her animated antics.

By 1934, under the watchful eyes of the motion picture industry, Betty began losing much of her sexuality, and with it much of her charm. She became an old maid type, sharing many of her cartoons with hapless supporting characters who usually stole much of the film from Betty. Her revealing black dress was replaced by a knee-length outfit that was often buttoned to the collar. She even lost her trademark garter belt and gained weight in her limbs. "Grampy," Betty's crackpot inventor companion, was added to the series, and he gave the later

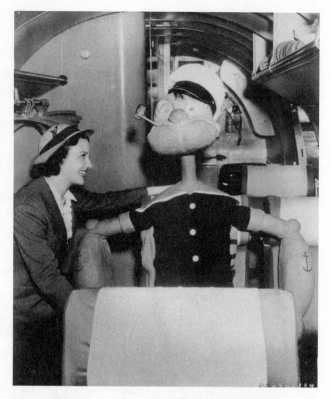

Paramount Pictures created a Popeye mannequin used for publicity purposes, such as being a passenger on an airplane.

films whatever spark they had. He was a favorite with the Fleischers and was used in ten films. The Fleischers tried adapting the comic strip characters "The Little King" and "Henry" to animated film by having them guest in two different Betty Boop cartoons. Oddly enough, though both characters were mute in the comic strips, the Fleischers gave them both speech in the Betty Boop cartoons. Neither character translated well into animation.

It has been stated that the Betty Boop series came to an end in 1939 because the studio was moving to Florida and Mae Questel, Betty's voice, could not make the move. The reasoning is obviously flawed, because Questel was also the voice of Olive Oyl ... a character who continued from Miami, with a new voice. As for Betty Boop, apparently she had had her day in the sun, and it was time for the Fleischers to move in other directions.

One of Fleischer Studios' most expensive projects was adapting the "Superman" series to animation. The budget for each cartoon was $90,000, a sum previously unheard of for an animated short. Paramount Pictures, who distributed and financed the films, gave their approval nevertheless, and the Man of Steel's color series was underway. Extensive rotoscoping was used in the Superman films so the characters wouldn't appear "Popeye-looking," though some sounded very

Above and opposite: Among the songs in this "Popeye Song Folio" is the well-known theme song, "I'm Popeye the Sailor Man."

Theme Song From Paramount's "POPEYE THE SAILOR" Cartoons

I'M POPEYE THE SAILOR MAN

Words and Music by SAMMY LERNER

I'm Pop - eye the Sail - or Man, I'm Pop - eye the Sail - or Man, I'm strong to the "Fin - ich" 'Cause I eats me spin - ach I'm Pop - eye the Sail - or Man.

★ *Symbols for Guitar*

much like a Popeye cartoon because the sailor man's voice, Jack Mercer, was often used for various characters in the Superman cartoons. The Superman series became an outstanding success, and their filming is regarded today as a significant event in the history of animation.

Other cartoon series produced by Fleischer included "Color Classic" (1934–1940), "Stone Age Cartoons" (1940), "Gabby" (1940–41, based on the character who appeared in the Fleischers' animated feature "Gulliver's Travels"), and "Animated Antics" (1940–41). Paramount Pictures also pushed the Fleischer team into producing an animated feature to compete with Walt Disney. The studio's first feature, "Gulliver's Travels," released in 1939, was a moderate success, and Paramount encouraged the Fleischers to produce another. "Mr. Bug Goes to Town" was the Fleischers' second cartoon feature, and mainly because it was released as a second-string picture, it flopped.

At this time, Max and Dave Fleischer were not getting along, and change was in the wind. In 1942 Paramount Pictures took control of the studio, renamed it Famous Studios. The "Superman" series continued for only a few more cartoons, but "Popeye" would stay in production until mid–1957.

Overshadowed by Walt Disney for so many years, Fleischer Studios has recently been receiving the critical praise it long deserved. The joy, humor and outstanding creativity of the people who worked at Fleischer Studios, characteristics they freely gave to their animations, have won them a place in the hearts of Popeye cartoon fans all over the world.

"The Fleischer Popeye Slight"

On October 27, 1992, the A&E network produced a special titled, "Cartoon Madness: The Fantastic Max Fleischer Cartoons." The event was hosted by noted film critic, Leonard Maltin, who professes great affection for the Fleischer Popeye films. If that is true, it was not evident in the special. The TV promos for this special featured a brief scene from the black and white Popeye film, "A Date to Skate" (1938) but Popeye's mention on the special was limited to scant minutes with footage from "Popeye the Sailor Meets Ali Baba and His Forty Thieves" (1937). The footage used had an unsynchronized audio track. (This takes place during the fight scene toward the conclusion of the film and the unsynchronized audio track occurred when the film print was struck for television.) Fleischer's "Superman" series also got just a blip on the television screen while the majority of Fleischer's other shorts were shown in their entirety. Needless to say, Popeye fans were outraged and a letter was sent to Mr. Maltin regarding Fleischer Studio's most successful series being slighted. To his credit, he did reply to Popeye fans via a letter to "The International Popeye Fan Club" dated November 30, 1992.

In the letter Maltin states, "the truth of the matter is that the Max Fleischer show you saw was produced by and for Republic Pictures, which own all of the Fleischer films except Popeye. Because of rights complications, it was not possible to obtain the great Popeye shorts, except for the same few public domain titles, we have seen over and over again."

Unfortunately, that explanation has a few holes in it. During the 1980s, there was a half-hour show called "That's Hollywood" narrated by Tom Bosley. An episode was produced saluting cartoon characters who made it to the big screen. Popeye was included and was represented by the concluding scene from "Popeye the Sailor Meets Sindbad the Sailor" (1936). The scene had excellent video and audio quality and was long enough to get the required information out to the viewing audience. A scene from "Sindbad" could have been used or the complete "A Date to Skate" cartoon, which, along with eight other Fleischer "Popeye" films are in the public domain. This slight was due to the fact that it was produced for Republic Pictures, who, despite the subject matter of the special, did not want to devote needed time to a character they didn't own the rights to. To add further insult, when this special was released on home video, the sailor man was featured prominently on the cover.

"The Doors"

No, this section isn't about the musical group, but rather what Popeye fans have often referred to as the best cartoons from the sailor's film career. "If a Popeye cartoon doesn't have those doors, why watch it?" is usually the way the Fleischer Popeye films are singled out.

For years, as my attention was usually focused in on the "Popeye the Sailor" opening graphics, followed by the title of the particular episode, I thought the doors were from a barn. They looked like the barn doors you would see in an old movie, which someone would slide open in a hurry to let the horses out if there was a fire. It was only recently when a friend of mine said to me, "You call yourself a Popeye fan; those aren't barn doors, those are ship doors." In all the time I spent watching these films, I failed to notice the crashing waves alongside the opening "Popeye the Sailor" graphic and doors. I also missed the anchor and coil of rope pictured in the opening sequences. While I dubbed them barn doors, others have called them the sliding doors or simply, the doors. Technically, they are ship doors and this proves one should never call himself an expert in any field. In the case of Popeye, I'm always learning something new. To set the record straight, not all of the Fleischer cartoons featured the ship doors, and as to whether all the best "Popeye the Sailor" films came from this era has always been a subject of debate.

Famous Studios (1942–1957)

Many ex–Fleischer animators and writers joined the newly formed Famous Studios, so there was no noticeable change when the Popeye series changed studios. In fact, many of the early Famous Studios Popeye films are as good as the cartoons produced by Fleischer.

Many of the themes Fleischer had introduced were continued by Famous especially, in keeping with the times, war themes through 1945. The very first Famous cartoon, "You're a Sap, Mr. Jap," features Popeye doing battle with a

Pictured are the opening titles for the Famous Studios Popeye cartoons. Popeye's head would be seen emerging out of a star followed by the Popeye the Sailor logo. This same logo would later be used for the King Features Syndicate television cartoons.

A 1942 model sheet of Popeye. Note that in the early animated films featuring him in his white sailor's uniform, his necktie was very long. A model sheet was used to help guide different animators working on the same picture.

pair of Japanese spies who claim to want a truce. Popeye eats his spinach pretty early in the cartoon, and the remaining minutes are taken up with one spy's plans to do away with himself to "save face." He decides to eat several strips of firecrackers and drink gasoline! At the cartoon's finish, the Japanese sub sinks into the ocean, with the sound of a toilet flushing on the soundtrack. This film hasn't been aired on television in years.

Famous went on to produce numerous war-themed cartoons. "Scrap the Japs" (1942) has Popeye fighting Japanese spy planes as well as a Japanese battleship. At the cartoon's conclusion, the Japanese soldiers become squealing mice who are trapped in a mouse cage of giant proportions. This cartoon is not aired on television anymore. "Spinach fer Britain" (1943) still is screened on television and features Popeye bringing in a rowboat full of spinach to Britain. Instead of Japanese spies, the sailor has to fend off two bumbling Germans who continually shout, "Heil Hitler!" The German spies are made out to be very foolish and are no match for Popeye once he eats his spinach. At the cartoon's finish, Popeye toots a "V" for victory from his corncob pipe.

Popeye takes a look inside the mouth of a Japanese spy. From the first Famous Studios Popeye film, "You're a Sap, Mr. Jap" (1942).

The Famous Studios version of Olive Oyl graced the cover of this November 1947 edition of *Rexall* Magazine.

"Seein' Red, White 'n' Blue" (1943) is the ultimate in the Popeye cartoons produced during World War II. Bluto wants to get injured to avoid the draft, but Popeye is in charge of the draft board. Popeye and Bluto wind up on the same side in this cartoon, fighting against Hitler, Mussolini, Hirohito, and the devil himself. A gang of Japanese spies, pretending to be little children in an orphanage, clobber Popeye and Bluto until Popeye eats his spinach. Popeye also gives Bluto some spinach (and shoves the can down his throat). Together, the pair beat up the spies. Popeye tells them, "Your emperor [*sic*] in Japan is gonna feel this." He then swings such a massive blow that his fist travels around the globe and bops Hirohito, who says, "It should happen to Hitler." Popeye's fist obligingly circles back to Germany and punches Adolf so hard that his mustache falls off. Mussolini grabs Hitler and cries, "Adolf … speak to me! Waaaah!" Hitler replies, "Booooo!" This cartoon has appeared on television in an edited, colorized version.

Some of Famous Studios' war-themed cartoons dealt with the Home Front. "A Jolly Good Furlough" (1943) has Popeye returning home from the Navy for a little rest. He starts off by getting run over by Olive's car; then his little nephews knock him silly with their "Home Defense" set-up,

Popeye rings the bell to win a box of sweets for his sweetie in "Quick on the Vigor" (1950). By this time the plot line of Popeye and Bluto battling it out for Olive Oyl was driving most of the films.

which includes an air-raid shelter, phony spy planes, and gas masks filled with bees. Popeye gets so upset that he cuts his leave short and goes back to the Navy. "Ration fer the Duration" (1943) also features Popeye's nephews as the sailor tells the lads to plant a victory garden to help the war effort. Popeye then dreams that he meets a giant who is hoarding items that Uncle Sam could use, such as rubber and sugar. Popeye does battle with the giant, then wakes up from his dream to see the garden his nephews have planted, which sprouts tires, nipples, shoes, and other items that will help the war effort along. "Me Musical Nephews" (1942) makes reference to Popeye being "away" (off at sea on military duty), and the whole premise of "The Hungry Goat" (1943) was the animal not being able to find any tin cans to eat because of the scrap-metal drive at that time.

Some war references are secondary to the plot. In the first color cartoon produced by Famous Studios, "Her Honor the Mare" (1943), Popeye's nephews try to sneak a horse into the house. In one scene, the nephews tell Popeye that the painter is coming up. The boys hoist the horse to their room in painter's clothing with a man's face painted on his behind. The face is Hitler's kisser! "We're on Our Way to Rio" (1944) featured traveling sailors Popeye and Bluto stopping in Rio to see the sights. "Mess Production" (1945) featured iron workers Popeye,

Failing to teach her how to drive, Popeye provides Olive with a safer mode of transportation as depicted on this foreign movie poster. The illustration was taken from the 1955 cartoon, "Car-azy Drivers" which was a reworking of "Wimmin Hadn't Oughta Drive" (Fleischer, 1940).

Olive, and Bluto producing products for the war effort and its aftereffects. (Olive's employment in this cartoon reflected another Home Front theme, the fact that many women worked in such industrial plants during the war.)

Though Famous Studios did carry on with some of Fleischer's popular themes, several of the early Popeye films played fast and loose with traditional Popeye elements. Though necessarily triumphant in his war adventures, Famous' Popeye in other cartoons was often portrayed as a buffoon rather than a hero, letting his nephews and his little sailor pal, Shorty, get the better of him.

The films where Popeye spent most of his screen time becoming a victim of various assaults were under the direction of Dan Gordon. Gordon took the series in a different direction eliminating the spinach and allowing Popeye to act as a straight man to the antics of his nephews and other menaces. As a child, watching these cartoons, I was never thrilled with the film's contents where Popeye took a thrashing often worse than what Bluto gave him.

In "Happy Birthdaze" (1943), Olive throws a birthday party for Popeye, who brings Shorty along. Shorty manages to flood Olive's bathroom, hit Popeye over the head with a golf ball, sling a hockey puck in Popeye's mouth and end up in the furnace with Popeye. When Olive discovers the big hole Shorty made in her floor, she thinks it's Popeye's fault. Angrily, she pushes Popeye's birthday cake through the floor, and it lands on Popeye with the candle sticking out of his oversized pipe. As Shorty sings, "Happy birthday to my pal," the scene grows dark and we hear a gunshot coming from Popeye's direction, making for a gruesome finish. "The Hungry Goat" (1943) features a goat on the lookout for food who takes a liking to the boat Popeye is working on. Popeye's attempts to stop the goat from eating parts of the boat are useless as the sailor gets bopped about at every turn. The admiral of the boat is watching the goat's antics from a movie theater (which is playing "The Hungry Goat" on the screen). As Popeye runs after the goat, a little boy seated next to the admiral says, "Aw, why don't Popeye eat his spinach and sock him one?" "Me Musical Nephews" (1942) has Popeye's nephews driving their tired uncle crazy by playing homemade instruments

Popeye serenades his beloved Olive Oyl in a publicity still from the early Famous Studios era cartoons.

late at night. Popeye goes nuts at the end of the cartoon and jumps off the movie screen and out of the theater the cartoon is playing in. "Woodpeckin'" (1943) features Popeye trying to find a good tree to build a mast with. The sailor picks a tree that houses a woodpecker. After the two battle over the tree, Popeye realizes that he shouldn't take the bird's home. He allows the bird to live in the tree, which gets planted in his ship.

The last black and white Popeye cartoon was 1943's "Cartoons Ain't Human." In this film Popeye makes an animated cartoon featuring himself and Olive as stick figures. Popeye's nephews also appeared in this cartoon.

The first color cartoon for Famous Studios' Popeye series was "Her Honor the Mare" (1943). In this cartoon Popeye's nephews attempt to keep a horse as a house pet. Popeye's sailor uniform was navy blue in this film, and it would appear in this color a few times during the run of the remaining cartoons. "Mess Production" (1944) was the first cartoon where Olive had a different hairdo. She was now featured with a big clump of hair at her forehead.

Many of the pre–1950 Famous Studios Popeye films were remakes of early Fleischer material. "For Better or Nurse" (1945) was a remake of "Hospitaliky" (1937); "House Tricks" (1946) was a reworking of 1938's "The House Builder-

Upper"; "Barking Dogs Don't Fight" (1949) was a remake of 1937's "Proteck the Weakerest"; and 1949's "The Fly's Last Flight" was a remake of 1941's "Flies Ain't Human." "Popeye's Premiere" (1949) was the first of three cartoons to incorporate footage from the three two-reel Popeye specials produced by the Fleischer Studios. "Popeye's Premiere" featured footage from Aladdin"; 1950s "Popeye Makes a Movie" featured footage from "Popeye Meets Ali Baba and His Forty Thieves"; and 1952's "Big Bad Sindbad" used footage from "Sindbad the Sailor." The best of the three was "Big Bad Sindbad," in which Popeye (in his original sailor's uniform to match the old scenes) tells his nephews about his encounter with the burly sailor.

Many of the comic strip Popeye cast who appeared in the Fleischer series appeared very little in the Famous Studios cartoons. Wimpy was in only a handful of films: "Popeye Makes a Movie" (1950), "Penny Antics" (1955), "Assault and Flattery" (1956), and one of the last cartoons produced for the theater screen, "Spree Lunch" (1957). Swee'pea appeared in "Baby Wants Spinach" (1950), "Thrill of Fair" (1951), "Child Sockology" (1953), and "Nurse to Meet Ya" (1955). Swee'pea's character design was altered so that the lad looked like any ordinary child and not the character presented in the comic strip or Fleischer films. He appeared in a red baby's gown and bonnet with one strand of curly hair on his forehead. Poopdeck Pappy was in two cartoons, "Popeye's Pappy" (1952) and "Baby Wants a Battle" (1953).

By the mid–1950s, the basic plot line of the series was Bluto stealing Olive from Popeye, who would then eat his spinach and save Olive. While the standards on the animation remained high throughout the production of the series, the repeated plot lines began to wear thin. By 1956 the series was ready for a close despite some interesting films: "Assault and Flattery" (1956), in which Bluto sues Popeye for the injuries the sailor has given him over the years; "Insect to Injury" (1956), in which Popeye battles an army of termites; and "Nearly Weds" (1957), in which Popeye and Olive almost get married. With the 1957 film "Spooky Swabs," Popeye's movie career as a cartoon character came to a close. Most of the Fleischer and Famous cartoons had sold to Associated Artists Productions for television syndication the year before.

It should be noted that the discontinuation of the Popeye series had nothing to do with the sailor's decline in popularity in theatres. The Popeye animated series was still Paramount Pictures' most financially successful property. Paramount Pictures was going through a difficult period and the idea of selling their backlog of animated cartoons to the still relatively new medium of television was a way to get a quick infusion of cash.

The Voices Behind the Faces

Popeye

One of the most amusing things about watching a "Popeye" cartoon from any year or produced by any studio is the voice of the one-eyed sailor performed by Jack Mercer. Alas, Mercer hasn't received the wide media acclaim that others in his field have. This lack of recognition is a shame, for one of the reasons for the character's enduring appeal in animation has been Mercer's vocals.

Popeye's original voice was that of William Costello, who played "Gus Gorilla" on the "Betty Boop" radio show. Costello had a gruff-sounding Popeye voice that was very suitable to the character in the early cartoons. However, studio chiefs at Fleischer began to feel that in order to ensure the success of the series, Popeye's character needed to be softened up a bit. At about the same time, Costello was becoming difficult to work with. Eventually he asked for a vacation in the middle of production, and the Fleischers fired him.

Costello's long career included stage work with Ginger Rogers and mainly as a drummer in the Paul Whiteman stage band when Bing Crosby was a singer with the orchestra. Throughout his musical career, he worked with 101 orchestras. He also recorded songs from the early Popeye films. He passed away on October 11, 1971, at the age of 73.

Jack Mercer was also a talented cartoonist. Pictured is a cartoon of Popeye by Mercer.

A new Popeye voice had to be located at once. A few in-betweeners did the voice, but none was suited for the character's long-term success. Jack Mercer was working as an in-betweener at the Fleischer Studios when Lou Fleischer overheard him doing a Popeye impression. Lou thought, "This is the new Popeye," and rushed to announce he had found the sailor man's new vocal artist. Mercer, however, was not far from advancement to full animator and at this time, animators were in very short supply. Although hesitant to accept this new role, Mercer became Popeye's new voice.

Mercer had always wanted to be an entertainer and came from a show business family. His parents had even used Jack, as an infant, in their vaudeville act. Jack went on to play child parts in theater and became a tap dancer. Mercer's parents encouraged him to find another profession, fearing that in the theater it would be too difficult for him to find steady employment. But when Mercer began his work in Fleischer's animation department, he looked upon it as still being in show business.

After Mercer assumed the Popeye role, he discovered that doing the voice

Jack Mercer with Hanna-Barbera's 1978–1983 version of his famous alter ego.

wasn't that easy. Mercer would record several takes, only to discover that his voice was becoming very hoarse. It took a little while, but soon Mercer became accustomed to Popeye's manner of speech, and the "Popeye" series (under the Fleischers) received a boost thanks to Mercer's ad-libbing and mumbles.

Popeye, however, wasn't the only character that Mercer voiced for the series. He also provided the vocals for Popeye's father, Poopdeck Pappy; Popeye's nephews (who spoke words in turn to complete one sentence; for example, "But," "we," "don't," "like," "spinach"); Bluto; Popeye's pal Shorty (in the first two cartoons Shorty appeared in); and, in the King Features TV cartoons as well as the

1936 film "Popeye the Sailor Meets Sindbad the Sailor," J. Wellington Wimpy. Mercer also supplied the voices for any extras which were heard in the Popeye cartoons. If Popeye was chatting with a policeman or a clerk, that character's voice would be done by Mercer.

When Famous Studios took over the Popeye series from the Fleischers, Mercer continued performing his regular Popeye duties as well as voicing cartoon characters who appeared in Famous Studios "Harveytoon" film series, including "Little Audrey," "Casper the Friendly Ghost," "Herman and Katnip," "Sing-a-Longs," and "Baby Huey." By this time in his career, Mercer had also become a writer for hundreds of the animated cartoons produced by Paramount Pictures, including Popeye cartoons.

When Famous Studios stopped production on "Popeye," Mercer continued providing the vocals for cartoon characters associated with films produced by Paramount Cartoon Studios. He also continued his association with Popeye by providing the voice for the spinach-eater on several record albums throughout the 1950s, 1960s and 1970s. Many record albums billed Mercer as "the original Popeye voice." By this time, William Costello's association with the character was long forgotten, though Costello's cartoons continued to be broadcast on television and he made personal appearances as the sailor.

Mercer became the voice for "Felix the Cat" and all the animated characters who appeared in the feline's adventures for the small screen from 1959 to 1962. Mercer's vocals were used for "The Professor," "Rick Bottom" (who sounded just like Mercer's version of "Brutus" on the Popeye records), "The Master Cylinder" and "Poindexter." Mercer once said that "Felix" had a wimpy-sounding voice. Mercer's voice can also be heard in a few "Adventures of Hercules" TV cartoons, and he later returned to voice both Popeye and Wimpy for the TV special "The Man Who Hated Laughter," which aired as part of "The ABC Saturday Superstar Movie."

In 1978, Hanna-Barbera would revive Popeye for Saturday mornings for CBS, and Mercer would return as both voice artist and writer. He found writing for these new, nonviolent cartoons a little difficult and didn't feel that they had to be cleaned up. Mercer felt that Popeye was the underdog and only defended himself when he needed to.

Mercer's Popeye voice roughed with age, but this seemed to suit the Hanna-Barbera character design. When the Hanna-Barbera series ended production, Mercer continued to voice the sailor in a series of television commercials, as he had during the 1960s following the syndication of the King Features Syndicate "Popeye" cartoon series. During the early 1940s when Jack Mercer was serving in the armed services, others filled in on the Popeye voice, most notably Harry Welch, who later recorded the sailor's vocals on a series of children's records. The non–Mercer voiced Popeye cartoons for Famous Studios are: "Shape Ahoy" (1944); "For Better or Nurse" (1944); "House Tricks" (1946); "Service with a Guile" (1946); "Klondike Casanova" (1946); "Peep in the Deep" (1946); "Rocket to Mars" (1946 Mercer started this cartoon but Welch finished it.); "Rodeo Romeo" (1946); "The Fistic Mystic" (1947); "The Island Fling" (1947); "Abusement Park" (1947).

Over 50 King Features comic strip characters appeared in a 60 minute special, "The Man Who Hated Laughter," that aired as part of the "ABC Superstar Movie." This special was also known as "Popeye Meets the Man Who Hated Laughter."

In some of the above films, a one-line piece of dialogue in Mercer's voice was used. For example, Welch voiced Popeye for the cartoon "This Island Fling," but when the sailor opens up a treasure chest and says, "Gee, thanks for the tip pal," that line is Mercer's. The same occurrence happens in the cartoon "The Fistic Mystic" as Popeye jumps upon a mattress with spikes.

After Mercer's passing in 1984, Maurice LeMarche voiced Popeye for the 1987-88 series "Popeye and Son," but Mercer was a tough act to follow and no one has really been able to duplicate his vocals for the character. When reporting Mercer's passing on "Entertainment Tonight," Rob Weller put it best: "Popeye gained his strength from spinach, but his personality was shaped by Jack Mercer." In a sense, Jack Mercer will never be gone as long as television stations continue to run the several hundred cartoons to which he brought so much life.

Mrs. Virginia Mercer, until her passing in 2000, frequently sent letters to various newspapers and magazines, which featured stories on other men claiming to be the voice of Popeye. Unfortunately, there were many that claimed to be the sailor's voice with erroneous facts on which to base their claims. It is

Harry Foster Welch, performed live Popeye shows, which was one of his talents.
The Popeye art was drawn by Joe Musial.

astounding that the media would even publish these claims without checking facts. For example, when William Costello, Popeye's original voice passed on in 1971, the *New York Times* ran his obituary which stated, "who for 25 years was the screen voice of Popeye the Sailor Man." When Harry Foster Welch's obituary was printed in *Variety* the paper referred to him as "creating the voice of Popeye." Mrs. Mercer wrote to *Variety* and clarified the situation by stating, "Welch had permission to dress as the character." Welch, indeed used the character of Popeye in several of his live shows including an appearance on "Pleasure Island," New England's version of a smaller scale, "Disneyland." Welch's debut appearance as Popeye broke attendance records up to that point in the park's history. While both Costello and Welch did have real associations with the Popeye character, Mrs. Mercer often had to deal with men who stated that they were Popeye's voice just by wearing a sailor's suit and puffing up their cheeks in public!

Olive Oyl

Mae Questel was Max Fleischer's first choice for Olive Oyl's voice. Questel also provided the voice for Fleischer's other popular female character, "Betty Boop." Questel has claimed she also provided Popeye's vocals while Jack Mercer was in the service.

Mae's parents encouraged her to study dramatics and singing. Questel later won a Helen Kane lookalike contest and was signed to Paramount to perform in the RKO chain of theaters in 1931. Max Fleischer saw her act and asked her to do the voice of Betty Boop, and later, Olive Oyl. Mae went on to voice many of the female characters in animated films produced by Paramount Pictures.

When the Fleischer studio moved to Miami, Mae was unable to go with them. Margie Hines replaced Questel as the voice of Olive Oyl and was equally effective performing the vocals. Hines also provided Olive's voice in the early Famous Studios Popeye films, but Questel returned to the part in 1944 after Paramount's animation studio moved back to New York.

Mae Questel, with Jack Mercer and Jackson Beck, would provide all of the vocals for the 220 Popeye TV cartoons that would be produced by King Features Syndicate in 1960 and 1961. Aside from Olive's voice, Questel also provided vocals for Swee'pea and the Sea Hag in these cartoons! Questel also became known as "Aunt Bluebell" in a series of paper towel commercials during the late 1960s and the 1970s.

Questel recalled the origins of the Olive Oyl voice: "Max Fleischer showed it to me (the storyboard). I thought there is an actress that sort of reminds me of a scrawny lady that's always using her hands and I thought, that should sound like Olive Oyl and it was a crackly kind of voice: Yoo-hooooo! Here I yamaamm-hm-hm-hm-hm! It's Olive Oyl and of course, Max seemed to like the voice and we used it!" As for the other characters, she voiced in the TV cartoons, she recalled, "Since then I have been Swee'pea and the Sea Hag, who is a witch, who says, "Go forth, Popeye, and do what I tell you! You! I'm gonna kill you!" Beyond her voice work, Questel also appeared in feature films, *A Majority of One* (1962), *It's Only Money* (1962), *Funny Girl* (1968), *Zeling* (1983), *National*

Mae Questel with many of the characters she's provided voices for over the years: Popeye, Spooky the Tuff Little Ghost, Winky Dink, Bimbo, Betty Boop, Casper the Friendly Ghost, and Olive Oyl. Questel also provided the voices for Swee'pea and the Sea Hag for the 1960-61 King Features television cartoons.

Lampoon's Christmas Vacation (1989) and *New York Stories* (1989). Questel's passing in 1998 was mentioned in the major news magazines, recalling the actress who gave Betty Boop and Olive Oyl spark and personality. Questel still pops up in feature films, and there is no mistaking her Olive Oyl voice.

In later years, Marilyn Schreffler would provide the voice of Olive Oyl for Hanna-Barbera's "All New Popeye" cartoons and for "Popeye and Son."

Jackson Beck, the voice of Bluto and Brutus.

Schreffler was very effective in saying Olive's trademark line: "Help ... Popeye ... Help!"

Bluto/Brutus

William Penell was the voice of Bluto for the early Fleischer cartoons. Gus Wickie, a baritone member of a vocal quartet used by Paramount Pictures, later assumed the voice. Wickie's trademark laugh, "Oh-ho-ho-ho," from the 1930s Fleischer films is often recalled by Fleischer fans. After Wickie, the studio used a few in-betweeners until Jack Mercer and Pinto Colvig took over Bluto's voice as well for a handful of films.

After Mercer, the voice went to a few more in-betweeners before Jackson Beck settled in the role. Beck started voicing Bluto in 1944 with the Famous Studios cartoon "The Anvil Chorus Girl." Beck recalled how he got the job voicing Bluto, "They gave me an idea of what I was supposed to do. I don't think anybody sat me down and had me listen to a cartoon. I don't really remember. I suddenly walked in there, and they said, 'Let's hear you do a gruff voice.' They liked what I did. I came into a room, and they said, 'That's it, you're hired!' I'm sure I didn't hear the other guys (previous Bluto voices) do it, except that I probably had seen a Popeye cartoon in a movie house, so I had a rough idea. So I did it from then on. You know I did Bluto for many, many years and I enjoyed every darn minute of it!"

Beck was also the radio announcer for the "Superman" radio program and later handled the same job for the 1966 "Superman" cartoon series. Beck would also provide the voice for Brutus, the Bluto replacement who would appear in the King Features TV cartoons of 1960-61. He also went on to do voices for many male characters in cartoons produced by Paramount Pictures (a job he shared with Jack Mercer). Beck's voice could also be heard on the "King Leonardo" cartoon series as well as "Underdog" and "Tennessee Tuxedo." Beck's voice has been used for countless television commercials, and he has appeared on the small screen in various character roles.

In the late 1970s and into the 1980s, television actor Allan Melvin, who played "Sam" on "The Brady Bunch," would provide Bluto's voice for both the "All New Popeye Hour" and the "Popeye and Son" cartoons by Hanna-Barbera.

The Lost Famous Studios' Popeye Cartoon

The following was researched and written by Tom Bertino, a member of "The International Popeye Fan Club" and printed in the organization's news magazine in the Summer 1992 edition:

I saw a new Popeye cartoon, a Famous Studios production that nobody had ever seen, unfold before my eyes almost. The cartoon I refer to never, in fact made it to the final stages of production. But through the miracle of good luck, an elaborate 140-panel color storyboard survived in the basement of a Famous animator. I have seen the entire set of drawings and would like to present to the club members a Popeye cartoon that they have never seen— one that nobody, in fact, ever will see. The fact that Popeye appears in his blue navy uniform and Olive retains her comic strip look, indicates that the board dates from around 1943 to 1945. As you will see, the most likely reason the picture never reached the screen was a censorship problem. The whole concept, and some of the specific dialogue and imagery would have been quite out of bounds in those days. It's a shame. It would have made a great cartoon.

We open at a tourist attraction, "Dante's Cavern," where Bluto is the ticket taker. Popeye and Olive enter, with Popeye's nephews in tow. Bluto flirts with Olive, who lingers at the gate. Popeye re-enters and whisks her away. Inside, we see a vast cavern dotted with dangerous looking stalactites. The kids ask, "Uncle Popeye, what made this place like this?" "Well kids," Popeye replies, "years ago Olive and me was skiing right over this mountain." In a flashback we see Popeye and Olive enjoying a skiing vacation, finally piling up in a snow drift at the bottom of the mountain. As they poke their heads out of the snow, Bluto appears as the Devil, complete with horns and a flowing red cape! He sings: "I am the King of Hades and I want the prettiest of ladies to be my Queen!"

Olive gushes, "You big handsome devil!" Bluto snaps into action and he scoops Olive up and whisks her back down the smoky tunnel. Popeye declares, "I must save Olive from that devil!" As he reaches the hole, an elevator car shoots up, driven by a little devil. "Going down?" Popeye jumps in, and the car goes into a fast fall. As the temperature rises, the car burns up. "Somebody must be talking about me," mutters Popeye, as he plummets. "My ears are burning." He falls into a pit of molten lava, where another devil is taking a bath, scrubbing his back with a pitchfork. The devil hoists Popeye out with his fork and complains in a sissy voice, "Can't a guy have some privacy?"

Popeye charges through hell's fiery halls, finding himself in the vast throne room. There sits Olive, crowned Queen of Hades. As Bluto kisses her, she melts ("I'm just butter in his hands"), but quickly pulls herself back together and gives Bluto a kiss that makes him burst into flames. Popeye charges forward with blood in his eyes but Bluto thrusts out a hand of friendship, offering a seat. As Popeye settles down, he realizes he's sitting in an electric chair! The juice shoots through him, and he dances around with flames running down his back like an Indian headdress.

Popeye and Bluto then engage in a tug of war with Olive in the middle, which ends when Bluto gives Popeye a poke with his sharp devil tail. Bluto then transforms into a blowtorch and gives Popeye a blast. The sailor grabs a hose to put his enemy out, but the hose shoots fire and Bluto loves it. After a little more grappling, Popeye is clearly overheated. Bluto signals a devil Good Humor Man, who supplies Popeye with a popsicle—a Tabasco popsicle! Bluto

A storyboard sketch of Hades (Bluto) and Popeye from the unfinished Famous Studio's production (courtesy of Tom Bertino).

is tired of toying by this time and one punch leaves Popeye dangling at the end of a rope, over a pit of fire and devils with pitchforks.

As Popeye struggles, Bluto and his Queen sit down to dinner. Dinner consists of logs and coal, washed down by gasoline! For after dinner entertainment, a humanoid flame does a striptease using puffs of smoke as fans! This is all too much for Olive, who, by now desperately wants to escape Bluto. Bluto pulls her closer and transforms into a blast furnace. Meanwhile, the burning rope to which Popeye clings is dropping him closer and closer to the mass of pitchforks waiting below. Popeye pulls out a can of spinach and eats its contents. The power travels up the rope, mends it at the instant it breaks, then returns to Popeye, and encases him in a suit of ice armor. With a blast of ice-cold breath, he freezes the entire pit. He then shimmies up the rope to save Olive, who is being pursued by Bluto in the form of a rampaging fire-belching steam locomotive. One blast of Popeye's freezing breath slams him into a wall, where he is reduced to a large can of "Canned Heat." This done, Popeye blows his breath all around the cave, literally, "freezing hell over!" What's left is a glistening ice cavern, where the devils now enjoy winter sports.

We now return to the present, where Popeye is concluding his story. The nephews are skeptical that he could have gone through this experience and not even gotten burned, and one of then proceeds to give him a hot foot. Popeye jumps in pain and lands with a thud. He looks up, and we see what he sees: his nephews as four sizzling little devils. The cartoon ends on this image.

The content and imagery of this cartoon certainly took the Popeye-Olive-Bluto romance triangle in quite a different direction. A few years back, thanks to Mr. Bertino's research, I was able to identify sketches from this cartoon being sold by an animation firm, but under the Famous Studios' entry, "I'll Be Skiing Ya" (1947).

Popeye and the Pastor

I can't say that I have ever met a Popeye fan who dresses in a sailor's uniform, eats spinach right out of a can or smokes a pipe, but there are people who incorporate the sailor's traits in their daily life. One such individual is Steve Bierly, a pastor, whose favorite "Popeye" films are the cartoons produced by Famous Studios. He was born in 1955 and was a graduate of Roberts Wesleyan College. Ordained in 1982, he is the author of two books about the ministry. He remembers watching Popeye on TV every day, even several times a day. A lifelong Popeye fan, having grown up in the era when the cartoons were continually broadcast on television, he would begin each day at the seminary by getting up to watch the cartoons being broadcast on a Boston station very early in the morning. Bierly is a pastor at the Reformed Church in America in Hull, IA. He discovered that Popeye, Olive Oyl, Bluto and the rest of the cast of characters can actually be used to teach spiritual lessons as well as entertain. On Bierly's website and in his articles published in the news magazine of The International Popeye Fan Club, he has written several essays linking Popeye and spiritualism, such as the following:

I Yam Popeye the Sailor Man

One of the many reasons that Popeye and his supporting cast have remained favorites of mine over the years is that I can relate to them. Seriously! I know the ways that they think and feel, because at various points in my life, I have thought and felt the same things. I have found myself imitating their actions, for better or worse. At times, I even wanted to be them. When I was a young boy watching Popeye cartoon after Popeye cartoon, the sailor was my hero. He, like Bugs Bunny, had the ability to take whatever anybody dished out and come out on top. And Popeye has super strength, too! How cool was that! The fantasy of every child. Popeye also had a "magical" way to escape danger or difficulty which seemed at first too much for him. When the going got too rough, he would eat his spinach and, suddenly, the tables would be turned and everything would work out all right.

What kid wouldn't want that? I certainly did. I would have given anything to be able to instantly be a better athlete, or to suddenly gain the muscles needed to beat up the school bullies, or to be able to do my chores and homework at super speed. Even as adults, we have the tendency to want someone or something to enter our lives and instantly make everything okay. A hard fact of life, though, is that some problems take quite a while to solve and wounds, emotional and physical, need time to heal. And sometimes, we, ourselves, hold the key to the solution of our problems. We need to make changes, or take risks, or make amends, etc. A quick fix just won't do it. Yet still the fantasy endures.

As I grew older, and even today, one thing I came to appreciate about Popeye was his determination to do what he believed was right no matter what other people thought, said, and did, no matter if anyone would join him or not.

Olive is smitten with Bluto, "The Fistic Mystic" (Famous Studios, 1947). Footage from this cartoon was later used in "Penny Antics" (Famous Studios, 1955).

> At my best, I have done this, too. And as a pastor, I'm duty bound to preach the Word of God as best I can understand it, even those parts of it that go against popular notions. Thanks for being one of my role models, Popeye!

Bierly feels that Famous Studios' redesign of Olive Oyl gave her an exuberance of life, innocence, faith in Popeye, despite impossible odds and a love for romance without letting guys take advantage of her. Famous Studios gave Bluto a confidence, intelligence, ability to focus on his goal, and a suave manner, which made the character so much more than just a gruff, blowhard bully. In Bierly's preachings and children's sermons he uses the examples of Popeye initially losing Olive because he was neglectful or Olive being smitten with another man so easily in discussions about what true love involves and what not to do when trying to win someone's heart. Youth workers have also contacted Bierly about how to use Popeye during weekend retreats.

An Animator's-Eye View

Between them, Fleischer and Famous Studios produced 234 Popeye films from 1933 to 1957. Many animators poured their best efforts into these works, including Robert Bentley, Frank Endres, Al Eugster, George Germanetti, William Henning, Seymour Kneitel (who also wrote several scripts for the series), Abner Matthews, Thomas Moore, Joe Oriolo, Sidney Pillet, Morey Reden, Gordon Sheehan, Ben Solomon, Dave Tendlar, and Myron Waldman.

Gordon Sheehan had just been hired by Fleischer when the first Popeye cartoon was gearing up for production in 1933. Popeye's animation debut was Sheehan's first experience in motion picture animation, a business in which he would continue for more than 50 years. In an article called "Vintage Popeye Is Good Popeye," which appeared in the newsletter of the International Popeye Fan Club, Sheehan reflected on his years at Fleischer and Famous, and on the history of the cartoon series:

> As an ex–Popeye animator with the old Max Fleischer Studios, I am frequently asked, "Why are the POPEYE animated cartoons that were produced in the 1930s and early 1940s so much more entertaining than those produced in the late 1940s and the 1950s?"
>
> I could be facetious and reply that the quality of the Popeye films started deteriorating as soon as I left the studio in 1944 (then Famous Studios), to take a job animating war-time films for the U.S. Navy. But this would be a ridiculous statement since I was only one of the several animators working at that time on the fabulous little spinach-devouring sailor character.
>
> Of course a lot of the seasoned Popeye animators and assistants were in the service during the war years 1941–1945, most of them with the Army Signal Corps or the Navy Photographic Center in Anacostia. This had a definite weakening effect on the quality of the war-time Popeyes. But then, most of these fellows returned to Famous and Popeye at the end of the war, with the exception of a few.
>
> Some say that it was after Max and Dave Fleischer lost their studio to Paramount in 1942 that the Popeye films started to become decadent. Yet, Paramount kept the same old producing staff pretty well intact after the changeover. Seymour Kneitel (Max's son-in-law), Izzy Sparber, and Sam Buchwald were still holding the reins for the studio just as they did during the Fleischer era.
>
> The average movie watcher seems to think that persons with the largest screen credits (usually the producers) are almost entirely responsible for all the wonderful things that happen in animated films (Disney, Lantz, Schlesinger, etc.); this is far from true. The main function of the producer really is getting together a large staff of talented, creative people whose contributions can make or break an animated production. I think this was quite true at Fleischer (with no intention of belittling Max or Dave's abilities and expertise). The Fleischers arranged the production schedule and had the final say on choosing the stories. But once a story had been approved and assigned to an animation group, it was pretty much up to the fellows at the animation boards, the head animator and his team of animators and assistants, to turn out a good film within a limited budget.
>
> Which leads me to my opinion of what made Popeye so great in the 1930s and early 1940s era, and so mediocre after that. I think the early esprit-de-corps and the pride of the early Popeye-producing animators were the key factors of success of the series in its first decade of production. As this spirit waned in the later 40s the series became less and less appealing, until it finally faded into obsolescence.
>
> Another reason for the dwindling quality of the Popeye films, some would say, was the increasing costs of labour. Most animators were paid a modest,

but above the per capita average salary, during the 30s and early 40s. With the organizing of the union wages increased year by year, and producers started to use every short-cut trick and gimmick conceivable to cut down on the animators' production time. Today the average animated cartoon is extremely limited in action and attractiveness compared to the full animation of the "good old days." But to get back to the constantly increasing salaries of animators, the prices animated shorts sold for increased too, so this should have largely offset the increased wages.

There were five animation groups when I started animating at Fleischer Studios in New York in 1935. Not all groups were working on Popeye. Some were specialists on Betty Boop, the Bouncing Ball, Color Classics and other Fleischer productions. But all five were in good-natured competition for quality with each other. Each group numbered about seven: the head animator, three key animators, and three assistants.

And all five groups were also competing with the rival studios, most of which were in California; the leader being, of course, Disney. This competition paid off for the Fleischer animators when the Popeye cartoons, even though produced on a much smaller budget, started to surpass the great Mickey Mouse at the theatre box office in the 1930s.

In those days every animator took pride in his productive capabilities. Fleischer animation groups were fun groups. About a week before one picture would be finished animating, a new story script would come in from the writing department. The head animator would make a story-board on 11 × 14 inch paper, roughly laying out the action for the entire story. When finished, the story-board would be tacked upon a wall and the whole group would gather around as the head animator explained the entire story. Then the comments would start from everyone in the group, assistants and all. There were suggestions for making certain scenes funnier by adding gags or funny actions. Imaginative little things that, while not adding much to the cost of production, greatly enhanced the humour of the presentation, a sort of "humour think tank!"

None of the animators were accomplished actors and most would have been scared to death on any stage, but each animator acted out, however crudely, any complex action he might encounter. And Popeye was active. There were never many held poses, such as seem to be the backbone of contemporary animated cartoons. There was in each animation room a large piece of carpet, which could be rolled out onto the floor whenever an animator wanted to "get the feel" of a falling down or rolling around action. And there was a big full-length mirror for the animator to observe his natural body movements while roughly acting out a scene. And, of course, each animator and assistant had his own personal mirror attached to his desk so that he could mimic himself doing mouth actions and facial expressions.

All pictures were given a strict budget and bonuses were given to the group that came under this budget. This helped too to make each group work as a team although sometimes, but not often, to the sacrifice of quality.

If dance steps or a special funny walk were needed for a cartoon character to perform, the veteran former star vaudevillian dancer, Jack Ward, was called in. Jack would go through the routine, freezing occasionally for the animator to make quick pencil sketches to be later transposed into the cartoon character's action. The famous songwriter and showman, Sam Timberg, and his assistants were always available to the animators when songs and music had to be adapted to animation action.

Later on, after the cartoon cels were photographed, Jack Mercer, the voice of Popeye, would study the finished film before recording and write puns and side remarks that didn't require lip-sync. When recorded, these ad-

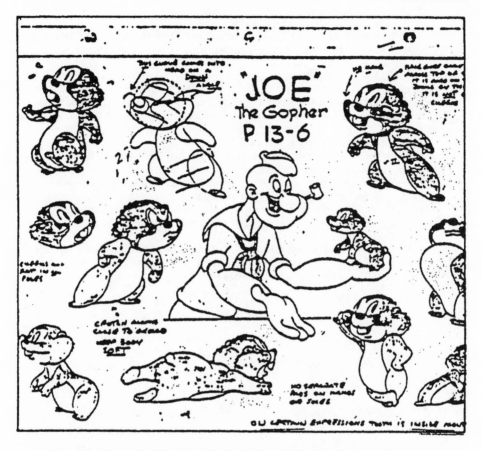

A model sheet for "Joe the Gopher" from "Gopher Spinach" (1954).

lib gags would appear as Popeye mumbling to himself. They richly enhanced Popeye's personality and provoked additional laughs from the audience.

Popeye animators were constantly observing and studying ways to improve their craft. The Trans Lux Newsreel theatre was directly across the street from the studio and twice weekly it featured the best of the competitors' cartoons. Most of the animators, whenever there was a change in programs, made a habit of grabbing a quick sandwich at lunchtime and ducking across Broadway to catch the Trans Lux hour show, to study what Disney and the other rival cartoon studios were coming up with. There was also a nearby movie house just off Broadway on 46th St. that showed a full hour of animated cartoons for a quarter. This too was patronized regularly by most of the animators for purposes of studying the latest trends in animation, and many animators went to the regular movies just to study the pantomime and comic artistry of such masters as Wallace Beery, Charles Chaplin, Ben Blue and the host of other greats. The animators would usually sit in the last row of the theatre, jotting down notes and making quick sketches of the actions on a cheap pad, later to be incorporated into the antics of Popeye or some other cartoon character. Nowadays it would have been much handier to sit in one's home, watch TV and leisurely study the great actors and actresses on the re-run movies.

I think things started to change in Popeye films when some do-good crusaders, during the 1940s, [were] starting to preach that Popeye was too violent to show to child audiences. Less action and more so-called "child psychology" was written into the scripts at the expense of laughs. This took the heart of the old "action" animators.

Later, I heard that Popeye cartoon production was farmed out to small individual studios, most of whom didn't keep the original Popeye character the same, and were only interested in knocking out films in the cheapest way possible, attempting to improve the script or adding any humour, capitalizing only on the Popeye name. Humour, which takes special effort, imagination and enthusiasm, became secondary.

Probably the most enjoyable job I ever had in my life was animating Popeye. I never thought of him as being violent as some critics have complained. He was always actively trying to do what was just and right. When he socked someone, as he did frequently, he wasn't doing it for sadistic spite or vengeance. He did it to solve a problem that had to be solved at the time to maintain justice. He got across a message of right and wrong, not by preaching, but by action.

I was sorry to see the animated Popeye series fade, but it is consoling to know that TV re-runs and home movies still keep the popularity of the "good old" Popeye films alive for new generations of kids to enjoy.

PART
THREE

Popeye on Television

SEE

Susie's Show

4:00 to 4:30 PM
Monday through Friday

channel **2** WBBM-TV
CHICAGO'S SHOWMANSHIP TELEVISION STATION
◉ **CBS TELEVISION**

In September of 1956, Paramount Pictures sold the Popeye film library to Associated Artists Productions for television syndication (while the remaining Famous Studios films were wrapping up production). In theatrical release, the cartoons opened and closed with the Paramount trademark, a mountain with stars around it, preceding the "Popeye the Sailor" title. The mountain, and in some cases, the "Popeye the Sailor" titles, were replaced with the A.A.P. title slide to indicate the television syndicator.

The films premiered in New York and Chicago on September 10, 1956. They were seen weekdays on WPIX, hosted by Captain Allen Swift (who later recorded Popeye children's records impersonating the sailor's vocals) and on WBBM's "Susie's Show." In Los Angeles, Tom Hatten of KTLA-TV also presented the films on weekdays, initially from 7:00 to 7:30 P.M. and later in the afternoons. For years, Uncle Gus of WMUR-TV channel nine in Manchester, New Hampshire, hosted "Popeye Theatre" (later retitled, "The Uncle Gus Show").

Practically every station in the United States carried the Fleischer/ Famous Studios cartoons, usually with an adult host. According to children's host historian, Tim Hollis, the shows included: "Popeye and Cactus" (Louisville, KY), "Popeye and Janie" (Indianapolis, IN), "Popeye and Pete" (Minneapolis, MN), "Popeye and Randy" (Louisville, KY), "Popeye and

Left: Eleven-year-old Susan Heinkel's "Susie Show," seen on WBBM-TV, became one of the first three programs in the United States to introduce the theatrical Popeye cartoons to television audiences. The drawing of Popeye, pictured on this ad was by Bud Sagendorf.

Donald Klauber, Station Sales Manager of Associated Artists Productions, Inc., tells:

"Why Popeye had to race to Texas!"

"Kids were clamoring, advertising sponsors waiting! A big TV station's popularity — and profits — were at stake!

"As usually happens, when KDUB-TV in Lubbock, Texas, finally signed up Popeye — one of America's hottest daytime programs — they needed those films in a real hurry!

"So we raced Popeye there — via Air Express!

"But launching a TV cartoon series is only a small part of our story. We use Air Express for 50,000 theater dates for our full-length feature films — with only 600 prints!

"We could not run this business as economically without Air Express!

"A 15-lb. shipment, New York to Lubbock, Texas, costs only $9.47 with Air Express — $1.36 less than any other complete air service.

"What's more, Air Express uses radio-controlled trucks to rush many of our shipments to and from airports — and, whenever necessary, a private wire system to trace shipments instantly. It really pays to use Air Express regularly!"

 *Air Express*

30 YEARS OF GETTING THERE FIRST *via U.S. Scheduled Airlines*

CALL AIR EXPRESS ... *division of* **RAILWAY EXPRESS AGENCY**

TIME, AUGUST 19, 1957

The 234 "Popeye" movie cartoons soon became one of America's hottest daytime programs.

the Admiral" (Binghamton, NY), "Popeye Cartoon Theatre" (Mobile, AL), "The Popeye Club" (Atlanta, GA), "Popeye Playhouse" (Miami, FL), "The Popeye Show" (Traverse City, MI), "Popeye, Tick and Tock" (Colorado Springs, CO), "Popeye's Cartoon Circus" (Louisville, KY), "Popeye's Firehouse" (Chicago, IL), "Popeye's Funhouse" (Syracuse, NY), "Popeye's Pals" (Jacksonville, FL) and "Popeye, Wallaby, and Friends" (Butte, MT).

The ratings for the cartoons went through the roof and recouped ten times their purchase cost. According to the Associated Artists Productions press book, the following rating shares were logged in for the "Popeye" series in 1957:

Boston	WBZ-TV	20.7
Buffalo	WBEN-TV	14.4
Chicago	WBBM-TV	14.0
Columbus	WBNS-TV	13.9
Denver	KBTV	23.3
Duluth-Superior	WDSM-TV	25.2
Los Angeles	KTLA	12.0
Miami	WTVJ	15.9
New York	WPIX	14.9
Phoenix	KPHO-TV	16.6
Portland, ME	WSCH-TV	15.2
Providence	WPRO-TV	19.5
Sacramento	KCRA-TV	10.7
Salt Lake City	KUTV	14.2
San Diego	KFSD-TV	15.5
San Francisco	KRON-TV	10.6
South Bend	WSBT-TV	14.9
Spokane	KREM-TV	18.7
Tulsa	KTVX	14.9
Wichita Falls	KFDX-TV	13.6
Youngstown	WFMJ-TV	20.0

Stations were also glowing due to the quick selling of advertising time slots during the Popeye cartoons, represented by this release from WPIX (New York, NY):

Popeye Sails with "SRO" Signal Flag
September 10
With Monday Through Friday Sellout
A month and a half before television station WPIX-11 launches its exclusive rights to "Popeye the Sailor," Fred M. Thrower, vice president and station manager, announces a Monday through Friday sell out.

The Popeye package was also added to children's shows already on the air. WBZ-TV was having great success with "Boomtown," hosted by Rex Trailer. The show was given a boost with the addition of the Popeye series. During the early 1970s, my brother and I visited the show. While all eyes were glued on the game

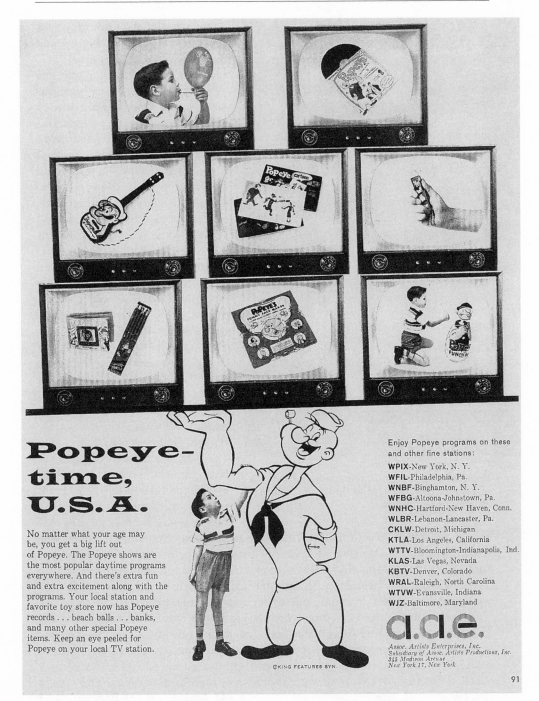

The success of the movie cartoons on television spawned hundreds of new items bearing the likeness of the sailor and his crew.

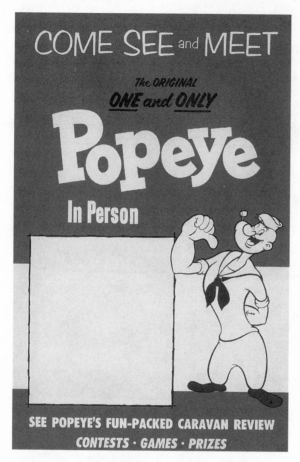

COME SEE and MEET
The ORIGINAL
ONE and ONLY

Popeye

In Person

SEE POPEYE'S FUN-PACKED CARAVAN REVIEW
CONTESTS · GAMES · PRIZES

Popeye's popularity on television led to bookings of a live Popeye at various carnivals and children's functions.

being played in the studio, my back was turned watching "Popeye and the Pirates" (Famous Studios, 1947) on a small television monitor. The Saturday morning this episode was aired, Popeye was the only cartoon aired throughout the entire show! Popeye products were popping up based on the success the animated films were having on the small screen—everything from costumes, pencils, wallets, punching bags, dolls and candies, to household items, books, jewelry, greeting cards and toiletries. Popeye also became a touring live act with Harry Welch and other entertainers putting on one-man Popeye shows. I visited one of these shows in the mid–1960s and watched Popeye give a one-man show. As a child, the thought of seeing a live Popeye must have been horrific for me as I cried and cried when my parents tried to get me to shake the sailor's hand. I did walk away with a nice Popeye Halloween mask.

King Features Syndicate may have owned the rights to the Popeye characters but they did not receive any money from either the sale or syndication of the 234 theatrical cartoons to television. What money King Features Syndicate did make was from licensing the characters for various products due to their television exposure. Al Brodax got his first taste of show business by working in the mailroom of the William Morris Agency. He later became one of the producers of a Broadway production after critiquing one of Sherwood Anderson's short stories. The show was called *Winesburg, Ohio* which lasted for 13 performances. During the 1950s he was promoted from mailroom to agent and one of the clients on his list was the Hearst Corporation, copyright owners of the one-eyed sailor. Hearst asked Brodax to start their television and motion picture division. As Brodax recalled, "Popeye at that time was running very high in the ratings. These were the Popeyes distributed by Paramount, the old Max Fleischer Popeyes. So I thought it would be a good idea, a good business move, to make an announcement that we were making 220 new Popeyes, all in color, as some of them were black and white and they were up for grabs. The Popeyes were produced within

THE MOST IMPORTANT EVENT OF THE YEAR

© King Features Syndicate, Inc.

To every child, the most important event of the year is his birthday. Imagine the excitement a child would feel if his birthday were celebrated on TV by Popeye the Sailor.

Well, that's exactly what's happening to millions of kids in 1964.

As part of POPEYE'S BIG BIRTHDAY YEAR, TV stations from coast to coast are throwing Birthday Parties each month on their Popeye cartoon shows . . . with Popeye games, Popeye prizes, "Popeye's Birthday Song" and Popeye's personal greeting to all the kids whose birthdays are that month.

Many children will hold their own parties at home while they watch Popeye's TV birthday special . . . just for them.

You too can take part in the wonderful excitement of "POPEYE'S BIG BIRTHDAY YEAR." How?

Retailers: ask your wholesalers for more Popeye items.
Wholesalers: ask manufacturers for more Popeye merchandise.
Manufacturers: ask us.

 KING FEATURES SYNDICATE
235 East 45th Street, New York, N. Y. 10017
Tel. 212 MU 2-5600
Chester Weil, Director of Special Services

Local TV stations were offered the opportunity to celebrate Popeye's 35th birthday in 1964. The artwork on this ad features the TV-cartoon versions of Popeye, Olive Oyl, Swee'pea, Brutus and Wimpy.

eighteen months and anyone with a modicum of experience in animation would deem that an impossible task. But thanks to the Hanna-Barbera technique of limited animation and my naïve approach, it somehow all worked out." Brodax contracted five animation studios to produce the Popeye cartoons. These studios were already into production with other cartoon series as the early 1960s were a boom for limited animation on television. Many Segar creations, not featured in the Fleischer/Famous Studios cartoons, appeared in these TV Popeyes, including "The Sea Hag," "King Blozo," "Alice the Goon," "Rough House," "Toar" and "The Whiffle Bird." Though Paramount Pictures was incorrect in their assumption that they owned the rights to the name, "Bluto," King Features Syndicate still felt it necessary to change the brute's name to "Brutus."

Many animation historians have called these 220 "Popeye the Sailor" cartoons produced by Brodax, "junk," "garbage" and "horrible." This simply isn't the case. The sheer number of cartoons produced during 18 months guaranteed there would be several poor films, but you can't put a blanket description on the entire series. People have often wondered why King Features Syndicate allowed such a short span of time for such a massive production. When it was decided to produce these new Popeyes, the sailor's popularity on television was unprecedented by any other cartoon figure. How long would this last? Was it just a fad that would eventually crash and burn? As Brodax stated, the production schedule was more of a business decision and was perhaps less concerned about the quality of each individual cartoon. King Features' official announcement for the production of the series was that children were getting tired of watching the theatrical Popeyes and wanted to see new ones. While that statement is debatable, it certainly is a fact that while King Features did not make any money from the Popeye cartoons syndicated by Associated Artists Productions, they would make a bundle from the sale of their TV Popeyes. The addition of these TV cartoons also helped keep Popeye in the public eye in comparison to the newspaper comic strip, which was losing papers as time went on. The TV cartoons also created a surge in licensing and by 1963, 454 films featuring the spinach-eating sailor were broadcast in over 150 television markets.

The Studios

As five different studios produced the 220 Popeye cartoons, each studio's work should be judged separately.

Gene Deitch and William L. Snyder

William L. Snyder was one of the first Americans to do business in postwar Eastern Europe. He imported European films through his production company, Rembrandt Films, founded in 1949. In 1959, he teamed with Gene Deitch, the former head of UPA Studios, to produce cartoons in Prague, which included "Tom and Jerry" for MGM and for Al Brodax, "Popeye" and "Krazy Kat." Their 28 Popeyes, which credit Snyder as producer and Deitch as supervising producer,

Failing in his attempt to keep Olive fat, Brutus decides to lose weight too! From
"Weight for Me" (King Features, 1960; produced by Gene Deitch and William Snyder; animated by Halas and Batchelor).

vary in animation quality. For example, "Hag Way Robbery," features simple character designs with the overlooking of detail. In one scene, Olive is carrying Swee'-
pea but the lad has no arms. In "Sea No Evil," it's another case of very simple
character designs. There is a scene where Popeye is paddling his boat back to land,
but, though his arms are moving, the background behind him isn't. "Voice from
the Deep" features too many abrupt scene changes to really enjoy the story. The
better animated cartoons were "The Lost City of Bubble-On" where Popeye discovers bubble creatures living under the sea; "There's No Space Like Home,"
featuring the rare time Brutus, knowing what Popeye's strength giver is, feeds
the sailor spinach to stop aliens! In the cartoon, "Beaver or Not," Popeye deals
with two unwelcome beavers. The Snyder/Deitch Popeyes benefited in a big way
in terms of animation with the addition of John Halas and Joy Batchelor. Halas
and Batchelor remain world renowned for their contribution to British and international animation film culture. They released their first feature-length color animation film *Animal Farm* in 1954. Their work on the Popeyes, for the most part,
featured excellent animation. You can't fault the animation in the films which they
are credited with, including: "Potent Lotion," "The Billionaire," "Model Muddle,"

Popeye, his arms tied, uses his teeth to open a can of spinach. From "Potent Lotion" (King Features, 1960; produced by Gene Deitch and William Snyder; animated by Halas and Batchelor).

"Matinee Idol Popeye" and "Weight for Me." The stories in these TV Popeyes were pleasant enough and comical, as in the example of "The Billionaire," where Olive buys her own beauty salon to make herself beautiful so Popeye will have to marry her. Upon seeing her improved looks (she looks like a gorgeous blonde), the sailor laughs and Olive's new face falls off, revealing her old self. Popeye remarks, "Don't be sad Olive, I likes ya ugly!" In "Which Is Witch," a cartoon animated by Halas and Batchelor, a robot Olive falls in love with Popeye and ends up keeping his pipe at the conclusion of the film. The Sea Hag, who created the robot to capture Popeye, ends up defeated thanks to the Olive double and says, "Foiled again and all on a count of you … and stop smoking that stupid pipe!" The trademark of these TV Popeyes is the eerie and haunting sounding background scores.

Larry Harmon

Larry Harmon, who while at the University of Southern California, planned to be a gynecologist, but soon found himself going into one show business job after another. According to a 1966 article in *TV Guide*, he was a movie actor (75 pictures), TV producer, director, scriptwriter, composer, musician, talent agent, voice specialist and puppeteer. In 1956, he secured the TV rights to "Bozo the Clown," the once popular recording figure for Capitol Records. Harmon's animation studio began producing 5½-minute Bozo cartoons (which would later total 156) to be featured with a live Bozo the Clown in a circus format. The format was a smashing success and soon nearly every television station had their own local Bozo. Al Brodax contracted Harmon to produce 18 TV Popeyes. (The crew under Harmon who worked on these also handled "Mr. Magoo" and "Dick Tracy" for UPA.) Harmon's cartoons featured very simple character designs. The stories, "Foola-Foola Bird" and "Childhood Daze," for example, were entertaining, but the simplification of the character designs became distracting. In Harmon's cartoons, there would often be scenes where Brutus' short sleeve shirt would suddenly become long sleeved and then back to short. When the characters spoke, their heads would often bob back and forth in rapid motion. In the Harmon cartoons, Popeye often appeared to be drinking his spinach as the vegetable looked and sounded like liquid. Memorable entries in this series include: "Ace of Space," where Olive is kidnapped by an alien creature, "Dead-Eye Popeye" featuring Popeye battling the McBride Boys (Brutus' look-a-likes) and "Caveman Capers,"

Olive is delighted that Popeye has won a car race driving his "Hoppy Jalopy" (King Features, 1960; produced by Larry Harmon).

a look back at how Popeye began his spinach diet. Harmon's first cartoon, "Muskels Shmuskels" is nowhere near as polished as his final entry, "Crystal Ball Brawl." During the 1960s and 1970s, many companies, which produced Bozo toys also, used Popeye. The two would often appear together on the same product. The various live-action Bozo programs would air Popeye cartoons if the TV station that owned the Bozo franchise also acquired the sailor's film and TV package.

Gerald Ray

According to "Bullwinkle" historian, Keith Scott, Ray got his early training at UCLA, Chouinard Art Institute, and Disney. He made a trip to Washington and studied with Don Graham, a Disney craftsman. He first worked with Jay Ward on "Crusader Rabbit" as animator and director. In that same position, he worked at UPA before rejoining Ward to work on "Rocky and His Friends." He directed several segments of "Fractured Fairy Tales." He later formed a commercial studio in Mexico City where he lived and worked for many years. It was during this period that he was contracted by Brodax to produce 10 TV Popeyes for King Features Syndicate. As in the case of the Gene Deitch Popeyes, an older audience can tell that these were produced overseas. Though the animation wasn't bad,

The Sea Hag plots with Toar in "The Last Resort" (King Features, 1960; produced by Gerald Ray). The Sea Hag and Toar first appeared in Segar's "Thimble Theatre" comic strip. Though played as a buffoon in this cartoon, Toar was a monstrous brute in the comic strip until becoming Popeye's pal.

it had a look to it quite similar to the early "Rocky the Flying Squirrel" episodes which, in Popeye's case, took a little getting used to. The scripts were clever and you could tell Ray and his crew had a fondness for Popeye. Ray's first effort, "Where There's a Will" features an amusing scene when Brutus, furious that a reading of a will has left him one can of spinach, beats up Popeye and throws the can in the sailor's direction. As the spinach-eating theme begins, Brutus looks at the audience and says, "Whoops, I shouldn't have done that." "The Last Resort" features E.C. Segar's, "Toar," a monstrous brute in the 1930s comic strips, he's played for laughs in this cartoon as the Sea Hag's sidekick. "Jeopardy Sheriff" had Poopdeck Pappy attempting to capture a gang of bank robbers to prove to his son that his stories to Swee'pea weren't just "whoppers." It was in Ray's cartoon "Popeye's Junior Headache" that viewers were introduced to Olive's bratty niece, "Deezil," who beat the tar out of Popeye while he was attempting to babysit. "Baby Phase," Ray's final entry, was a delightful cartoon featuring Swee'pea as a "world famous juggler." Each of Ray's cartoons ended with one of the characters singing to the tune of the Popeye theme song: "At home or vacation, spinach is me salvation, says Popeye the Sailor Man" ("The Last Resort"); "It's bad to be tardy, to a hamburger party, says Wimpy the Burger Man" ("Egypt Us"); or "I may tell a whopper but I am the Popper of Popeye the Sailor Man" ("Jeopardy Sheriff"). Besides "Rocky and His Friends," Ray is best known for his work on "King Leonardo and His Short Subjects," also known as "The King and Odie."

Jack Kinney

Al Brodax told me that Jack Kinney's studio was given 101 of the TV Popeyes to produce because he "was a well respected Disney animator." Kinney was a sequence director on such films as *Pinocchio* and *Dumbo* and directed *Der Fueher's Face*. He was a director for the popular "Goofy" series for Walt Disney. He left Disney in 1959 to form his own animation company. His TV work included UPA's "Mister Magoo" and "Dick Tracy" cartoons. His studio was also involved

Is Popeye feeding Wimpy essence of spinach or essence of hamburger to stop his
growing? It doesn't matter because the same sequence was used for both scenes
in this ghastly animated mess, "Popeye and the Giant" (King Features, 1960; produced by Jack Kinney). Animation director Hugh Frasier is responsible for many
of the poorly animated TV Popeyes produced and directed by Jack Kinney.

with producing episodes of "The Alvin Show" and the pilot episode of "Barney
Google and Snuffy Smith" for King Features Syndicate."

Kinney's TV Popeyes feature scripts with funny gags and puns. In "After
the Ball Went Over," Popeye actually loses a ping pong match to Brutus and when
asked by Olive if the sailor wants anything special, he looks at the audience and
says, "yeah, a new writer to puts me spinach back in the script." "Popeye the
Lifeguard," features the sailor surrounded by lovely ladies and saying to
Olive, "No more pretty girls for me Olive, only you," to which Olive gives a dis-
tressed look to the audience. In "Popeye's Testimonial Dinner," Popeye is celebrated as a hero but a bawling Brutus convinces the audience that the brute is
just "misunderstood." The scripts were the bright spot in the Kinney cartoons
but the animation was so poor in so many, that as an adult, they are difficult to
enjoy.

Kinney had several animation directors working for him. The quality of the
animation in a Kinney film depended on who the animation director was. By far
the worst offender was animation director, Hugh Frasier. His efforts, which
include: "Popeye and the Giant," "Time Marches Backwards," "Old Salt Tale,"
"Popeye the Popular Mechanic" and "Invisible Popeye," feature scenes with ter-

Harvey Toombs   Hugh Frasier

Harvey Toombs   Rudy Larriva

Ed Friedman   Eddie Rehberg
Volus Jones

Ken Hultgren   Alan Zaslove

Pictured are the different visual designs of Popeye's face, with the name of the animation director responsible for it in the TV Popeyes produced by Jack Kinney. The quality of the animation in a Kinney Popeye depended upon who was credited as animation director.

rible animation. "Old Salt Tale" has too quick scene changes. In the last scene, Popeye is wearing a swimsuit and less than a heartbeat later, his white sailor's uniform. Why didn't anyone catch and correct that? "Time Marches Backwards" is horrible with the constant screeching of Olive's, "Help-help!" It is enough to make you stick your head in the oven. "Double Cross Country Feet Race" is a dreary mess, with a portion of the cartoon out of sync with the audio track. I remember watching an episode of "The Flintstones" where Fred, with a long white beard, was sitting in a chair. Suddenly, Fred gained a third arm and sure enough, Hugh Frasier was listed as one of the animators on this episode. It reminded me of the time Olive Oyl gained an eye at the bottom of her nose at the conclusion of "Old Salt Tale."

Animation director, Eddie Rehberg is credited for "Popeye in the Woods," "Popeye's Pizza Palace," "Popeye's Museum Piece," "After the Ball Went Over," "The Golden Touch," "Forever Ambergris" and "Frozen Feuds," among others. Rehberg's cartoons feature annoyingly quick scene changes, most notable in the scene where Wimpy is handed a bill and then makes out several IOUs in "Frozen Feuds" and in "After the Ball Went Over." However, the animation in "Popeye and the Herring Snatcher" and "Popeye's Museum Piece" is tolerable.

Animation director, Harvey Toombs produced fine animated

Alice the Goon and Brutus fall in love with each other, thanks to "Popeye's Hypnotic Glance" (King Features, 1960; produced by Jack Kinney). This TV Popeye featured a good storyline and animation, credited to animation directors Ed Friedman and Volus Jones.

efforts including: "Popeye in the Grand Steeple Chase," "Popeye the Piano Mover," "Bell Hop Hop Popeye," "Tiger Burger," "Spinachonare" and "Popeye's Car Wash."

Ed Friedman and Volus Jones' well animated cartoons included: "Wimpy's Lunch Wagon," "Popeye's Pep-Up Emporium," "Swee'pea Through the Looking Glass," "Weather Watchers," "Olive Drab and the Seven Swee'peas" and "The Super Duper Market."

Animation director, Ken Hultgren, is credited for the terrible "Sea Hagracy," but the animation improved with his other efforts including: "Popeye and the Spinach Stalk," "The Green Dancin' Shoes," "Jeep Jeep," "The Black Knight," "The Golden Type Fleece" and "The Blubbering Whaler."

Animation director, Rudy Larriva's animation was well executed in such efforts as "Jeep Tale," "Private Eye Popeye," "Popeye the White Collar Man," "Paper Pasting Pandemonium," "The Square Egg" and "Popeye's Cool Pool."

"Down the Hatch" and "Spinach Shortage" are credited to animation director, Alan Zaslove. He and other animation directors, who worked on one or two cartoons, rounded out the productions "produced and directed by Jack Kinney" (as listed on the credits). The moments of bad animation in the Kinney cartoons

is enough, unfortunately, to blot out any remembrance of the good quality Kinney efforts. The fact remains that there are good ones. Just make sure to check the name of the animation director before deciding to continue to watch the cartoon. Interestingly enough, Kinney's studio produced one of two pilots for the TV Popeye series, "Barbecue for Two." This well-animated, fast-paced cartoon featured Popeye, Olive, Swee'pea and Wimpy as they appeared in the comic strip at the time. Popeye wore his black shirt with red collar while Olive reverted back to her homely appearance. The conflict in this cartoon was created by Popeye's next door neighbor, referred to as "Junior," just prior to having his lights punched out by the sailor. "Junior" looked like Brutus.

Top: Olive Oyl admires "The Square Egg" (King Features, 1960; produced by Jack Kinney). This cartoon is credited to animation director Rudy Larriva. For this series of TV cartoons Olive retained the facial design from the majority of the Famous Studios films but her clothes were based upon the comic strip version. *Bottom:* Popeye often had both eyes open in the Jack Kinney TV Popeyes as seen in this illustration from an animation cell from "Popeye Revere" (King Features, 1960; produced by Jack Kinney). The animation director for this cartoon was Ken Hultgren.

Paramount Cartoon Studios: Directed by Seymour Kneitel

In 1956, Paramount took full control of their animation studio and renamed it Paramount Cartoon Studios. They continued production, until mid–1957, on the theatrical "Popeye" cartoons and their other series. While continuing to produce animated films for the big screen, Paramount Cartoon Studios, contracted by Al Brodax, worked on King Features Syndicate's "Beetle Bailey," "Barney Google and Snuffy Smith" and the TV Popeyes. The 63 cartoons (including one of the pilots) this studio produced were among the best in the series. Individuals who worked on the theatrical Popeyes were involved with their production, which enhanced the

This animated sequence of Popeye holding his can of spinach then pouring the contents in his mouth was used often in the TV cartoons produced by Paramount Cartoon Studios. However, the sequence was always carefully woven into the existing action. The musical score, provided by Winston Sharples, when this sequence took place heightened the anticipation of what would happen after Popeye ate his spinach. This scene is from "Strikes, Spares an' Spinach" (King Features, 1960; produced by Paramount Cartoon Studios).

films. Experienced animators and writers, Martin Taras, Gerry Dvorak, WM. B. Pattengill, Irving Dressler, Dante Barbetta, Jack Mercer, Morey Reden and Jim Logan contributed to the cartoons. "Myskery Melody," "It Only Hurts When They Laugh," "Me Quest for Poopdeck Pappy," "The Valley of the Goons," "Poppa Popeye," "What's News" and "Wimpy the Moocher" were all based on Segar's "Thimble Theatre" comic strips. You can't watch "The Valley of the Goons," "Gem Jam," "County Fair," "Hamburgers Aweigh" or "The Medicine Man" and find fault with the animation, because there isn't any. These were cartoons, though not produced with the budget of the earlier theatricals, still produced with care. Winston Sharples' musical scores, heard in the Famous Studios cartoons, helped heighten the excitement in these TV Popeyes. Many cartoons, like Gerald Ray's batch ended with Popeye singing lyrics to his theme song, for example, "Even down to the end you're still the best friend of Popeye the Sailor Man" ("From Rags to Riches to Rags").

When these cartoons were released to the television market they were snatched up quickly by stations still having success with the older films. The films grossed three million dollars during their initial release and, as Brodax stated, "The project was a success and brought joy to scores of kids as well as to the bookkeepers at the Hearst Corporation." His mentioning of "kids" is an important point regarding the reputation of this series.

My first exposure to the films was in the mid–1960s on "The Three Stooges & Popeye" program from Providence, RI. Just before school, from 7:00 A.M. to 7:30 A.M., I was treated to either one "Three Stooges" short followed by a theatrical "Popeye," four TV Popeyes or a mixture of TV and theatrical Popeye films. As a kid, all I noticed was that some cartoons were in black and white, Popeye's suit varied, Olive's hairdo and dress changed and Bluto became known as Brutus. The

Top: Popeye breaks into a sweat, trying to figure out how to spell cat. From "The Spinach Scholar" (King Features, 1960; produced by Paramount Cartoon Studios). This was a delightful entry in the series which helps to disprove the notion that all of the TV Popeyes are terrible. *Bottom:* "I'm strong to the finich when I eats the spinach of Popeye the Sailor Man," Swee'pea sings at the conclusion of "The Baby Contest" (King Features, 1960; produced by Paramount Cartoon Studios). Swee'pea eats Popeye's spinach to save the sailor from becoming Brutus' permanent punching bag.

lack of quality in the TV Popeyes went unnoticed by me; I was just thrilled that there was more Popeye to watch! Having been in contact with many Popeye fans over the years, I have found I'm not alone in my thoughts. Of course, as I grew older, I noticed that a great deal of the TV Popeyes weren't worth the enthusiasm I gave them at the age of seven or eight. These TV productions were not produced with the adult audience in mind as in the case of the movie cartoons. They were cranked out for the children, who at the time, wanted to see more Popeye. This isn't to say that children deserve to watch crap, but in order to complete production of these cartoons in 18 months, several clunkers, as well as many good ones, became a part of this series. What has also hurt the reputation of the films is the fact that many stations would air a Fleischer cartoon, followed by a TV Popeye. How can you compare the two? But many animation historians do, without taking into account the business decisions that brought the television episodes to life. These TV Popeyes, despite how one may feel about their quality, had a long broadcast life in the United States, airing on independent stations well into the mid–1990s and continuing to air internationally.

The Continuity Factor

Regarding the fast-paced production of the TV Popeyes, Al Brodax stated, "With strict controls over model sheets, writing teams and the utilization of domestic and foreign studios and most importantly, the voices of Jack Mercer and Mae Questel as Popeye and Olive Oyl, I completed the project within bud-

Top: Note how Popeye's facial design from "Interrupted Lullaby" (King Features, 1960; produced by Gene Deitch and William Snyder) looks very close to the full figured image of the sailor from the animator's model sheet. *Bottom:* Notice how the image of Popeye's face from the animator's model sheet, though facing in the opposite direction, looks very much like the sailor's facial design from the last scene of "I Bin Sculped" (King Features, 1960; produced by Gerald Ray).

Apparently for the pilot cartoon for the TV Popeye series produced by Jack Kinney, "Barbecue for Two" (1960), the standard model sheets were not used as both
Olive Oyl and Popeye are depicted like their comic strip counterparts. This would
be the only TV Popeye cartoon featuring the print designs of the characters.

get." A model sheet features drawings of a cartoon character. This sheet is then
distributed to the various animators to ensure consistency during the production
of the cartoon. Looking at the model sheet of Popeye that was distributed, it is
evident from the Gene Deitch/William L. Snyder cartoons and the Gerald Ray
productions that those studios paid the most attention to it. While there are traces
of the model sheet drawings in a few of the Jack Kinney cartoons (Popeye's facial
expressions at the conclusion of "Popeye's Picnic" and Popeye's walking in the
hot sun from "Deserted Desert"), the animators drew their own interpretations
of Popeye, Olive Oyl, Brutus, Wimpy, Swee'pea and the rest of the cast. The
closest Larry Harmon's studio came to matching the model sheet of Popeye was
keeping him in his white sailor's uniform. Paramount Cartoon Studios had the
experience of producing the theatrical Popeyes so the model sheets weren't that
essential. Not only Popeye, but the majority of the main characters featured in
the TV productions had model sheets created. These model sheet poses were also
used on merchandise during the 1960s to mid–1970s. The model sheets apparently weren't distributed prior to the production of the two pilots for the TV
Popeyes. Jack Kinney's "Barbecue for Two" features the comic strip designs of

the characters and Olive Oyl is wearing her short sleeved shirt and high heels from the Famous Studios productions in Paramount Cartoon Studio's, "Hits and Missiles." After the completion of these two pilots, which were budgeted at $25,000, according to Al Brodax, Olive wore her comic strip attire while keeping the facial design of the Famous Studios films and Popeye wore his white sailor's uniform. While Popeye's closed eye often opened up in the Famous Studios films, it was more evident in these TV productions, which I have yet to see indicated on a model sheet of the sailor during this period. The recording of the soundtracks was done quickly as Brodax recalled, "I recorded all the soundtracks in New York to create a uniform sound, and I had a kid waiting downstairs with a chauffeur to take him to the airport to send the tracks to places like Czechoslovakia, Los Angeles and some went to Australia." Jack Mercer was often found voicing several cartoons in one day as evidenced from this partial listing of his recording schedule, which lists the date of the recording, the number of cartoons completed per day and the studio the films were for:

The cover to a "Popeye and His Pals" candy box by the Phoenix Candy Company. The image of Wimpy was drawn by Bud Sagendorf, used in the comic strip and comic books. The image of Olive Oyl, however, is taken from the animator's model sheet of the character used to produce the TV Popeyes. This illustration of Olive would pop up frequently on various products during the 1960s through the 1970s.

1960

3/8	3	Gene Deitch
3/14	5	Charles Shows (Larry Harmon)
3/15	5	Charles Shows (Larry Harmon)
3/21	7	Jack Kinney
3/22	9	Jack Kinney
3/24	7	Jack Kinney
4/21	4	Seymour Kneitel (Paramount)
5/5	8	Jack Kinney
5/6	8	Jack Kinney
5/13	4	Gene Deitch
5/16	5	Charles Shows (Larry Harmon)
5/17	5	TV Spots
6/6	2	Seymour Kneitel (Paramount)

The TV Version of Popeye Goes to School

In 1971, King Features Syndicate was responsible for a safety film, produced by Abe Goodman, which was distributed to school systems across the country. In the film, which combined animation and live action, Popeye instructs people on various street safety topics. Here is how Popeye introduced the film:

> I'm Popeye the Sailor Man, beep, beep
> I'm Popeye the Sailor Man, broom, broom
> I'm very discreet what I does with me feet
> I'm Popeye the Sailor Man, beep, beep, broom, broom.
> Tha's the words, look where you are going.
> Mateys, I has been asked ta weighs anchor awhile
> by some friends of mine (he is referring to the police)
> They is friends of yours too.
> They says for me to speak some words of wisdom
> about the subject of looking. Now being a sailor
> I has a sharp eye, two of them (He opens his closed eye.)
> like you!

Popeye proceeds to introduce the audience to the policemen who will demonstrate some of the safety issues in the film. Popeye was presented as he appeared in the 1960-61 TV cartoons. The animation was excellent, credited to long time Fleischer and Famous Studios animator, Myron Waldman. Waldman had the following to say regarding his association with the "Popeye" cartoons: "Popeye was another character who was created to help revitalize Betty Boop. I don't think any of us knew that he was to become the studio's shining star. There's no doubt that Popeye and Olive fit right into the Fleischer style. Olive was perfect. She had no elbows and oh those knees! I animated one of the early Popeyes 'Can You Take It' (Fleischer, 1934) with Thomas Johnson. A lot of people have said that this film helped define his character." The safety film won a Gold Award at the New York International Film and TV Festivals.

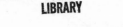

KING Features

EDUCATIONAL DIVISION

235 EAST 45TH STREET, NEW YORK, N. Y. 10017   AREA CODE 212 — 682-5600

LOOK WHERE YOU ARE GOING

(Popeye Safety Film)

Operating on the philosophy that the best way to teach children is to talk up to their level and be amusing, this film shows youngsters the basics of sidewalk safety. Shot on the busy streets of New York, with Popeye as the lecturer, real groups of city school children are shown that (1) Policemen are their friends and are around to help them (2) Each traffic sign has a different shape and different meaning, which should be followed for the child's safety. Children are shown the proper ways to cross streets, individually and as a group, as well as the proper way to ride a bicycle in the road. In the most dramatic and graphic portion of the film, utilizing a New York City police car and a doll-replica of one of the girls in the group, Popeye shows what can happen to a child crossing improperly with an oncoming car going 40 mph. Popeye leaves the children smiling with a review of all his lessons and the warning to "keeps the eyes peeled at the sign."

The letter given to school systems showing the safety film, "Look Where You Are Going," starring Popeye the Sailor Man.

Smooth Sailin', POPEYE 'n' BRUTUS

Herb Messinger as Popeye and Brett Pearson as Brutus from Popeye's Physical Fitness Campaign, which took place in 1962. The characterizations of the pair were based on the TV Popeye cartoons produced by Al Brodax. Popeye was the first character to have additional TV cartoons produced due to the popularity of a theatrical animated series.

Popeye's Network Debut

Popeye first appeared on network television as part of "The ABC Saturday Superstar Movie." This ABC Saturday morning series, featured well known characters, from animation, film and television featured in hour-long adventures. King Features Syndicate hired cartoon veterans Jack Zander and Hal Seeger to bring to life many of King Features Syndicate's comic strip favorites. For many, this production would be their debut in animated form. Popeye, Olive Oyl, Wimpy, Swee'pea, Brutus, the Katzenjammer Kids, the Captain, Mama, the Inspector, Quincy, Tiger, Lil' Iodine, Steve Canyon, Flash Gordon, Maggie and Jiggs, Snuffy Smith, Henry, the Little King, the Phantom, Mandrake, Lothar, Tim Tyler, Blondie, Dagwood, Hi and Lois, Beetle Bailey, the Sarge, Dale Arden, Jughaid, Loweezy, Sparkplug, Daisy and Dot were all a part of this 60-minute program, which premiered on October 7, 1972, and would be rerun during the 1973-74 season. I had the pleasure to speak with Jack Zander regarding the production of the cartoon. He recalled getting a phone call from King Features Syndicate asking if he would be interested in producing a cartoon featuring many of their comic strip stars. Zander received a script from the syndicate, and he hired a few writers to punch it up. The money King Features invested into the production meant that it would be produced with limited animation. According to Zander, the main concern from the syndicate was to ensure that the characters looked like their strip counterparts. Despite this, Popeye was sporting his captain's hat, rather than his sailor's hat, which he had been wearing in the comic strip for several years.

The plot concerned Professor Morbid Grimsby and his assistant, Brutus, who used an evil computer to kidnap the comics and hold them captive on his secret island forever. The comics are tricked into taking a vacation on the *S. S. Hilarious*. When the ship suddenly goes missing, the White House calls in the adventure characters to locate them. The comic characters strike a deal with Grimsby. If they make him laugh, he will have to let them all go. When Grimsby catches site of his reflection in a mirror, he laughs and sets everyone free. The characters board the Professor's submarine to escape the island, which is actually a reactivated volcano. The submarine gets lodged between two boulders and, despite the presence of the adventure heroes, it is Popeye who saves the day by eating his spinach and using a swordfish's nose as a drill to free the submarine before the volcano erupts. The final scene has all of the characters, including the Professor, at the White House awaiting the president. He is delayed in his office, laughing at the newspaper comics section. The production was later edited down to a half hour for syndication, but I don't recall it being aired on television in this form. The artists and writers behind the comic characters' strips were credited at the end of the cartoon. Oddly enough, Popeye artists and writers were not among them, which gave the impression that he was mainly thought of as an animated cartoon character by this time. Jack Mercer and Bob McFadden's voice work was featured in the film, which was written by Lou Silverton. The original music score was provided by Elliott Schiprut. A coloring book was produced in 1972 by Artcraft based on the special.

A cast shot of Popeye and his gang by Hanna-Barbera, before the actual production of the cartoons. Popeye's captain's hat was later changed to a sailor's hat, and the general visual design of Bluto was altered.

The All New Popeye

The CBS network had already revived familiar cartoon favorites to their Saturday morning lineup including "Mr. Magoo" and "Mighty Mouse" before the decision was made to produce new Popeye cartoons. Both Jack Mercer and Mae Questel had to audition for their old voice parts and while Mercer was hired, Questel wasn't. Art Scott, who was head of special programming hired Marilyn Schreffler whom he thought was a better Olive than the original. Allen Melvin was hired to voice Bluto. Apparently King Features wasn't bothered any longer by the legalities of the previous name change to Brutus. Other cast members of Segar's "Thimble Theatre" strip would be featured in the new cartoons including Popeye's look-a-like nephews who no longer sounded alike. Art Scott said that interest in a new Popeye series was sparked by the Broadway success of "Annie" and the talk of a Popeye feature film. Scott stated that they would be

Opposite top: Promotional picture for Popeye's first prime-time animated special, "Sweethearts at Sea" (Hanna-Barbera, 1979). This cartoon, which aired in February 1979 as a Valentine's Day special featured Popeye, Olive, Wimpy, Bluto, Eugene the Jeep, and (pictured here) the Sea Hag. *Bottom:* Newspaper ad for "Sweethearts at Sea."

A publicity photo from one of the early Popeye cartoons for "The All New Popeye Hour" entitled "A Bad Knight for Popeye" (1978).

returning to the original animated concept. "We're trying for some sort of compromise between current network standards and the old Popeye standards. Hanna-Barbera, who had great success with 'Yogi Bear' and 'The Flintstones,' is getting roughly $90,000 for a half-hour of animated material. The current budget is better than what they spent in the 60s but nothing like what was spent on the originals. There are other problems with updating Popeye, too. The original series was born in a violent era when prize fighting was a national craze. Popeye and Bluto would go toe to toe and really slug it out. We can't have people punching each other, so we have other ways of showing competition. Network and antiviolence network strictures are so tough that Popeye can't even roll up his sleeves. It makes it awfully hard on the writers."

One of the main writers on this series was Jack Mercer, who felt that the violence issue was ridiculous when the old cartoons were still playing to large audiences daily. Mercer would think of some of the old gags and clean them up. Many of the animators working on these new cartoons also were involved with the Fleischer films. J. F. D'Angelo, then president of King Features Syndicate, and Lee Polk, vice president of King Features Television Productions, Inc., informed the press that the series was scheduled to begin in September 1978 and would telecast over a two-year period.

I recall watching the first episode of "The All New Popeye Hour," which began with an "Adventures of Popeye" cartoon, followed by a "Popeye's Treasure Hunt" segment (the length of two "Adventures of Popeye" cartoons), "Dinky Dog," a cartoon about a huge dog unrelated to Popeye, and another Popeye adventure. I was surprised that, other than Popeye wearing his sailor's hat, the character designs of the cast except for Bluto and the nephews, went back to the Fleischer period.

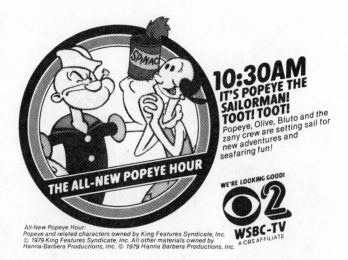

All-New Popeye Hour:
Popeye and related characters owned by King Features Syndicate, Inc.
© 1979 King Features Syndicate, Inc. All other materials owned by
Hanna-Barbera Productions, Inc. © 1979 Hanna Barbera Productions, Inc.

Advertisement sent to TV magazines to promote "The All New Popeye Hour."

Bluto was now wearing a striped, short sleeved shirt and captain's hat. His eyes were open but squinty and his nose was small. His beard was wide enough so that his teeth would show through to help convey expression. Though the nephews wore uniforms similar to their "Uncle Popeye's," they also sported sailor's hats rather than the rounded sailor's caps they wore in both the Fleischer and Famous Studios films. The nephews, being created by the Fleischer Studios and under the ownership of Paramount Pictures, were absent from the 1960-61 TV Popeyes. Apparently, CBS and Hanna-Barbera didn't run into any legal conflicts in reviving them, though the name of one of the nephews was changed to "Papeye." I suppose "Poopeye" was taboo on network television. Popeye and his crew, including the E.C. Segar design of the Sea Hag, were featured in 1970s stories. Popeye learns to disco in "Spinach Fever." Olive wants to be a Dallas Cowboys cheerleader in "Olive Goes Dallas." "Close Encounters of the Third Spinach" was a take off of the film *Star Wars*, with the sailor as "Pop-Star." This is the only film, thanks to Jack Mercer flubbing a line that Popeye calls his bearded foe, both Bluto and Brutus in the same film.

"Ballet Hooey" was a throwback to the Fleischer cartoons, meaning, expect the unexpected. Popeye prepares to eat his spinach to stop Bluto from bursting his basketball after the two sailors have created havoc during Olive's ballerina performance. As Popeye gets set to have the spinach fall in his mouth, Olive's head pops in the scene and says, "I'll take that." She eats the spinach and proceeds to teach the boys a lesson for ruining her ballet!

"Popeye's Finest Hour" put Popeye back into a white sailor's uniform, as he is incorrectly enlisted in the Navy. This time, Popeye's rival is Bluto's nephew, who looks just like his uncle. The plot of this cartoon was an older sailor, Popeye, adjusting to the younger men of the Navy. Popeye manages to use his spinach muscles to save the fleet and becomes an honorary admiral. Also featured on the

"Private Olive Oyl" cartoons featured the antics of Olive and Alice the Goon in the armed service. These cartoons appeared on "The Popeye and Olive Comedy Show." Pint-sized Sgt. Blast was their frustrated superior officer. Wimpy, Swee'-pea, and Eugene the Jeep appeared in a few of the "Private Olive Oyl" cartoons, but Popeye and Bluto did not. Joanne Worley of "Laugh-In" fame provided the loud voice for Sgt. Bertha Blast.

program were creatively written health and safety tips. The nephews would often be enticed to danger by a street-smart wolf, Mr. No-No. Popeye would arrive and set the lads straight. Regarding drinking, Popeye would sing, "Ya cants get much sicker than by drinking hard liquor says Popeye the Sailor Man ... toot! toot!"

In one tip, the wolf entices the nephews with a bag of cocaine. I have to admit this was a bit unnerving for me to see in a Popeye cartoon, yet, the safety message behind the segment was very effective.

Olive Oyl was much more independent in the new cartoons. She often figured the way out of a situation and in "The Loneliness of the Long Distance Popeye," she didn't wait for the sailor to show up. Olive pulled herself out of Bluto's grip and flipped the bully over her shoulder. This series was a big success in the ratings and was renewed for a second year. The addition for the second season was "Popeye's Sport's Parade," which alternated with the treasure hunt segment. In 1980, the show was trimmed to a half hour and called "The Popeye and Olive Comedy Show." "Private Olive Oyl"—cartoons about Olive and Alice the Goon in the army—was the first segment. Sgt. Bertha Blast, voiced by Joanne Worley, was forever in peril over the antics of Olive and Alice. The second cartoon, "Prehistoric Popeye," featured the cast as cave people. The final segment was a new "Adventures of Popeye" cartoon. The safety tips continued to appear during the

When "The All New Popeye Hour" was turned into the half-hour series "The Popeye and Olive Comedy Show," one of the regular segments was "Prehistoric Popeye," which featured the characters as cave people.

half hour. The year 1983 had produced enough cartoons for syndication, so the series went off the network. I recall watching the last network telecast on a Saturday morning only to have the new Popeyes appear on a local Boston station in syndication the following Monday. During the sailor's five years on CBS, 192 additional cartoons were produced along with 81 health and safety tips.

Why "Popeye and Son"?

In 1987, CBS brought Popeye back to the network in a new series called, "Popeye and Son." Fans who may have recalled the late 1950s Sunday "Thimble Theatre" strips featuring Swee'pea in a sailor's uniform sharing comical situations with Popeye, might have thought this was the inspiration for the title. Alas, Swee'pea was nowhere to be seen in this version. Instead, Popeye and Olive had married. Popeye, wearing a funky Hawaiian shirt, blue cap and blue pants, owned a gym. Olive, dressed in a gym suit had a new mop top hairdo. They were the parents of "Junior," a tyke who looked like neither of his parents, until he ate spinach. When he ate the vegetable, he would get Popeye forearms. The gimmick of the stories was that Junior hated spinach and would yell "yuck" after consuming some.

The advertisement reads:

DON'T BE BULLIED BY THE COMPETITION

POPEYE BEATS THE COMPETITION

	32	32	29	31	32	
						THE ALL NEW POPEYE BEATS EVEN THE MOST FORMIDABLE OPPONENTS
19		23	22	28		
CASPER AND THE ANGELS		DAFFY DUCK	THE JETSONS	SCOOBY AND SCRAPPY-DOO	13	☑ POPEYE ☐ COMPETITION
					YOGI SPACE RACE	

SOURCE: NTI

Popeye received a larger average share than each of these popular cartoon shows when he ran against them in a five-year period from 1978 to 1983. In fact, Popeye beat *all* his network competition in this period 75% of the time! With *The All New Popeye* in your corner, you can't help but come out a winner.

ALL NEW POPEYE
NOW AVAILABLE OFF-NETWORK

♔ King Features Entertainment
A subsidiary of The Hearst Corporation

As soon as the Hanna-Barbera Popeye cartoons left the CBS network, King Features Syndicate promoted them for immediate worldwide syndication. The drawing of Brutus used for this ad was by Popeye comic strip artist/writer Bud Sagendorf. Sagendorf was Segar's assistant on the original "Thimble Theatre" strip.

A dapper looking Bluto, looking more like "Brutus" from Bud Sagendorf's comic strip of the period, was married to a short frumpy woman named "Lizzie." They had a bully named "Tank" for a son and he hated Junior. While Wimpy, the Sea Hag, Eugene the Jeep and the Goons appeared in episodes, the spotlight was clearly on Junior and his friends including, "Woody" and "Dee-Dee." "Granny," Popeye's grandmother, who first appeared in the comic strip in 1961, makes her animation debut in a cameo appearance.

Popeye and Olive were married for the "Popeye and Son" cartoon series, which aired on CBS Saturday mornings from 1987 to 1988.

To illustrate how far this series veered from the original Popeye concept, in one cartoon, Bluto goes back to a store to return a ring he has picked out for his wife because Junior saved his money to buy the very same ring for his mother. Though Hanna-Barbera did an excellent job with the animation, the series didn't appeal to Popeye fans and the show was cancelled at the conclusion of the 1987-88 season. The series consisted of 13 episodes with two cartoons per show. Despite the fact the series only lasted for one season, it spawned several rack toys (items you would see on a spinning rack), jigsaw puzzles and a lunch box. "Popeye and Son" items have been merchandised overseas as of 2000 and King Features Syndicate still licenses these designs of the characters to interested parties.

Eugene the Jeep, Popeye's son Junior, and Junior's pal Woody go surfing. The beach was often used as a backdrop for Junior's adventures with his friends on "Popeye and Son."

Popeye Meets the Stooges

During the late 1950s and throughout most of the 1960s, two television programs were always mentioned by PTA groups as being harmful to children: "Popeye" and "The Three Stooges." Parents feared that their children would attempt to beat up the neighborhood bully after eating spinach or poke each other in the eye as the Stooges often did. What parents failed to remember is that neither the "Popeye" cartoons (from the Fleischer/Famous Studios period) or the "The Three Stooges" shorts were meant to be screened on television daily. These were originally watched in theatres before the start of a feature film with adults as their main target audience. Stations responded to the parents' concerns by pairing up the shorts with the cartoons. "Popeye and the Three Stooges" was a big hit on many local television stations for several years. The children had scored a victory! Moe Howard, leader of the Three Stooges, would often defend the violence in the shorts by stating they were no more violent than Popeye films. It has also been recorded that Popeye theatrical films were the most popular syndicated series in the country after debuting on television in 1956. The sailor was knocked into second place after "The Three Stooges" shorts first appeared on television. Popeye retained his title as the most popular animated cartoon series in syndication for several years.

Popeye and the Mouse

Mention Mickey Mouse to many Popeye fans and they will get angry. You will find very few fans of the sailor's films that are followers of Walt Disney's famous creation. This has to do with many historians giving Mickey Mouse the title, "World's Most Successful Cartoon Character." When one checks the facts, this title simply doesn't apply. Popeye and Mickey's careers are often linked. Mickey Mouse made his debut in the classic "talkie" cartoon, "Steamboat Willie" in 1928, while Popeye first walked into the "Thimble Theatre" comic strip in 1929. While Popeye was later adapted to animation, Mickey

Bluto and Olive Oyl as they looked in the "Popeye and Son" series. The character design of Bluto was very similar to Bud Sagendorf's comic strip version of "Brutus."

Mouse was worked into a newspaper comic strip. Both have had literally hundreds of thousand of items produced bearing their likenesses. The fact that there have been so many Mickey Mouse products produced over the years makes some think he has hundreds of animated cartoons to his credit. Mickey Mouse was one of the first animated cartoon characters to have his film career ended because the writers couldn't develop any more plots revolving around his sweet nature. "He was so awfully nice that it was hard to write stories for him. Donald Duck, Goofy, Pluto and the others overshadowed him," said Roy Disney, Jr., in 1988. While Popeye cartoons were continually in production, Mickey Mouse's last regular series entry was as early as 1942. His next film was released in 1947, followed by two in 1948, and one each year from 1951 to 1953. What revived Mickey's career was the debut of "The Mickey Mouse Club" in 1955, but even in this popular series, he was usually seen as only the host of the show. The Walt Disney Company wisely began using Mickey Mouse as their symbol for their many ventures, which kept him in the public eye. No one can deny that Mickey Mouse is popular with millions today as a popular cartoon symbol, but for the sheer volume of animated cartoons produced starting in the 1930s to the 1980s, Popeye still holds the record as the most successful animated cartoon character for both film and television.

Olive and Bluto are astonished at the racial stereotyping of indigenous islanders found in this cartoon (no, actually they're looking at Popeye's feats of strength). This is a scene from "The Island Fling" (Famous Studios, 1947) that features such native people but an edited print has been broadcast on television.

Popeye and the Censors

Despite the wide syndication of the films by Fleischer, Famous, and King Features, not every scene from every Popeye cartoon is still shown on television. Scenes or entire cartoons have been pulled from broadcast for reasons that would not have occurred to the makers of those films. For example, portrayals of Japanese soldiers that strike today's viewer as offensive and racist were standard fare in World War II America. Today, the World War II cartoons featuring Japanese villains are rarely seen on television.

In recent years, another group of cartoons has been largely unavailable on the television screen—what might be called the "island native" group. Famous Studios made at least three cartoons using caricatures of blacks that, while not uncommon in old animated films, are largely viewed as unacceptable for broadcast today. For example, the 1945 cartoon "Pop-Pie Ala Mode" is no longer aired. In this cartoon, Popeye lands on an island full of hungry cannibals. The natives have a desire to eat Popeye and attempt to roast him in a stewing pot. The cannibals are portrayed as brown with big pink lips. Oddly enough, footage from this

Popeye feeds Bluto spinach so they can defeat Japanese spies disguised as orphans. Popeye's fist will also smack Prime Minister Tojo and Adolf Hitler in the clever film "Seein' Red White n' Blue" (Famous Studios, 1943) that has long been banished from TV screens due to racial stereotypes.

cartoon appears in the 1948 cartoon "Spinach vs. Hamburgers." In some prints of the 1948 cartoon, the footage is left alone, while others remove it.

The appearance of a brown, big-lipped native was the reason why 1947's "The Island Fling" was kept off the air for many years. In this film, Popeye and Olive land on the island of Robinson Crusoe (who is actually girl-hungry Bluto). Footage of a female native mooning over both Bluto and Popeye has been cut, for the most part, from the now edited television print that has aired on Ted Turner's cable stations, WTBS, TNT and Boomerang. Though the editing is done nicely, it is obvious that scenes have been cut from the cartoon; still, it's good that it's back on the air in some version.

"Popeye's Pappy" (1952) is another cartoon featuring a tribe of man-eating, brown natives and also has vanished from the airwaves. In this cartoon, Popeye goes in search of his Pappy, who now is king of an island. The natives rescue Pappy from his son, Popeye, who wants to take him back home to his wife. The natives decide to cook Popeye in a pot, but when Pappy begins to get some fatherly feelings towards his son, he eats a can of spinach and both swabs beat up the hungry natives.

Like the other "island native" cartoons, this film had much airplay after its syndication debut in 1956. In fact, many programs geared strictly to children aired

Popeye, dressed in drag, tries to attract the attention of a pirate from "Popeye and the Pirates" (Famous Studios, 1947). What Popeye used to create his bosom has been (possibly) forever edited out of the film.

all of the above-mentioned Popeye cartoons until changing sensibilities caused them to be either shelved or edited.

One scene from a Popeye cartoon has forever remained a mystery as the film has been aired in edited form since its syndication debut. In "Popeye and the Pirates" (1947), Popeye dresses up as a woman to attract the attention of a pirate. When he thinks he's rid of the pirate, Popeye starts to take off his dress; then, suddenly, the scene cuts to Popeye in his white sailor suit, running from the pirate. Could it be that a scene where Popeye shows off some ladies' underwear has been forever snipped? Perhaps only the people who watched this cartoon on the movie screen have seen the whole picture.

In the 1956 cartoon, "I Don't Scare," there is a scene where Bluto is blown skyward, as he falls to earth, Popeye's forearm extends and his muscle forms the number 13. Then, he bops Bluto with his mighty fist. Because the motion conveyed to illustrate Popeye gaining the 13 number in his muscle has often been used after the sailor has eaten some spinach, people have wondered if the scene of him eating the vegetable in this film was cut out. While it is a possibility, by listening to the music in this scene, I can't detect any cut. Perhaps Popeye didn't need his spinach to flex his muscle in this film.

Popeye the Endorser Man

Popeye has appeared in a number of animated television commercials over the years. During the 1960s, the King Features television designs of Olive, Popeye, and Brutus appeared in an animated commercial promoting Popeye and Brutus "Soaky" figures. The segment was animated by Paramount Cartoon Studios. "Start" brand orange juice used Popeye to promote their product, and the King Features TV version of the sailor was featured in a couple of

Left: Scenes from the infamous Minute Maid commercial that aired in 2001, featuring Popeye, Olive Oyl, Bluto and Wimpy. This commercial sparked a wave of controversy throughout the media as to whether or not Popeye and Bluto were more than just ... friends? In truth, there have been animated cartoons where the pair were pals rather than enemies. No one questions the sleeping arrangements of the Three Stooges, so let's leave Popeye and Bluto alone. *Above:* Popeye was used in two animated commercials promoting "Start" brand orange juice in the early 1970s. The second advertisement featured Olive Oyl, who did damage to Popeye's arm, after drinking "Start" orange juice and gained strength. The animated commercials claimed that "Start" orange juice contained "more iron than spinach," however, the brand was not as enduring as Popeye's favorite vegetable. Popeye was also used in print campaigns to promote the orange juice.

King Features trade advertisement promoting Popeye for use in product merchandising.

Popeye's Famous Fried Chicken & Biscuits has been around for several years using the characters to help promote their food. Originally, the name "Popeye" for the chicken franchise referred to Gene Hackman's character "Popeye Doyle" in the movie *The French Connection.*

their animated commercials. During the mid–1970s, the comic strip designs of Popeye, Olive, and Brutus were featured in an animated commercial promoting their likenesses on pillows and bedsheets by Burlington House, Inc. Also during the 1970s, a Navy-uniformed Popeye made a cameo appearance in one of the "Dr. Pepper" commercials singing, "I'm Popeye the Pepper Man." Popeye was seen on a ship with a bevy of girls dressed in sailors' outfits.

Allens Popeye brand spinach has been on supermarket shelves for years.

The Nintendo Company featured Popeye in three commercials for the Popeye arcade game during 1983 and 1984. The first featured Popeye and Brutus
brawling over the use of the game, with Olive watching the fighting pair. The
second featured Popeye talking with the audience, and the third had Popeye bop-
ping the announcer talking about the game.

Popeye popped up in ads with Sonny the Coo-Coo bird for Cocoa Puffs
cereal. In these commercials, Popeye and Sonny get stranded on an island and
the sailor can't remember what makes him "tough." A can of spinach washes
ashore and Popeye gets his strength back.

Recently Popeye, Olive, Swee'pea, Wimpy, and Bluto (based on the Fleischer
studio designs) appeared in a series of television commercials showing the sailor
gaining strength by eating Quaker Oatmeal. In each cartoon, Olive Oyl says to
Popeye, "Popeye, your spinach?" Popeye replies, "Can the spinach ... I wants
me Quaker Oatmeal!" These simple ads stirred up a surprising amount of controversy. First, while Popeye fans were glad to see these well-animated commer-

Popeye, Olive, and Bluto (referred to as "Brutus" in this print version) were featured in a well-animated commercial for marine conservation during 1991.

cials on the air, they couldn't understand why Popeye would turn his back on
spinach. Couldn't he enjoy both? "Oatmeal is good food, like spinach," said Jeff
Brown, vice-president of King Features Syndicate, in 1990. "The essence of Popeye is good nutrition. That's why we've positioned Popeye in the campaign. Look,
I'm not a dietitian but we really don't think it's a problem for Popeye to eat something besides spinach once in a while." The people at Quaker Oats simply said
that they got permission from Popeye's owners to use the character as their

In 1989, Popeye was the official mascot for the Boy Scouts of America.

spokesman and to utter, "Can the spinach." However, another problem occurred during this campaign. At the conclusion of each commercial, Popeye would sing, "I'm Popeye the Quaker Man." Also, little comic books featuring "Popeye the Quaker Man" were tucked into the oatmeal packages. Real Quakers strenuously objected. Elizabeth Foley, spokesperson for the Quaker church, stated, "They had Popeye solving disputes and conflict through violence. This is completely obnoxious and offensive. We are an organization of pacifists. To portray us as a church that beats up on other people is not OK." Quaker Oats responded by saying that they looked upon the ads as humorous and never intended to spark any controversy.

Quaker children even got involved and suggested that Popeye display his strength in a more Quakerly fashion. "Courage and strength can be shown in a peaceful manner," they stated. The Quakers suggested that Popeye and Bluto decide to work together and build a homeless shelter. Paul Hendricks of King Features Syndicate said that the concept of Popeye and Bluto working together wouldn't be totally out of character as long as it wasn't saccharine-sweet. He added that Popeye is basically a nice guy. See what happens when you take away Popeye's affection for his spinach?

Popeye's association with Quaker Oats didn't last very long after this controversy occurred. Oddly enough, he did pop up in one later commercial endorsing prizes found in the oatmeal packages, but in this animated commercial he was seen without his beloved pipe. The pipe has often been taken away from Popeye in recent years. Even in some early illustrations, the pipe has been air-brushed out so that children will not be encouraged to smoke!

Olive Oyl and Swee'pea appeared in an ad for "Solo" laundry detergent. In 1991, Popeye, Olive, and Bluto appeared in a spot promoting marine conservation. Bluto is seen dumping trash in the water. Popeye uses his spinach muscles to create a whirlpool that spins the trash back at Bluto. However, Popeye still notices trash in the ocean and tells the audience that he can't clean up the water alone ... he needs their help.

In the mid–1990s, Popeye was used as the spokesperson for a television spot for Blue Cross and Blue Shield. Frank Caruso, the vice president of licensing at King Features Syndicate, called me one evening because he needed to know which TV Popeyes featured scenes with Swee'pea in peril, that would make up the ad. Scenes from the cartoon, "Pop Goes the Whistle" (Paramount Cartoon Studios, 1961), were used.

Wimpy was used in a commercial for Bagel Bites. At the beginning of the ad you see just his hand snatching bagel bites in a family's home. Finally, Wimpy is located, hiding in a closet, saying, "I would gladly pay you Tuesday for a Bagel Bite today." The ad closes with a scene of Wimpy licking his mouth from the 1960 TV Popeye "Camel-Ears" (Jack Kinney). Wimpy also turned up in a spot for Burger King featuring scenes from a few Paramount produced TV cartoons woven together.

In 1995, the post office celebrated the 100th anniversary of the comic strip by releasing a set of comic strip stamps. Despite the fact several comic strip characters were used on the stamps, the post office chose Popeye to be placed on the front of the booklet promoting the stamps. He was also the star of a television commercial announcing their arrival. The sailor was chosen although, by 1995, the Popeye comic strip was running in only a few newspapers in the United States. It was a testament to his recognition as a pop culture figure, rather than comic strip character, which led to his being chosen by the post office. During the summer of 2001, Popeye, Bluto and Olive starred in a commercial for Minute Maid orange juice, which ignited a storm of controversy. The well animated ad featured Bluto pushing Popeye on a swing, Popeye burying Bluto in the sand, the pair getting tattooed by a pair of Wimpys, drinking Minute Maid orange juice together and riding by Olive Oyl on a bicycle built for two. Christian conservative groups got the word out that they felt Popeye and Bluto were acting too friendly. The advertisement was illustrating, when you drink Minute Maid orange juice, people act in unexpected ways. Minute Maid's spokesman Dan Schafer stated in response to the controversy, "The ad does not suggest any relationship other than that Popeye and Bluto are friends. If a consumer group connects with one of our ads, then that is fine; we target our ads very broadly, to orange juice lovers." Mr. Schafer's response is rooted in fact that there are "Popeye" animated cartoons which show the pair working together ("Seein' Red, White n' Blue," Famous Studios, 1943) or as friends ("Fightin' Pals," Fleischer, 1940). The animation designs for the characters in this ad went back to the Fleischer Studios period.

Popeye Toys Based on the Cartoons

Well before the first Popeye cartoons aired on television, many Popeye collectibles were available, all based on Segar's "Thimble Theatre" comic strip. These products continued to be produced into the 1950s. After the original Popeye theater cartoons debuted on television, these first Popeye items became such a smashing success that thousands of new collectibles were manufactured. Popeye was one of the first cartoon characters whose exposure on television would lead to the manufacture of related merchandise. The number of Popeye collectibles doubled in size following the release of the 220 King Features TV cartoons in 1961.

Despite having been produced to take advantage of Popeye's success in television, many collectibles feature the comic strip versions of the characters (which closely match the Fleischer Studios designs). Others feature the white-suited Popeye of the Famous Studios and later King Features cartoons. Many products billed Popeye as "TV's Most Popular Cartoon Star" or "TV Cartoon Favorite," showing that the manufacturer was capitalizing on Popeye's television popularity rather than on his appearances in the print medium.

Here is a rundown of some of the Popeye items produced since the mid–1950s:

"Popeye" Coloring Book #2925 (1958). Features Bluto on the cover. Back of book bills Popeye and Olive as TV's most popular stars.

"Popeye" Coloring Book #2834 (1959). Bills Popeye as "TV's most popular cartoon star."

"Popeye Activity Book" #2831 (1960). Message on cover reads, "Watch Popeye cartoons on TV."

"Popeye" Coloring Book #2834 (1961). Features King Features TV designs.

"Favorite TV Cartoon Characters to Color" Book #4924 (1961). Features both the comic strip and the King Features TV versions.

"Popeye Sticker Book" #2631 (1961). Popeye is billed as a "TV star."

"Popeye Secret Pictures" Book #3097 (1962). Features the King Features designs on the cover.

FROM COAST-TO-COAST . . . TELEVISION'S FAVORITE

jaymar Popeye

BOXED • MYLAR WINDOW • STAY-IN-TRAY
JIGSAW PUZZLES

7964—AUTHORIZED POPEYE
Based on the famous newspaper, movie, and TV Series, another Jaymar first.
PACKED: 4 doz. assorted
WEIGHT: 33 lbs.   SUBJECTS: 4
BOX SIZE: 7¾"x10"x2¼"

Popeye
FUNNY
FACE
MAKER

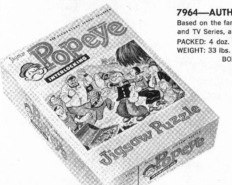

3104—AUTHORIZED POPEYE
Four 10"x13" "Stay-in-Tray" Inlaid Puzzles in Mylar window box.
PACKED: 1 doz.   SUBJECTS: 4
WEIGHT: 20 lbs.
BOX SIZE: 10⅛"x13⅛"x⅝"

2363—AUTHORIZED POPEYE
Stay-in-Tray Puzzles diecut for little boys and girls.
PACKED: 6 doz. assorted   SUBJECTS: 4
WEIGHT: 29 lbs.   SIZE: 10"x13"

1096—FUNNY FACE MAKER
Creates over 10,000 funny faces. Fun for young and old.
PACKED: 2 doz.   BANDED: 1 doz.
WEIGHT: 9 lbs.   SIZE: 11" x 11"

JAYMAR SPECIALTY CO. • 200 FIFTH AVENUE • NEW YORK, NEW YORK

The success the theatrical Popeye films were having on television during the late 1950s was often used as a promotional tool when advertising new products. Pictured is an advertisement for jigsaw puzzles and a "Funny Face Maker" by Jaymar.

Popeye, Olive (holding two Soakies of Popeye and Brutus), and Brutus in a Soaky television commercial from the early 1960s. These are the 1960-61 King Features TV versions of the trio.

"Popeye Sticker Fun" Book #2631 (1963). Features the King Features designs on the cover.

"Connect the Dots" Book #3097 (1963). Features the white-suited Popeye riding a horse on the cover.

"Popeye Color by Numbers Book" #2959E (1963). The white-suited TV Popeye is illustrated on the cover.

"TV Coloring Book" #2834 (1964). The white-suited TV version of Popeye is pictured at the wheel of a ship.

Note: All coloring and activity books listed above were produced by the Samuel Lowe Company.

Popeye Cartoon Kit by Colorforms (1957). One of the first Colorform sets. Featured the Famous Studios versions (white-suited Popeye and Bluto) of the Popeye cast. Olive was also featured in her Famous Studios design.

Popeye Costume by Collegeville (1950s and 1960s). Featured either the comic strip (Zaboly version) or King Features TV design.

Popeye Family Dolls and Handpuppets by Gund (1950s–1960s). The Gund company produced several Popeye family dolls. Usually the rubber head of the character stayed the same while the body style varied. The cast used were

Popeye, Olive, Wimpy, Swee'pea, and later Brutus. The Gund company also produced Popeye marionettes.

Popeye and Olive Oyl Bike Bobbers (1960s). Little figures of Popeye and Olive to attach to a bike's handlebars. Based on the King Features TV designs.

Popeye and Olive Push Button Puppets by Kohner Brothers (1960s). Little push button puppets based on the King Features TV designs.

Popeye Soaky by Colgate (1960s). A cartoon character soap container based on the King Features TV design of Popeye. The Woolfoam Corporation also produced this item based on the King Features TV design. A Brutus Soaky was also produced by Colgate using the King Features TV design.

Popeye Tricky Walker by Jaymar (1960s). King Features TV design.

Popeye Magic Slates by Samuel Lowe (1960 and 1963). The slates, at various times, pictured the comic strip and King Features TV designs.

Give-a-Show Projector by Kenner (used Popeye as one of their slides from 1960 to 1970). This toy often featured Popeye as the main attraction on the box. At least six different Popeye slides were produced. All used the comic strip designs of the Popeye cast, except that two slides featured "Bluto" and three depicted the King Features TV version of "Brutus."

Popeye Presto Paints by Kenner (1961). Pictured the comic strip versions, though Popeye's face on the box cover is illustrated as he appeared in the King Features TV cartoons.

6 delicious flavors in every box, each in its own pure plastic bag—ready for the kids to freeze whenever they want a frozen treat!

Store without refrigeration, 'till ready to use. So economical, too! Now at your favorite food store.

"Pop-Ice" was a fruit flavored product which used Popeye's face on the box for many years during the 1960s.

An excellent example of how both the films and the TV cartoons influenced a Popeye toy. *Left:* This Give-a-Show projector slide, produced by Kenner Toys in 1962, uses the King Features TV version of "Brutus." *Right:* A 1966 Give-a-Show slide features a Fleischer Studios design of "Bluto." Several of Kenner's Give-a-Show Projector slides used the names "Bluto" and "Brutus."

The instruction booklet to Colorforms' 1966 "Popeye's TV Cartoon Kit" featured the 1960-61 King Features Syndicate designs of Popeye, Olive, and Brutus.

Popeye Wrap-a-Round Playmates by Payton Products (1961). King Features TV designs of Popeye, Wimpy, Olive, and Brutus.

Popeye Sun Cards by Tillman's (1962). King Features TV designs.

Popeye Lunch Box and Thermos (1964). The King Features TV design of Brutus is pictured on the lunch box alongside the comic strip versions of the Popeye cast.

Popeye 14 Paints by the American Crayon Company (1965). King Features TV designs of Popeye, Olive Oyl, Swee'pea, and Wimpy.

Popeye Sparkle Paint Set by Kenner (1966). This set pictures a mixture of both the comic strip and King Features TV designs of Popeye, Olive, Eugene the Jeep, Swee'pea, the Sea Hag, Brutus, and Wimpy.

Popeye's TV Cartoon Kit by Colorforms (1966). King Features TV designs of Popeye, Olive, Swee'pea, and Brutus.

Popeye Dancing Toy by Hasbro (1967). A little wind-up dancing figure of Popeye based on the King Features TV design.

Popeye the Sailor Bendy Figure by Lakeside (1967). A blue-suited Popeye Bendy based on the King Features TV design. The companion toy to this was a Popeye Bendy Face (1968).

Popeye Paint and Crayon Set by Hasbro (late 1960s). The illustration on the box cover shows the King Features TV designs of Popeye and Swee'pea fishing. It actually looks as if it was pulled from one of the 1960s cartoons.

Popeye and Olive Oyl Dolls (big and small) by Dakin (1960s and 1970s). Though Popeye is wearing his black shirt and red collar, his facial design is based on the King Features TV cartoons, as is Olive Oyl's.

Popeye Candy Boxes by the Phoenix Candy Company (1960s and 1970s). The 1960s versions show the King Features TV cartoon designs while the 1970s boxes show character designs from "The All New Popeye Hour" by Hanna-Barbera (1978–83).

Popeye Drinking Glass by Deka (1971). King Features TV designs.

Brutus, Olive, and Popeye Coca-Cola Glass (1977). King Features TV designs.

Popeye Board Game by Parker Brothers (1983). King Features TV designs.

Popeye and Son Jigsaw Puzzles by Milton Bradley (1987). Featuring the character designs from the "Popeye and Son" cartoon program.

"Popeye and Son" Lunch Box by Thermo-Serv (1987).

"Popeye and Son" Toys including stamp sets, pop-maker, play money, grabber, and chalk board.

In 1994 and 1996, I helped produce two "Popeye" trading card series by Card Creations. Each one depicted both the different comic strip and animated cartoon versions of Popeye with background information regarding the image featured on each card. Around 1996, more and more Popeye items no longer used poses drawn by Bud Sagendorf or E.C. Segar style art. In their

"Popeye and Son" toys included several blister rack items including this "Lot's [*sic*] of Bills" by JA-RU (1987). Pictured on the product are Popeye, Junior, Eugene the Jeep, Wimpy's nephew, Bluto and Olive Oyl as they appeared in the "Popeye and Son" television series.

place were poses taken from animator's model sheets from the Fleischer Studios. Popeye was now being billed as "Classic Popeye since 1929."

Though the Fleischer design of Bluto was also being used, King Features Syndicate was calling him "Brutus," which continued to cause confusion over the name of Popeye's bearded foe. The return to the Fleischer style was popular enough to attract more companies wanting to use the Popeye cast in this version, which included:

"Legend of the Fridge" Magnets of Popeye and Olive (1996).

Square-shaped Magnets by Ataboy (1998).

Postcards by Pyramid (1998).

Beanies of Popeye, Olive, Swee'pea, Wimpy and Brutus by Highlight Stars (1999).

Racing Champion's "Street Wheels," Popeye, Olive, Swee'pea and the Jeep, Wimpy and Brutus racing cars (1999).

The design of the Popeye cast has since gone back to the Fleischer Studios period for many new products since 1996. Pictured is a Popeye postcard by Pyramid (1998).

Banks and Mini-lunch Boxes by Tin box Company (2000).

Popeye Golf Club Cover (in the shape of a handpuppet) by Winning Edge (2000).

Popeye Beanie with Golf Club by Winning Edge (2000).

Popeye, Olive, Wimpy, Swee'pea, The Jeep and Brutus Beanies and Keychains sold exclusively at CVS (2000).

18-inch Popeye Taking Doll by Precious Kids (2000).

Popeye Bendable by Precious Kids (2000).

Popeye and Olive Pull Back Boat by Precious Kids (2000).

Action Figures of Popeye, Olive (with Swee'pea), Wimpy (with the Jeep), Bluto and Peacoat Popeye by Mezco Toys (2001).

Grayscale Figures of Popeye, Olive and Bluto, which can interlock to form a 7-inch tall diorama by Cipriano Studios (2001). These are faithful renditions of the trio as they appeared in the mid-to-late 1930s Popeye films by the Fleischer Studios.

12-inch Popeye Action Figure by Mezco Toys (2001).

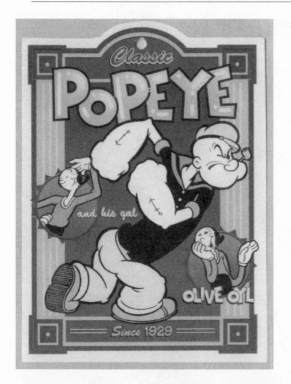 

Left: The tag to the Popeye Family CVS dolls depicted Popeye and Olive as they appeared in the Fleischer Studios cartoons. These dolls, as well as other newer products, billed the sailor as "Classic Popeye, since 1929." The dolls appeared in CVS stores across the country in 1999 and 2000. *Right:* The Vandor Company has produced a number of Popeye items including a cookie jar which plays the sailor's theme song, released in 2003.

Classic Comic Strip Statues of Popeye, Olive, Wimpy and Bluto by Dark Horse (2000, 2001).

Action Figures of Popeye (white sailor's uniform), Bluto (white sailor's uniform), Poopdeck Pappy, the Sea Hag and her vulture, Storm Gear Popeye by Mezco Toys (2002). The Popeye and Bluto action figures are based upon their appearances in the later Fleischer cartoons and the Famous Studios films.

The Vandor Company produced several ceramic items, including **mugs, cookie jars, salt and pepper shakers and bobbing head figures** in 2003.

Popeye Brand Enriched Bread was launched in April of 2003.

Baby Popeye and Friends, infant versions of the Popeye cast created by Frank Caruso, have been seen on birthday party sets, figurines and baby products.

Other products bearing the likeness of the characters from the Fleischer cartoons included: tee shirts, children's vitamins, Christmas ornaments, satin beaded candy boxes, banks, cookie jars and teapots. Outside of the United States, during the late 1990s to the present, new items bearing the images of the Fleischer versions

The Mezco company had great success with their line of Popeye, Olive, Wimpy and
Bluto action figures in 2001 so a second set was released in 2002 and a further series
is scheduled for 2004.

Left: Baby Popeye & Friends logo. *Right:* A Popeye balloon in a Pennsylvania Thanksgiving Day parade.

were being produced, which included: a coffee table, coat rack, CD holder, end table, coloring books and stationery products.

Popeye on Video and DVD*

Popeye cartoons from all the studios that produced them have appeared on video and DVD for several years. The first cartoons put on video were the three-color Fleischer specials which are in the public domain. These three appeared on many, many labels with varying degrees of quality on video and DVD. On video, several Popeye theme tapes were issued featuring cartoons from the 1960-61 series. These theme tapes also featured "Snuffy Smith," "Beetle Bailey," "Cool McCool" and "Krazy Kat." Public domain Famous Studios cartoons have been released in and outside of the United States. Hearst Entertainment has released several Popeye titles using the Hanna-Barbera cartoons from 1978 to 1983 and a series of "Popeye and Son" episodes for both video and DVD. Several episodes from the Hanna-Barbera productions, as of 2003, have only been released outside of the United States.

Here is a listing of Popeye titles currently available on video:

The information in this section is current as of the time this book went to press in April 2004.

Life-sized Popeye, Olive, and Brutus at the beach boardwalk in Santa Cruz, California.

Fleischer Studios

Popeye the Sailor Meets Sindbad the
  Sailor
Popeye the Sailor Meets Ali Baba's
  Forty Thieves
Aladdin and His Wonderful Lamp
Let's Sing Along with Popeye (actu-
  ally a "Screen-Song" cartoon)
Little Swee'pea
I'm in the Army Now
The Paneless Window Washer

I Never Changes My Altitude
A Date to Skate
Customers Wanted
With Poopdeck Pappy
I-Ski Love-Ski You-Ski
Eugene the Jeep
Spinach Roadster
Blow Me Down
Females Is Fickle

(Note that many of the Fleischer black and white cartoons have been put with other studios' titles and titled, "Cartoon Collections" and are of varying quality and part of bootleg collections.)

Famous Studios

You're a Sap, Mr. Jap
Me Musical Nephews
Seein' Red, White n' Blue
She-Sick Sailors
Big Bad Sindbad
Ancient Fistory
Floor Flusher
Taxi Turvy
Bride and Gloom
Greek Mirthology
Fright to the Finish
Private Eye Popeye
Gopher Spinach

Cookin' with Gags
Popeye for President
Out to Punch
Insect to Injury
Parlez-Vous Woo
I Don't Scare
Shuteye Popeye
A Haul in One
The Crystal Brawl
Patriotic Popeye
Spree Lunch
Spooky Swabs

King Features TV Cartoons

Dead-Eye Popeye
Ace of Space
Two-Faced Paleface
From Way Out
There's No Space Like
   Home
Astronut
Egypt Us
Jeopardy Sheriff

Out of This World
Westward Ho-Ho
Hill Billy Dilly
Pest of the Pecos
Tiger Burger
Aztec Wreck
Invisible Popeye
Jingle Jangle Jungle
Forever Ambergris

Round the World in 80
   Days
Sea Hagracy
Voice from the Deep
Sea No Evil
Skinned Divers
Irate Pirate
Hag Way Robbery

(additional titles released outside of the United States)

Retro style designs of the Popeye family which were introduced in 2003. These designs have appeared on pins, magnets and bendable figures.

Hanna-Barbera Cartoons

Top Kick in Boot Camp

Computer Chaos

Snow Fooling

Infink-try

Goon Hollywood

Goon Balloon

Private Secretaries

Troop Therapy

The Great Speckled Whale

Shark Treatment

Popeye the Sleepwalker

A Goon Gone Gooney

Popeye Goes Sale-ing

Pappy Fails in Love

Ships That Pass in the Fright

Popeye Snags the Sea Hag

The Game

Popeye's Roots

Westward Ho-Ho

Chilly Con Caveman

Come Back Little Stegosaurus

Mother Goose Is on the Loose

The Midnight Ride of Popeye Revere

Vegetable Stew

Neanderthal Nuisance

Popeye of the Klondike

The Spinach Bowl

Pedal Powered Popeye

Olive's Shining Hour

The Loneliness of the Long Distance
    Popeye

Popeye's Self-Defense

The Umpire Strikes Back

The Decathlon Dilemma

Take Me Out to the Brawl Game

Olive Goes Dallas

(additional titles released outside of the United States)

In the United States in 1999 Rhino Home Video, as part of their "Saturday Morning Funnies" series, issued two videos featuring the Hanna-Barbera Popeye cartoons later released in DVD format. Nostalgia Family Video, located in Baker City, OR, issued two "Popeye" videos. Volume 1 featured eight black and white titles in the public domain, "Little Swee'pea" (1936), "I'm in the Army Now" (1937), "The Paneless Window Washer" (1937), "I Never Changes My Altitude" (1937), "A Date to Skate" (1938), "Customers Wanted" (1939), "With Poopdeck Pappy" (1940), "Me Musical Nephews" (1943) and a Popeye "Soaky" commercial from the 1960s. Volume 2 in 2000, featured several public domain Famous Studios cartoons and the safety cartoon, "Look Where You Are Going." In 2003, *Popeye: A Biography*, a look at the sailor's career, produced by Michael Atkinson was released by Midnight Matinee Video from Boston, Massachusetts.

Where Are the Classics on Video and DVD?

During the late 1990s several companies continued to release the same public domain "Popeye" cartoons produced by the Fleischer and Famous Studios on video and DVD. Why the rest of the library from these studios has not been made available on video or DVD has been a constant source of frustration, not only for Popeye fans but animation scholars as well.

Unfortunately, the reasoning behind this is a misunderstanding between King Features Syndicate and whoever owned the "Popeye" theatrical series during any period since their release to television in 1956. One of the reasons King Features Syndicate produced their own "Popeye" series for television in 1960 was the fact that they did not receive any money from the airings of the theatrical Popeyes on the small screen because they simply owned no part of them. This was clearly stated in a *TV Guide* article discussing the creation for the TV Popeyes in the August 27th–September 2nd issue (1960):

> Why, a new Popeye series for television? Apparently it's the result of a running battle between United Artists Associated, which syndicates the oldies and King Features. The newspaper syndicate firm owned no TV rights to the movie shorts. When they were released to TV, consequently, King Features did not share in the lucrative residual payments.

While King Features Syndicate earned money for allowing Paramount Pictures the use of their characters in the production of the animated films, no financial arrangement was made once the films were syndicated on TV. This arrangement still stands. What has changed is that United Artists no

Promotional art by Neil Tenczar for the video, *Popeye: A Biography* ©2003. Produced by Michael Atkinson.

longer owns the films and the medium has changed from TV to video and DVD. In 1983, United Artists had planned a video release of several early color Famous Studios "Popeye" cartoons but King Features Syndicate sent the firm a cease and desist letter claiming they were the only ones who could release Popeye on home video. The confused lawyers at United Artists panicked and acknowledged in writing that King Features had the rights to Popeye, and this letter has held up the release of the theatrical films on home video and DVD. It has often been printed that it is King Features that has solely held up the release of the cartoons on video and DVD due to the mistaken impression that they own the rights to the films. However, why didn't the lawyers at United Artists research their claim thoroughly? Whenever there has been background information written regarding the creation of the TV Popeyes, the ownership of the theatrical films has often been printed. Clearly this is due to a misunderstanding on the part of both parties, not just one. During the end of the 1990s, Warner Brothers acquired rights to the theatrical cartoons. One can only hope that they will not repeat the same mistake as United Artists or actively work out an arrangement with King Features to release these cartoons on video and DVD. As a representative from Warner Brothers told me in late 2001, regarding the desire to have these films released on video and DVD, "Oh good ol' Popeye—we get a lot of requests for him!"

The Colorization of Popeye

Several years ago, performers and fans of classic black and white programs have spoken out against Ted Turner's colorization process. Turner has claimed that anyone preferring to see a colorized program in black and white need only turn down the color knob on his television set. But with an animated cartoon, the colorized version may differ from the original whether viewed in color or black and white. In 1987 Turner began colorizing the 120 Popeye films originally produced in black and white by Fleischer and later Famous Studios. The color conversion was done by Entercolor Technologies and cost approximately $10,000 to $11,000 per cartoon depending upon length. Turner explained in a press release that coloring a cartoon is different from coloring a motion picture: "The process for coloring Popeye is a total film process, involving making all necessary color separations from the original 35mm masters. Then each cell is hand-colored. The color converted cells are transferred onto 16mm film. The effect is a new color negative." However, because the pictures are redrawn and hand colored, in several cartoons, movement and images that appeared in the originals are missing in the new prints. For example, if the person doing the redrawings forgot to draw Popeye's pipe in one scene, the pipe would be gone—whether the viewer turned down his color knob or not. Here are a few examples of Popeye cartoons distorted by the colorization process:

"Blow Me Down" (1933). In the black and white version, several objects are hurled at Olive Oyl's dressing room, creating a knocking sound. Olive, after hearing the sound, says, "Come in." In the colored film, the objects were not drawn, so Olive's words make no sense.

"I Eats My Spinach" (1933). In the opening scene, Popeye sings his theme song. While the action goes on around him, the voice goes out of sync, ruining the pacing of the scene. In the black and white original, the action and vocals are in sync. During the rodeo fight between Bluto and a bull, the bull's horns hit Bluto causing the brute's head to spin, which is heard on the soundtrack. In the colored cartoon, Bluto's head doesn't move. Toward the end of the cartoon, Popeye punches a bull. It flies into the air and falls to earth in the form of various

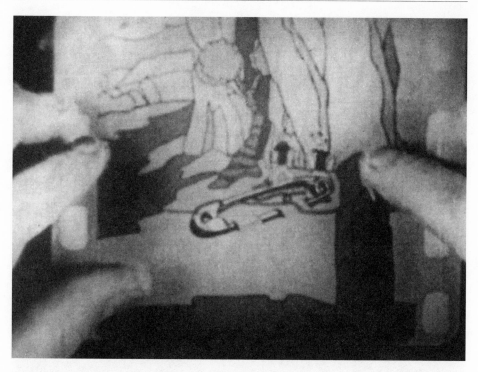

Scene from the black-and-white "Goonland" (Fleischer, 1938) shows two live-action hands joining the film together. This clever device was removed from the colorized version.

cuts of meat. In the colorized cartoon, Popeye punches the bull, and it flies up in the air, and then suddenly, Popeye and the bull vanish, only to appear a few seconds later.

"A Dream Walking" (1934). This film features dazzling 3-D backgrounds, and the black and white version is considered a classic, but the added color makes it look like standard fare. In the film are two brief scenes showing Popeye running behind Bluto. Each scene features a different backdrop. In the colored version, the same backdrop is used in both scenes.

"The Dance Contest" (1934). This cartoon featured the illusion of a moving ballroom, which is ruined in the colorized version.

"For Better or Worser" (1935). Bluto suffers a blow to the head and while we hear him shake it off, we don't see the action as it wasn't redrawn in the colored version. This cartoon is often aired with a sped-up soundtrack. Another classic ruined.

"You Gotta Be a Football Hero" (1935). Popeye eats his spinach and becomes a one-man football team with images of several ghostly Popeyes surrounding him. The ghostly images must have been scared away in the color version as they do not appear.

Colorization of the early Popeye cartoons has produced some amazingly careless errors, as seen in the two versions of the 1936 Fleischer cartoon "A Clean Shaven Man." The top photograph is from the black-and-white original, with Bluto walking into "WIMPY's BARBER S[HOP]." The bottom photo shows Bluto in the colorized film, walking into "WIMBY's BBER...."

"King of the Mardi Gras" (1935). Not only do Wimpy's hat and coat keep changing color, but Bluto is billed as "Bloto" on the circus tent. In the black and white cartoon, a bit of the tent partially covers the U in Bluto, but in the color version, I suppose it was easier to change the spelling of Bluto's name rather than to correctly trace the shape of the tent.

"Adventures of Popeye" (1935). The live action scenes featuring the two boys were left in black and white while the animation was colorized. The last five minutes of the film's audio, starting with Bluto and Popeye fighting on logs gets thrown out of sync with the animation in the colored print.

"The Spinach Overture" (1935). Popeye twirls his pipe; we hear it but don't see it.

"A Clean Shaven Man" (1935). Popeye and Bluto run to "Wimpy's Barber Shop" in the black and white version, which has been renamed, "Wimby's Bber" in the colored print.

"Bridge Ahoy" (1936). Olive and Popeye are tossing rivets to each other. In the colored print, for a split second, Popeye and Olive suddenly switch places because the cel of the pair was filmed in reverse. This error ruins the pacing of the scene.

"Little Swee'pea" (1936). The 3-D backgrounds all but vanish in the colored print.

"Morning, Noon and Nightclub" (1937). In the black and white films, the animators drew details to the posters seen in the cartoons. In this colored version, the posters look crude and childish.

"Learn Polikeness" (1938). At the end of this cartoon, Popeye toots his pipe. In the colored version, we hear the "toots" but the mouth movements have not been redrawn.

"Big Chief Ugh-Amugh-Ugh!" (1938). Popeye and Olive are riding a donkey and you hear a "thump" on the soundtrack, but you don't see the movement that goes along with this sound because it was not redrawn in the color print.

"Goonland" (1938). This classic cartoon features the film breaking and two human hands use a pin to repair it. The hands are missing from the color version and the film puts itself back together. When the Cartoon Network aired a special honoring 50 of the greatest cartoons ever made, this cartoon and "A Dream Walking" were featured. Many people were upset, however, that the network decided to air the colored versions of each film rather than the black and white originals.

"Child Psykolojiky" (1940). Popeye plays poker with his Pappy, but the chips keep vanishing and appearing in the colored version.

"Pip-eye-Pup-eye-Poop-eye and Peep-eye" (1942). Popeye's nephews have their names carved in their chairs. Because the names were redrawn so carelessly, in some shots we see only the letters "Pee" carved on Peepeye's chair.

"Olive Oyl and Water Don't Mix" (1942). In a brief scene, as Olive approaches Popeye and Bluto from behind, the back of Bluto's hair was not colored in making him bald.

"Many Tanks" (1942). Yet again, Popeye toots his pipe at the end of the film but the action was not drawn in.

"Me Musical Nephews" (1942). Popeye is wearing his white uniform in this cartoon but in the colored version, when his nephews start to say their prayers, Popeye is seen wearing his black shirt, blue pants and red collar for a split second.

"Too Weak to Work" (1943). Why are Popeye and Bluto's sailor knots colored red in this film?

"A Jolly Good Furlough" (1943). This is another cartoon with the portion of the soundtrack out of sync with the animation, due to being redrawn and colored.

"Woodpeckin'" (1943). Who can read the opening credits?

"Cartoons Ain't Human" (1943). Popeye holds up a very suggestive drawing and a human hand appears and marks it "Censored." In the color version, the hand is not used and the word "Censored" just appears.

These are only a few examples of the mishandling the black and white films have had to endure. In truth, children will probably not notice these errors, but it's a shame that the classic work of the Fleischer Studios has been represented by color prints featuring shoddy animation. Television stations generally feel that color episodes bring in larger ratings than black and white programs. This is the reason why the Popeye cartoons were redone in color. Yet there is almost certainly a big audience who still prefers to watch a black and white Popeye cartoon. Black and white programming is, after all, a part of entertainment history—just like Popeye himself.

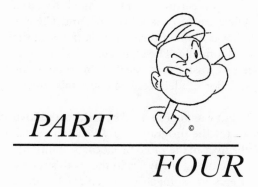

PART

FOUR

Radio and Records,
Stage and Screen

The Radio Program

The Popeye radio series began on September 10, 1935, on the NBC radio network. The program was aired three days a week and ran in a continuous format (like a soap opera), much as Segar's strip was running at the time. It featured the voices of Det Poppen as Popeye, Olive La Moy as Olive Oyl, and Charles Lawrence as Wimpy. Matey, a young lad, was another recurring character in the radio series and was portrayed by Jimmy Donnelly. The character of Matey was used instead of Swee'pea because Swee'pea wasn't very vocal at this time in the "Thimble Theatre" comic strip, and the sailor needed a lad he could talk to who could speak to him in return.

The NBC program lasted until 1937 but was later revived by CBS with Floyd Buckley in the Popeye role. The sponsor for the program was Wheatena cereal, and Wheatena became Popeye's strength-giver in the radio broadcasts. Thus any mention of spinach had to be rewritten, including the lyrics in the swab's theme song. "I'm strong to the finich 'cause I eats me spinach" was replaced with "I yam what I yam 'cause I yam what I yam."

During Popeye's radio career, a prizefighting craze was sweeping the nation, and Popeye's audience just followed that craze by tuning in to the prizefights that the sailor was having on the radio with his rivals. These famous fist fights became a trademark in Popeye's humor. Oddly, Bluto was not heard on these radio shows (as he only appeared once in Segar's "Thimble Theatre" comic strip in 1932).

In the long run, the radio program has become a forgotten footnote in Popeye's media career. However, in the 1970s, three different labels produced record albums featuring several episodes of the radio show. Each album had the same title: "Popeye." The dates and labels were as follows:

1976. George Garabedian Productions.
1977. Golden Age Records.
1979. Nostalgia Lane.

The episodes, all of which appeared on all three records, were "Popeye and the Runaway Trolley," "Popeye and Who's Who at the Zoo," "Popeye, Geranium and the Giant," and "Popeye Meets Robin Hood."

In the Fall 2000 issue of "The International Popeye Fan Club" news magazine, a listing was published of several episode titles of the radio program, heard in 1936 through 1937.

1936

The Heroes Return
The Auction Sale
Grand Opening
Popeye in Africa, Part 1
Popeye in Africa, Part 2

Wimpy's Disgrace
The Magic Carpet, Part 1
The Magic Carpet, Part 2
Popeye in Politics
Community Sing
Wimpy Land Slide
Unhand Me Villain

Rip Van Popeye, Part 1
Rip Van Popeye, Part 2
Rip Van Popeye, Part 3
Campaign Tactics
The Complete Anglers
The Unveiling
The Living Statue
The Barbecue
The Galley Slaves
The Old Mill
Popeye Goes Roller Skating
The Submarine
Old King Cole
Rest Cure in Yellowstone
Popeye's Halloween Program
Popeye in India, Part 1
Popeye in India, Part 2
Popeye in India, Part 3
Little Red Riding Hood
Mountain Land Slide
Popeye and the Three Bears
Humpty Wimpy
The Curiosity Shop
Popeye and Delilah
Popeye at Dancing Class
Carmen
Popeye and Pooka-Hauntess
Black Diamonds
Popeye in Toyland
Rounding the Horn
Popeye Plays the Piper
Popeye on Mount Olympus
Popeye in Porcelain
Popeye and the Birds

Popeye and Jack Frost
Popeye and the Old Man Pharaoh
Popeye and the Organ Grinder
Christmas Spirit
Sir Walter Popeye and Ka-Wan
The Bicycle Marathon
The Turkey Talks

1937

Noah's Ark
Sunken Treasure
Calamity Olive and Wild Bill
Sir Popeye, the Peerless
Popeye in the Gymnasium
Popeye and Alexander
William Popeye Tell
Scrap Iron Yard
Olive Who Lived in a Shoe
Popeye Makes Rain
Popeye Fights a Duel
The Horse Show
Popeye and Father Time
Popeye Does a Little Road
The Ainsheenk Marineer
Wimpy, Grand Lama of Tibet
The Ghost Ship
Matey Revere
Matey Hansel and Marjorie
Sir Isaac Wimpy Newton
Popeye Gulliver
Popeye Romeo and Olive
Don Quixote Popeye
China Clipper

Popeye the Recording Artist

The radio shows are not the only Popeye material that has been recorded. Due to the success the Popeye animated cartoons had on television, a number of children's recordings featuring the Popeye cast were produced. Many featured original songs and stories, while others were readings of scripts pulled from the 1960-61 TV cartoons. Jack Mercer (Popeye) and Mae Questel (Olive Oyl) often provided the voices for the albums; when Questel wasn't available, Mercer did Olive's voice, too, as well as the voice of Brutus. The albums were produced from the late 1950s well into the 1980s. A bit of the copy from the "Popeye's Favorite

Stories" album (1960) gives some indication of Popeye's popularity on television at the time:

> The stories were created by Dick Kleiner, who has the necessary prerequisite for the assignment—three children who watch every Popeye cartoon on television they can get. They even invent channels, in order to get more Popeye cartoons. The magic of Popeye's appeal, which seems to intrigue adults and children and even stray dogs, is hard to explain. So let's not even try; suffice it to say that it exists, that virtually everyone enjoys Popeye's adventures and that here in Popeye's Favorite Stories you'll find six brand new exciting funny stories.

Here is a rundown of the Popeye record albums produced to capitalize on the sailor's television success, and the songs/stories which appeared on each one:

"Popeye's Favorite Stories" (RCA CAMDEN, 1960). "Popeye the Skin Diver," "Popeye Goes to the Jungle," "Popeye Flies a Rocket," "Baby Sitter Popeye," "Popeye the Cowboy," and "Popeye and the Man from Mars."

"Popeye the Sailor Man and His Friends" (GOLDEN RECORDS, 1960s). "I'm Popeye the Sailor Man," "Popeye in Cartoon Land," "Strolling Through the Park," "Help! Help! and I Had a Hamburger Dream," "Home on the Range," "Television Night," "Never Pick a Fight," "Every State Is a Great State," "Take Me Out to the Ball Game," "The Emperor of Japan," "A Game for a Rainy Day," and "Why Do You Answer a Question with a Question."

"Popeye's Songs About Health, Safety, Friendship and Manners" (GOLDEN RECORDS, 1962). "Shake Hands," "A Friend Is Someone You Like," "I Have a Little Friend," "A Friendly Town," "Red and Green," "When You Ride Your Bicycle," "Never Play with Matches," "Swimming," "Lonely Tooth," "Sleepy Head," "Scrub and Scrub," "Ah-Choo," "Polite Ways Make Happy Days," "It Matters If You Have Good Manners," and "When You Go to a Show."

"Popeye the Sailor Man—4 Exciting Stories" (PETER PAN, 1970s). "Moon Struck," "Pollution Solution," "Oyle on Trouble Waters" and "A Child Shall Lead Them."

"Popeye the Sailor Man" (PETER PAN, 1976). "Skin Divers," "Jeep Jeep," "Fleas a Crowd," and "Where There's a Will."

"Popeye—4 Exciting Christmas Stories" (PETER PAN, 1977). "Christmas Pie," "Pearl Burgers," "Deck the Halls," "Santa Popeye."

"Popeye the Sailor Man" (PETER PAN, 1980s). "Popeye's Trained Fleas," "The Sunken Treasure Affair," "Popeye Meets a Jeep, Jeep," and "Popeye's Good Fortune."

Opposite: **Several "Popeye" record albums have been produced over the years. Many, including the one pictured at top, featured the voices of Jack Mercer and Mae Questel. The record pictured at bottom was based on a TV cartoon script; some others featured original stories or even a few of the 1930s Popeye radio programs.**

"Popeye; In the Movies" (PETER PAN, 1980s). "Popeye in the Movies," "Spinach on the Spanish Main," "Gold Fever," and "Who's Afraid of a UFO."

"Popeye the Sailor Man" (PETER PAN, 1980s). "Popeye the Astronaut," "Popeye's Secret Formula," "Popeye and the River Queen," and "Sweet Pea's Disappearing Act."

The Popeye Movie

Robert Evans, who produced such films as *The Godfather* and *The Odd Couple*, learned that Famous Music at Paramount Pictures collected royalties of $75,000 annually off the original "I'm Popeye the Sailor Man" theme song. This sparked an interest in Evans to produce a feature-length live action "Popeye" film. Robert Altman was to direct and writer and cartoonist Jules Feiffer was to script the feature. Both wanted to do a picture based on Segar's world—which may be the reason the film failed to be any more than a moderate success at the box office.

The script for *Popeye* had been kicking around for at least three years prior to its production. The film was originally slated to be called "Popeye and Olive Oyl" and to star Dustin Hoffman and Lily Tomlin. In early sessions on the film, Hoffman was enthusiastic; but about 50 pages into the script, he changed his mind and declared that Jules Feiffer's script was not taking the right approach. Robert Evans backed Feiffer and refused to hire a new writer. Hoffman left the project. Tomlin also bailed out, but her reasons are unknown.

It was at this time that Robin Williams was rapidly becoming the most popular TV star in the country with the success of the series "Mork and Mindy." Williams was wildly inventive and ad-libbed often on the series, as Jack Mercer used to do for the Fleischer Popeye cartoons of the 1930s and 1940s. Williams was more than physically right for the character of Popeye, looking a lot like Popeye would without the exaggerated features of comic strip art. In the role of Olive Oyl, Evans cast Shelley Duvall, another dead ringer for the character she was to play.

Beginning with these excellent choices, Robert Evans went on to assemble an outstanding cast to portray a host of Segar characters, including Poopdeck Pappy, J. Wellington Wimpy, Swee'pea, Nana and Cole Oyl (Olive's parents), Castor Oyl (Olive's brother), Geezil, and Bluto. Particularly fine in their roles were Ray Walston, who added lots of off-the-cuff muttering and swearing to his role as Poopdeck Pappy, and Paul Dooley, who convincingly mooched his way through the part of Wimpy. Wesley Ivan Hurt played little Swee'pea and was always a cute presence on the screen.

Makeup attempted to be true to the Segar characters while avoiding the sort of grotesquerie that can come from attempting to recreate comic strip art with live actors. Robin Williams' face was left pretty much alone (though his hair was dyed red to match the Popeye of Segar's colored Sunday strips). His arms and legs, however, were elaborately made up with sculpted latex forms that slipped on over his limbs. As for costuming, here the representation of Segar's work faltered. While costumes for Olive and the supporting characters were on target, Popeye was usually clothed in dark-colored bellbottoms and a white shirt with dark blue collar. His more familiar attire was seen in only one fleeting scene in which he battles with Bluto.

Popeye's hometown, called "Sweethaven" in the film, was lovingly created with detailed sets that effectively portrayed a Segar world. The "town" was built on the island of Malta by designer Walt Kroeger. Much of the action took place outdoors, where the sets were used to great advantage.

An honest attempt was made to capture the bizarre nature of Segar's original strip. A scene featuring a boxing match between Popeye and Oxblood Oxheart faithfully included Wimpy as the referee and, like the original, had Oxblood's mother tossed into the battle. The scene where Popeye first reunites with his long-lost Pappy is pure Segar (lifted from the original comic strip where Popeye sees his father for the first time in years). One interesting use of Segar material involves the discovery that Baby Swee'pea can predict the future, a talent that Olive and Wimpy make use of at the racetrack. This power was originally Eugene the Jeep's, from a 1936 "Thimble Theatre" strip.

The thing that hurts the film the most is the songs. Robert Evans wanted to do a comic strip musical, but the majority of the songs don't need to be there and are annoying. In one scene, Olive goes on singing about her boyfriend Bluto and how "large" he is. Most of the lyrics talk about how big in size the brute is, but it's a pointless song. Another pointless number is Bluto singing about how mean he is. While he's belting out the tune he's smashing the Oyls' home ... so it's evident he's mean! Shelley Duvall is a fine actress, but she can't sing too well and it's apparent. (Mae Questel did a much better job belting out a few songs in the animated cartoons.) Robin Williams screams his numbers, and the only song worthy of being in the picture is the closing (and expected) "I'm Popeye the Sailor Man."

On the other hand, the script does not offer much relief from the songs. The film attempts to explain the origins of the characters: why Popeye sailed to Sweethaven, why Pappy remained hidden all these years, the discovery of Swee'pea left in a basket by his mother and the growing attraction between Popeye and Olive Oyl. Why did the audience need to know the origins of characters that have been around for decades? This explaining took a lot of screen time and became boring. A Popeye tradition was smashed during the course of the film when Williams muttered, "I hates spinach." For a film attempting to be true to its origins, this was a doozy. It figured into the plot, however, because it provided an opportunity for Popeye to discover the vegetable as a source of strength: Bluto, hearing that Popeye doesn't like spinach, force-feeds it to the sailor. Popeye then gains his super-strength and promptly clobbers Bluto.

Whatever the flaws of its script, the major reason for the film's commercial failure is probably its attempt to recreate Segar's Popeye. Audiences came expecting to see the Popeye they knew best: the animated film star. No matter how wonderful Segar's strip was (and still is), Segar's Popeye is not the version that the mass audience knows. When characters like Olive's parents, the Tax Man, Castor Oyl and Geezil appeared on the screen, people no doubt just wondered who they were. The battle at the finish between Popeye and Bluto was very brief; fans of the elaborate animated battles were probably disappointed. And certainly, no one expected to hear Popeye say he hated spinach!

The film does contain a tribute to the Fleischer cartoons: the opening features the original Fleischer cartoon opening, with Popeye's voice saying, "Hey, what's this … one of Bluto's tricks? I'm in the wrong movie." That opening scene was animated by Hanna-Barbera, and Popeye's voice was by Jack Mercer. The opening probably led people to expect a live-action version of a Popeye animated cartoon. They didn't plan on seeing the story of Popeye or his first encounters with Olive, Wimpy, etc. These character relationships should already have been established. Perhaps a better idea would have been to build a plot around Popeye's battle with Sindbad or Ali Baba, rather than stringing Segar strips together and adding songs that didn't help carry the motion picture.

The movie opened to mixed reviews in 1980, though the casting of Williams and Duvall was almost unanimously praised. Many critics faulted the songs and script, and the film's expected box-office business never materialized. The film did spark new interest in the comic strip character of Popeye, and the strip (then being done by Bud Sagendorf) saw its low circulation figures boosted for a brief time. Merchandise based on the film hit stores, including a Colorforms set, puzzles, board game, storybooks, photo-novel books and activity books. Popeye merchandise, using the comic strip designs of the characters, resurfaced with the opening of the movie. Though *Popeye* pulled in $61 million at the box office, the film has enjoyed an afterlife as a popular video rental. Today, in Anchor Bay, Malta, the set from the movie still stands and tens of thousands of tourists visit each year. There is also a stage show featuring young employees dressed as the Popeye characters, a 15-minute film, "The History of the Popeye Village Film Set" and a musical revue. The movie was released on DVD in 2003.

Synopsis of the Movie

A brilliant sunrise buoys the spirit of a lone sailor in a battered, worn dinghy as he braves a sea squall in hopes of reaching land. As the sailor approaches land, the town of Sweethaven is basked in morning sunlight. The sailor stops in the town, which is just greeting the morning and new day. As the sailor walks the docks, a tax man, riding a bicycle, approaches him. "I'm the tax man and that'll be a 25-cent docking tax," he shouts. The tax man begins to tax the sailor for each item he brings to shore. "Altogether you owe the Commodore a dollar eighty-seven," the tax man says. When Popeye asks who the Commodore is, he's taxed a nickel for "question tax." Strangers gather to watch the sailor pay the tax man.

As the sailor passes by boarding houses, signs are put up stating, "No rooms for rent" and "No visitors." While walking, the sailor comes across a pipe. As he bends over to pick up the pipe, some movers almost drop a piano on top of the sailor, but it manages to swing by him. He walks on, smoking the pipe.

Opposite: **Two shots from** *Popeye,* **the live-action feature film starring Robin Williams as Popeye and Shelley Duvall as Olive Oyl. (Swee'pea was ably played by Wesley Ivan Hurt.)**

Robin Williams was more than physically right for the role of Popeye the Sailor. The film has had a long afterlife on home video.

The sailor goes by the Oyl residence, where there is a room for rent. He asks Nana Oyl, "You got a rom for renk?" Nana replies, "A what for what?" Nana Oyl shows the wandering sailor in while her daughter, Olive, is trying on hats for her upcoming engagement party with her suitor, Bluto. "I can't get engaged to Bluto ... I can't," she says, looking in the mirror with the ugly hat on her head. She then accuses the squint-eyed sailor of listening in on a private conversation she's having with herself. Nana introduces Olive to "Mr. Eye." "What kind of a name is Popeye ... pretty strange!" "Wot kind of a name is Olive Oyl? Some kinds of lubricants?" the sailor mutters under his breath.

Olive has trouble opening the room where Popeye will board. She yanks it open and goes flying into orbit. Meanwhile, friends and family gather in the dining room for dinner. They include Mr. Geezil, Castor Oyl, and J. Wellington Wimpy. Nana Oyl announces, "Mr. Eye!" Popeye replies, "That's Popeye." As the clan eats and talks, the food is passed from hand to hand, but Popeye can never get ahold of any. After the meal is over, an empty-plated Popeye says, "Well, it's never good to be full, ya know."

As night falls, Popeye dreams of finding his long-lost father, whom he's tracked to Sweethaven. He holds up an empty picture frame with the words "Me Poppa" written in it.

The next morning at Roughhouse's Eatery, Popeye tells Wimpy why he's here in Sweethaven. While Popeye explains his plight to Wimpy, some rough seamen overhear the pair's conversation and mimic Popeye's speaking voice. "Hey," shouts Spike, "You sure got a really nice-lookin' face, one-eye!" "I've seen better arms on a baboon," adds Slug. "You're a slimy lookin' shrimp," says Mort. "If you wants to know why you're so lomksome, go take a look in the mirror," adds Butch.

Popeye asks the brutes to apologize for their smart remarks, and when they don't, his fists go into action. "POW," "SMASH," "BAM" ... the men get tossed around the room.

That evening it's Olive's engagement party to Bluto, but she gets cold feet and runs off. Bluto grows very angry waiting for Olive. Meanwhile, Olive, intent on leaving town, runs into Popeye. While Popeye and Olive chatter, they discover a baby in a basket, left at their feet. A note pinned to the basket reads, "To da one-eyed sailor. I musk trusk someone wit' me baby until I frees meself o' certain finanskal obligationks which will take 25 years or so, at which time I shall reclaim him. Inna meantime, love him as only a mudder cud, Signed A Mudder."

In the film, the power to predict the future was given to the baby Swee'pea, though it originated in the comic strip as belonging to Eugene the Jeep.

Back at the Oyls', Bluto is screaming, "Where's Olive?" and destroying the house. Olive and Popeye arrive back at the Oyls' with the newfound baby, and Bluto sees the pair. "GRRRRRRRRR," Bluto growls as he approaches Popeye. Popeye tries to explain, but Bluto is in no mood to talk, and he punches Popeye about the boardwalk. Bluto punches Popeye into the water, and the sputtering sailor says, "Don't t'inks I blames ya, cause I doesn't."

The next morning, Popeye names the baby Swee'pea. "Sweetpea!" Olive shrieks. "You're bats!" "I found him in Swee'having so he is me Swee'pea. Dats is his name!" counters Popeye. Olive says, "That's the worst name I ever heard for a baby!" "Yeah?" says Popeye. "Wot does you wants t' call him—Baby Oyl?"

The Oyl family have discovered that Bluto has the means to kick them out of their house, and after Olive breaks off their engagement, he does just that. Their son, Castor, decides to enter a dangerous boxing match to win the tax money the family owes to get them back their home. Nana Oyl sees Castor in the ring and shouts to her daughter, "Olive, you've got to get your brother out of there!" It's too late, and Castor Oyl prepares to fight the mean Oxblood Oxheart. Castor is no match for the bully and gets thrashed around the ring. Popeye is upset that Oxheart is picking on Castor and bounces into the ring to take Olive's brother's place. Oxheart looks at Popeye. Turning to his pint-sized mother, who is standing at ringside, Oxheart says, "This one looks easy, Mom."

Magically, Swee'pea reassures Olive that Popeye will win—which, after using his twister punch on Oxheart, he does. Olive is amazed that Swee'pea knew Popeye would win. The next day, Olive informs Popeye of Swee'pea's prediction, and Wimpy overhears them talking. Popeye and Olive discover that they do care for one another. Wimpy decides to take Swee'pea for a walk, and Popeye goes off looking for the lad.

Nana discovers that it's "Derby Day" and Wimpy has taken Swee'pea to the races. Wimpy is using Swee'pea's powers to help him clean up at the racetrack. Bluto is spying on Wimpy and learns of Swee'pea's magical power to predict the future. Olive and Popeye find Wimpy, and though Popeye is angry, Olive is delighted. Popeye says to the pair, "Me chilt will not be exploitilkated fer ill-gotten games!" Popeye takes Swee'pea and leaves as Bluto calls Wimpy into his private office. Popeye decides to leave the Oyl home, which he won back for the family when he beat Oxheart in the boxing arena.

The tax man confronts Popeye and demands an unlicensed baby tax from the sailor. Enraged, Popeye pushes the tax man, who falls into the water while the town explodes into cheers and wild applause. During all the ruckus, Wimpy grabs Swee'pea and takes him to Bluto. Bluto says to Wimpy, "Here's your 30 hamburgers ... now gimme the kid!" Bluto adds, "You mention this to anyone and I'll feed you to the sharks!"

Olive spies Bluto taking Swee'pea to the Commodore. Olive meets up with Wimpy, who confesses to his crime, and they climb aboard the Commodore's boat to spy on Bluto. Bluto tries to convince the Commodore to use Swee'pea's power to obtain wealth, but the old man disagrees. Olive looks at the Commodore and says, "Look! He's got Popeye's arms! Popeye's eye! We better tell Popeye we found them!" Meanwhile, the Commodore tells Bluto he must come across any wealth "fair 'n' square!" Bluto gets angry and ties up the Commodore with a rope. Bluto decides to use Swee'pea's powers to lead him to an old sunken treasure which the Commodore knows about.

Olive and Wimpy go to Popeye and tell him about the kidnapping—"and what's more, it appears that your father is the Commodore!" Olive snaps, "He's a rat, a crook, a kidnapper, a bad father and a Commodore!" Popeye storms off to prove her wrong. The townspeople get wind of what's going on and follow Popeye to the Commodore's boat.

As Popeye approaches the boat he mutters, "Me Paps! I know he's in here. No, he ain't! But wot if he is?" As Popeye approaches his tied-up Pappy, Bluto escapes with Swee'pea. Popeye says, "Poppa!" Pappy replies, "I ain't nobody's poppa, ya one-eyed fish-faced sissipated sniffle-snaffer! I yam Poppa t' no male ner female chilt dat no court cud prove otherwise!" Popeye replies, "But Poppa, I yam yer one an' only exprang! Lookit, da same bulgy arms!" Pappy says, "No resemblinks!" Popeye states, "We got da same squinky eye!" Pappy shouts back, "Wot squinky eye? No resemblinks!" Popeye counters, "We got da same pipe, Pap!" Pappy rebounds with, "Ya idjit, ya can't inherit a pipe!"

Pappy decides there's only one way to decide if Popeye is his son. He orders the sailor to pick up an opened can of spinach on the floor. Popeye picks it up, and his father demands that he eat it. "Eat ik? Raw? I don't wan' no spinach! I hates spinach!" Popeye cries. Pappy then admits that Popeye is his son because when the sailor was a baby he wouldn't eat his spinach either!

Meanwhile, Bluto has captured Olive and taken off in search of Pappy's sunken treasure. Popeye and his father, along with Wimpy and the Oyl family, follow in hot pursuit. Bluto asks Swee'pea, "Is that where the treasure is?" Swee'-pea replies, "Weeeeeeeeeee!" Bluto realizes he's on the right course. Bluto arrives on Scab Island, and Pappy recalls that the treasure is hidden under the ocean.

Bluto takes a small rowboat and, with Swee'pea aboard, goes in search of the treasure. "Kid, we're gonna be rich, at least I am!" Bluto finds the treasure chest but confronts Popeye, who has dived in the water after him. "Bluto, ya may be bigger dan' me, but ya can't win cause yer bad! And ya knows good always wins over bad!" Popeye shouts. Bluto punches Popeye, who falls back into the ocean.

Popeye's pipe pops out of the water and, using it, the sailor searches for Bluto. While Bluto and Popeye mix it up, Pappy and Wimpy haul up the treasure. Under the ocean a big sea creature awakens and has its eye on Swee'pea in Bluto's rowboat. Popeye and Bluto begin a sword fight while the sea creature grabs one side of the rowboat. Pappy spots the danger to Swee'pea: "Hey, dere's an oktapussy down dere! He's goin' t' get da kid!" Pappy and Wimpy manage to hook on to the rowboat, and just as the sea monster drags the rowboat under the ocean, Swee'pea is snagged by the hook and pulled to safety.

The sea monster then begins to threaten Olive. Bluto has shoved Olive into a broken ship's funnel, and she's stuck, with her legs protruding. The monster grabs her legs. Meanwhile, Pappy opens up the treasure chest. Its contents include a can of spinach and Popeye's baby items. "Here's Popeye's shoes, and here's his spinach!" Pappy says with pride. They hear a cry: "Ohhh, help! Popeye! Octo-pus! Octopus!" The monster pulls Olive under the water. Bluto is still pounding on Popeye. Pappy says, "Ya gotta eat spinach!" Bluto ties a chain to Popeye as Pappy throws him a can of spinach, which bonks him on the head! Popeye sput-ters, "I don't wan' spinach ... I yam not gonna eat ik!" Bluto pops open the spinach can and says, "So you don't like it, eh? Well, now you're gonna eat it!" Bluto feeds the raw spinach to Popeye and pushes him into the ocean. Bluto growls, as Popeye goes under: "See ya in Davey Jones' locker!" He then turns to the little group on the rocks and hisses, "Now my treasure!"

Suddenly the water gurgles behind Bluto. As he looks down, a huge, huge arm skyrockets from under the ocean with a fist headed right for Bluto's jaw. KA-BOOM! Popeye wallops Bluto in the kisser, and then he dives into the water and beats up the sea monster, who frees Olive. He gives the sea monster his twister punch, and the beast goes flying into the air.

Olive says to a blushing Popeye, "Oh, Popeye. My hero!" The gang notices that Bluto has turned yellow and watches him swim away ... fast! Castor shouts, "Look at him swim!" Popeye dances about and sings his theme song. The gang sings along with Popeye, who skips and dances to the final frame—and toots his pipe at the finish.

The *Mad* Magazine Party

I had to see *Popeye: The Movie* twice. The first time I fell asleep. After leaving the theater I was angry about what the film was, compared with what it could have been. While it was proper to have the film based on Segar's original concepts, there should have been a balance with the animated cartoon versions more familiar to the public. I kept thinking to myself, "What would the animated Popeye think of this movie?" My answers came in a delightful parody of the movie that appeared in the 225th issue of *Mad* magazine.

Throughout this parody (entitled "Flopeye"), a cartoon figure of Popeye observes and comments on the action. In the beginning, he remarks:

> How about dis! Dey went an' made a pictur about me wid real people! Dat means I'm gonna be more famous den I wuz before. Yez can loin all about me! An' maybe I'll loin a t'ing or two! Like for instance, why I talks like such a moron!

The cartoon Popeye later gripes about the lack of plot, but he is really perplexed by the scene in Roughhouse's Eatery when Popeye beats up the local toughs:

> It amazes me how he can beat up anybody widout any spinach! I always eats spinach before I beats up anybody! Dis pitchur is sure confoozin'.

Later, when Bluto attacks Popeye at the Oyls' home, the cartoon Popeye comments that his movie counterpart was able to beat up several brutes a few panels before this—but now:

> I can't defend myself against one tub of lard like him? Dis pitchur makes less an' less sense as it goes on!

In the end, the cartoon Popeye loses patience and does exactly what most of the real movie's audience no doubt wished he would. The scene has switched to Pappy telling his son to eat spinach to save Olive and Swee'pea. The sailor says, "But I don't like spinach!" This really makes the cartoon Popeye angry, and he steps into the scene and shouts:

> What de hell is this! Since when don't I likes spinach? Everyone knows Popeye loves spinach! Everyone except the goofs who made this pitchur! Outta me way ... it's Popeye to the rescue!

As the cartoon Popeye rescues Olive, the movie version shouts at him:

> Well, what makes you so hot? What kind of a role model are you? You smoke, you squint! You curse, you mumble, and you mangle the English language!

Olive tells the cartoon Popeye he is wonderful. Popeye replies,

> Thanks ... an' now I'm gonna take care of de one poison dat makes me look like a bum!

Olive asks:

You mean Bruto?

Popeye replies:

No ... him!

and promptly knocks his movie counterpart right in the jaw. He then turns to the readers and says:

An' to all me fans ... if I gots any left after dis pitchur ... I apologizes profoosely! I means, I yam what I yam ... but dat guy wasn't even close!

This parody was written by Stan Hart, and it summed up the things many Popeye fans were angered about: Parts of the film were confusing, and the characters didn't jibe with people's expectations. Perhaps some cartoon characters are better off left out of the field of live action and should remain in the world of animated cartoons.

Popeye: The Play

The little-known existence of a stage musical about Popeye means Popeye has appeared in all the major media: print, films, television, live-action movies, radio and theater. Since 1984, Pioneer Drama Service has offered the play *Popeye* for rental by organizations that wish to put it on. The musical is based on "the popular comic strip" rather than on the more popular animated cartoons. The characters in the cast include Popeye, Olive Oyl, Wimpy, the Sea Hag, Brutus, and the Sea Hag's vulture, Bernard.

The script was written by R. Eugene Jackson, with music by Carl Alette. The two-act show runs 90 minutes and contains 24 musical numbers. A simple exterior set includes a sky backdrop, Wimpy's shop, ticket office, hag's shop, service window, ticket window, rope on which Olive swings (that must be fun for the performer playing Olive Oyl), and several pier pylons. The Sea Hag's pet vulture, Bernard, is a paper pup pet and takes flight on its own with the aid of a trick line.

Costuming is based on the comic strip designs of the characters. Popeye is pictured on the cover of the script in his black shirt with red collar and his captain's hat. Olive wears her comic strip attire, and Brutus is the Bud Sagendorf design.

The musical numbers are true to the characters and portray situations familiar to Popeye fans. Wimpy sings, "I'll Gladly Pay," a number about his longing for hamburgers. "Hanky Pank" relates in song Brutus's attempts to woo Olive Oyl. In "My Spinach Punch," Popeye sings the praises of spinach, and in "You Are Me Goil" he sings about his love for Olive Oyl.

The dialogue in the play captures the spirit of the comic strip characters, especially in the scenes between Olive and Brutus. Like the comic strip version

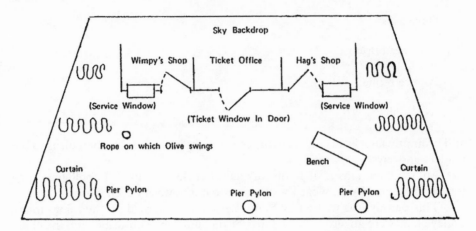

Diagram of the set for the play "Popeye the Sailor."

of Olive, the play's leading lady does not fawn over Brutus (Bluto) as much as she does in the cartoons. Lines of dialogue for other characters show them to be likewise consistent with the strip. For example, Popeye declares that "Them whut's evil gits whut's comin' to 'em sooner er later" (this sounds like pure Segar). He also assures Olive that he has "never struck a woming. They're too soft." Brutus hounds Olive for "one little kiss" and calls her "my little Olive-pimento."

Wimpy utters classic moocher's lines, such as, "Well, ahem, I seem to be a little short of cash at this particular juncture in my life. However I'm sure the money will come tomorrow."

The play is set in the present, on Liberty Island, U.S.A. Popeye is a tour guide on Liberty Island. Popeye tells the visitors of the historic treasures to be found in the Statue of Liberty. The Sea Hag overhears him and mistakenly thinks the treasures can be stolen. She and her son, Brutus, set out to discover where they are hidden. They capture Olive Oyl and Swee'pea, hold them hostage, and hide Popeye's stock of spinach. Wimpy, meanwhile, opens a hamburger stand on the island and has a near disastrous encounter with a group of lady tourists who are unable to find any meat in the hamburgers he is selling for a dime.

Brutus and Popeye have several confrontations, with Brutus usually on the losing end. Swee'pea is snared by the Sea Hag, who tries to force Popeye into handing over the treasure. Popeye tries to save the lad with his spinach, but the Sea Hag has sunk his stock in the ocean. Popeye emerges from the water with a spinach can on his head and sucks the green weed into his pipe. Brutus thinks Popeye is weak from lack of spinach and picks a fight but soon finds otherwise. As Popeye's sailor's code won't let him sock the Sea Hag, Olive does! Olive rescues Swee'pea from the witch's clutches and pounces on top of the hag. Wimpy, meanwhile, has managed to sell his phony hamburger business, and the play concludes with the tune "All's Well."

While the play is based on the comic strip, strong elements from the animated cartoons are included in the script. Of course the name "Brutus" is a creation of the television cartoons, and his wooing of Olive is reminiscent of the animated work. Olive being the one to pound on the Sea Hag, rather than having Popeye break his sailor's code, is also an idea from television; in several of the King Features television cartoons of 1960-61, Olive ate Popeye's spinach and took care of the hag with her scrawny fists. Popeye's description of how he eats his spinach at the close of the play also echoes the cartoons: "I sucked up a can to me pipe, snapped it open wit me teeth, and gobbled down the delicious green contents!" This is pretty much the same way Popeye got to his spinach in many a cartoon. There is also fanfare music whenever Popeye eats his spinach, which is, of course, right out of the animated cartoons.

To the Popeye comic books, one can trace the idea of Brutus being the Sea Hag's son. This was introduced in the Popeye comic books at the time the name "Bluto" was not being used in the print medium. Bud Sagendorf had drawn a character who looked like Bluto and called him the Sea Hag's son. Years later, George Wildman made "Brutus" the witch's sonny boy.

PART
FIVE

The Supporting Cast
of Characters

Olive Oyl

Olive Oyl made her debut in Segar's "Thimble Theatre" comic strip in 1919, predating Popeye's debut by ten years. Olive and her pint-sized brother, Castor, were the stars of the strip, but they both became supporting players when Popeye was introduced.

Olive Oyl made her animation debut in 1933, along with Popeye and Bluto. Her character design originally matched Segar's version. When Famous Studios took over production of the Popeye film series from the Fleischer Studios in 1942, they decided, starting with the 1945 cartoon "Mess Production," to redesign Popeye's girlfriend. Her hair became much fuller on the top of her head, and she developed—*gasp!*—a bust! "Mess Production" includes a nice shot of Olive applying makeup; in this shot her newly discovered improvements are clearly visible. She also began wearing a short-sleeved shirt, rather than her long-sleeved attire, and her trademark long shoes were replaced by high heels. Perhaps Famous Stu-

A model sheet featuring Famous Studios new visual design for Olive Oyl. Olive now sported a clump of hair at her forehead, a short-sleeved shirt, and high heels. Tom Johnson, whose name appears on this model sheet, was one of the animators from Famous Studios. Note the Famous Studios versions of Popeye and Bluto are also pictured.

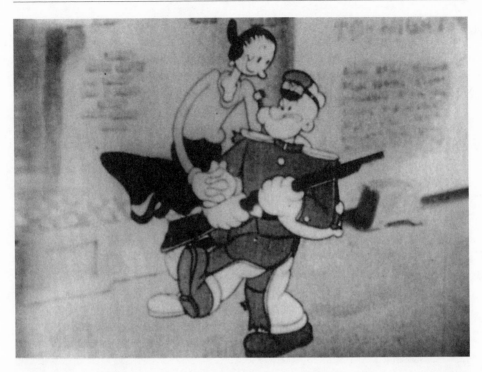

Olive Oyl and Popeye in "I'm in the Army Now" (Fleischer, 1936). Fleischer Studios' design for Olive was true to the original comic strip creation of E.C. Segar.

dios felt the need to make Olive a bit more attractive so the audience could see some kind of reason for Popeye and Bluto's brawls over her affections. Keep in mind that the bulk of the scripts for the Famous Studios cartoons featured the Popeye-Olive-Bluto romance triangle.

Olive was a very fickle character in the Famous Studios cartoons. In film after film, she would start off on a date with Popeye, spot another fellow (usually Bluto), and dump Popeye in favor of the other guy, until the new boyfriend wanted "a li'l kiss." Then she would scream for Popeye to save her, which he would obligingly do, and she would end up in Popeye's arms again. The 1950 cartoon "Quick on the Vigor" is a classic example of this plotline, with Olive and Popeye attending a carnival together ... together, that is, until Olive sees Bluto the weightlifter. She walks off with him, but has to call on Popeye to save her when Bluto's wooing proves too aggressive.

The principal variation on this theme was Bluto's line of work which changed from film to film. He appeared as a zookeeper ("Pitchin' Woo at the Zoo," 1944), a Superman imitator ("She-Sick Sailors," 1944), a circus ringmaster ("Tops in the Big Top," 1945), a steel worker ("Mess Production," 1945), a rodeo star named Badlands Bluto ("Rodeo Romeo," 1946), a "magical mystic" ("The Fistic Mystic," 1947), a wealthy nobleman ("The Royal Floor Flusher," 1947), a Tarzan type ("Safari So Good," 1947), a strongman ("All's Fair at the Fair," 1947), a prehistoric man ("Pre-Hysterical Man," 1948), an entertainment director for

Popeye, Olive, and Bluto as they appeared in Famous Studios' "Service with a Guile" (1946). Famous had not quite settled on Olive's new look; here she is wearing the old long-sleeved blouse, but she sports high heels and generally has a more gussied-up style than the Fleischer version of Olive.

vacationers ("Vacation with Play," 1951), a bull-fighter ("Toreadorable," 1953), and a smooth-talking television star ("Parlez-Vous Woo," 1956). Now and then, Olive's roving eye would settle on someone besides Bluto. In "Marry-Go-Round" (1943), Popeye wants to propose to Olive but can't bring himself to do it. His pal Shorty steps in to show him how to go about it, and Olive ends up falling in love with Shorty. (In a significant departure from the usual plotline, Popeye eventually gives up on Olive and takes an interest in Shorty's girlfriends.) In "Shape Ahoy," Olive is delighted to be rescued from a desert island by Frank Sinatra, who sings to her as they sail away on a raft (leaving both Popeye and Bluto behind). Olive falls for a pirate in "Popeye and the Pirates" (1947), and for a blond, muscle-bound lifeguard in "Beach Peach" (1950). In "Shaving Muggs" (1953), Olive tells Popeye and Bluto that she won't go out with either one of them until they get shaves and haircuts. Both sailors mangle themselves to try to please her, but in the end she goes off with a Captain VanDyke, who has long red hair and a full red beard. Another common plot device was Popeye and Bluto competing for some type of employment, with Olive Oyl the potential employer. In the cartoon "Farmer and the Belle" (1950), Popeye and Bluto compete to become Olive's farmhand. In 1955's "A Job for a Gob," Olive needs a ranch hand, and both sailors apply for the job. The usual progression in these cartoons is that

"Bride and Gloom" (1954). By now the redesigned Olive Oyl was firmly established in the animated films.

Bluto cheats and Popeye ends up with the position. However, in an early color Famous Studios film, this plotline took an interesting twist. In the 1944 cartoon "The Anvil Chorus Girl," Bluto and Popeye compete to become Olive's black-smith helper. Bluto beats Popeye up; Popeye eats his spinach and knocks the stuffing out of Bluto; and Olive decides to hire Bluto for the job. Bluto says to a departing Popeye, "So long, Popeye … I'll be seeing you." Popeye replies, "So long, Bluto … I'll be seeing you!" Olive has decided to make some time with Popeye while the hapless Bluto is left behind to run Olive's business. It seems that even when Bluto wins, he loses.

When King Features Syndicate took over production of the Popeye series for television in 1960, Olive retained her Famous Studios hairdo but wore her comic strip attire. She seemed much more closely attached to Popeye in these films than in the Famous Studios pictures, possibly because the character of Bluto, now renamed Brutus, was made a little darker in nature. Yet the relationship between Popeye and Brutus is supposed to be friendlier, at least in "Psychiatricks" (Paramount, 1960). Olive wants to stop Popeye's fighting outbursts and turns to Brutus for advice. Strangely, she says to Brutus, "Oh, Brutus … you're his best friend. What can we do to help him?" "Best friend"? Brutus? Do Popeye and Brutus do chummy things like bowling or fishing together when the camera isn't on them? (It's hard to imagine; however, the idea of the Bluto/Brutus

Popeye, Olive, and Wimpy as they appeared in the 1960 TV cartoon "Egypt Us"
(King Features; produced by Gerald Ray). King Features' design for Olive retained
the Famous Studios hairdo but went back to the old comic strip attire.

character being friends with Popeye goes back at least to the 1940 cartoon "Fightin'
Pals.")

Olive was more aggressive in the King Features cartoons because she had
her own bully to contend with. Segar's creation, the Sea Hag, was now featured
in many of the cartoons, and she often tried to push Popeye around. Popeye's
sailor code would not allow him to strike a woman ... so Olive usually downed
the spinach and did the job. This happened in the following cartoons: "Gem
Jam" (Paramount, 1960), "Hamburgers Aweigh" (Paramount, 1961), "Popeye's
Double Trouble" (Paramount, 1961), "A Poil for Olive Oyl" (Paramount, 1961),
and "Giddy Gold" (Paramount, 1961).

When Hanna-Barbera created "The All New Popeye Hour" for CBS Saturday morning television in 1978, Olive was less the victim (though she did her
share of screaming for help) and more a thinking character. Using those limbs
of hers, which could stretch to dazzling heights, she often saved Popeye's skin
from danger. During the "Treasure Hunt" segments, it was often Olive, not Popeye, who found clues and solved puzzles to lead them to different treasures. In
one episode, Olive competed for the title of Dallas Cowboys cheerleader ("Olive
Goes Dallas"); she also appeared as a stuntwoman ("Popeye Goes Hollywood"),
a track runner ("The Loneliness of the Long Distance Popeye"), and various
other guises including a truck driver, a ballet dancer, a decathlon runner, an
Olympic athlete, a member of the armed forces, and a small business owner.
Olive was truly a modern woman in these TV cartoons. She was often portrayed
more as a team player with Popeye than as someone he had to save from Bluto.

In 1980 Olive was given co-star billing for Hanna-Barbera's "The Popeye and Olive Comedy Show." She was featured in her own segment called "Private Olive Oyl." In these cartoons she teamed with Alice the Goon and had misadventures in the armed service. Olive's superior was Sgt. Blast, who just called her "Oyl!" Olive was forever goofing up, and Sgt. Blast wanted her out of the service. Yet no matter what Olive messed up, she always ended up the winner, giving Sgt. Blast a nervous breakdown.

Olive became a wife and mother for Hanna-Barbera's "Popeye and Son" series for the 1987-88 season. In this series, Olive sported a bunched-up hairdo and wore a gym suit. She was a devoted wife and mother and shared in her son's adventures on occasion.

Olive Oyl is every bit as famous as Popeye. She has often appeared by herself on products, advertisements, and toys. There was an Olive Oyl balloon in Macy's

Olive Oyl balloon in the Macy's Thanksgiving Day parade.

Thanksgiving Day parade for a few years, pulled by men in sailor suits. Olive and Swee'pea were featured in a commercial for Solo brand laundry detergent for many years, and her lanky body has often become a symbol for malnutrition! Like Lois Lane and Superman, Maggie and Jiggs, Blondie and Dagwood ... Olive Oyl and Popeye will be forever linked together.

Wimpy

J. Wellington Wimpy made his debut in Segar's "Thimble Theatre" strip in the early 1930s. His clever schemes to obtain food without paying for it have ranked him as one of the greatest character creations in comic strip history. Some historians in the comic strip field actually consider Wimpy to be a greater creation than Popeye.

Wimpy made his animation debut in Fleischer's 1933 cartoon "I Yam What I Yam," which was the first entry in the Popeye series. Throughout the cartoon, Wimpy, with knife and fork in hand, goes after a school of ducks despite the fact

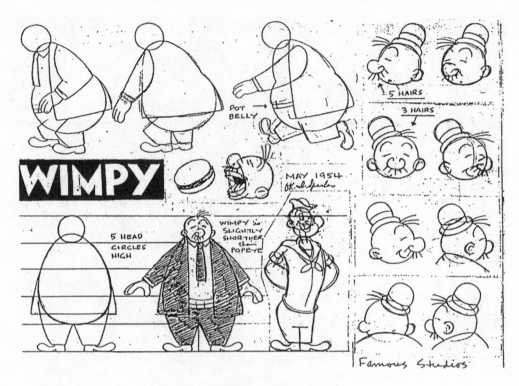

A 1954 model sheet for Wimpy, who, like Swee'pea, appeared in few of the animated films produced by Famous Studios.

that he, Popeye, and Olive are being attacked by Indians. Wimpy also uses one of his famous sayings in this cartoon: "Come on in for a duck dinner ... you bring the ducks!" In 1934's "We Aim to Please," Wimpy shows Bluto how to get served at Popeye's eatery without having to pay for it. Wimpy gets a hamburger and pickle while informing Popeye, "I'll gladly pay you Tuesday for a hamburger today." (Today, this is Wimpy's best-remembered phrase.) Popeye and Bluto begin to brawl in the cartoon while food spills over all the place. Wimpy walks in, sets up a table, and catches the food as it flies in the air. In 1936's "Bridge Ahoy," Popeye and Olive help Wimpy build a bridge when Bluto won't let the moocher ride his ferry for free. After Wimpy says to Bluto, "Oh, I'll gladly pay you Tuesday for a ride today," Bluto dunks him in the ocean. In an amusing scene, Bluto has Popeye all tied up and is using the sailor's face as a punching bag. Wimpy sees this from a distance, sticks out his chest, holds his breath and charges over. But it turns out that Wimpy headed in that direction only to dab some mustard on his hamburger!

Wimpy was often portrayed as an announcer in the Fleischer Popeye cartoons. In 1934's "Let's You and Him Fight" he was the ring announcer; in 1934's "The Dance Contest" he was the master of ceremonies. Also in 1934, in "The Man on the Flying Trapeze," he again assumed the role of announcer.

One of Wimpy's screen highlights was in the 1936 Fleischer cartoon, "What

Wimpy talking with Popeye, "May I borrow a penny for which I will gladly pay you back Tuesday," Wimpy asks Popeye in "Penny Antics" (Famous Studios, 1955). This film was a remake of "Customers Wanted" (Fleischer, 1939). In both cartoons, Wimpy was a key player.

... No Spinach?" Wimpy is Bluto's help in the bully's diner and naturally tries to mooch as much food as possible. Bluto stops him at every turn, but when Popeye strolls in for a bite, Wimpy sees a new chance for a free meal. Bluto and Popeye naturally end up fighting, and during the melee Wimpy runs into the safe Bluto has filled with food. At the cartoon's finish, Wimpy strolls out of the safe looking like a stuffed turkey!

Wimpy was Popeye's hapless helper in the 1938 cartoon "The House Builder Upper." Olive's house has burned down, and firemen Popeye and Wimpy try to rebuild what's left. Wimpy attempts to saw some wood, holding the saw in one hand and eating a hamburger with the other! In 1939's "Customers Wanted," Wimpy is the sole customer in Popeye and Bluto's arcade. Throughout the film, Bluto and Popeye show Wimpy scenes from their old pictures to keep him as their customer. Wimpy seems to enjoy Popeye's films, but says to Bluto regarding his scenes, "No ... no, I do not consider it worth the money!"

At the conclusion of the cartoon it is Wimpy accepting money as customers come charging in to watch Bluto and Popeye brawl.

The 1939 cartoon "Hello How Am I" features Wimpy in some unusual action. Olive invites Popeye over for a "hamburger dinner." Wimpy overhears

Popeye and Wimpy go swimming in a publicity still used to promote the King Features Syndicate television cartoons.

this invitation and, licking his chops, decides to dress up as Popeye to be on the receiving end of Olive's hamburgers. Wimpy actually beats up the real Popeye by hitting him over the head with chairs. But when Wimpy sees Popeye pull out his spinach, he knows he's had it. Popeye downs the spinach and bops Wimpy right out of his Popeye costume, after which Wimpy beats a hasty retreat.

Wimpy wasn't used very much in the Famous Studios cartoons, and when he was, it was in remakes of earlier Fleischer scripts. For example, Fleischer's "Customers Wanted" (1939) was remade as Famous Studios' "Penny Antics" (1955), while 1934's "We Aim to Please" was reworked as 1957's "Spree Lunch."

Wimpy gained the position of a judge in the 1956 Famous Studios cartoon "Assault and Flattery." Judge Wimpy hears the case of "Bluto vs. Popeye the Sailor," in which Bluto sues Popeye for all the beatings the bully has received at the hands of the spinach-eater. After hearing Bluto's testimony, Wimpy sobs, "Very touching ... very touching indeed" ... but he's sobbing because he's slicing an onion for his hamburgers.

Wimpy was seen in many of the King Features TV cartoons. In 1960s "The Billionaire" (Gene Deitch/William Snyder), Wimpy buys up several hundred cows and intends to put them through a grinder so he'll have a never-ending supply of hamburgers. When the cows look at him with those trusting eyes, the moocher just can't bring himself to do it. In "Egypt Us" (Gerald Ray, 1960), Popeye is off trying to save Olive from becoming a human sacrifice and leaves Wimpy to watch over their hamburger lunch. Popeye keeps running back and forth to make sure Wimpy doesn't eat the burgers, but by the time he and Olive run back to the burgers, they've become Wimpy's lunch. Wimpy sings, "It's bad to be tardy to a hamburger party ... says Wimpy the Burger Man!" In "Wimpy the Moocher" (Paramount, 1960), Wimpy claims to have found a pearl in a clam served to him at Rough House's diner. Wimpy gives Rough House the pearl in exchange for a plate of hamburgers. Rough House then rushes off to Geezil's hock shop to get money for the pearl, only to find out that the pearl is a fake that Wimpy bought from Geezil earlier. This cartoon was based on a "Thimble Theatre" strip from the late 1930s. In the comic strip, Rough House was often the target of Wimpy's schemes. "The Cure" (Paramount, 1961) has Popeye convincing Wimpy to give up hamburgers—but if he does, the Sea Hag will lose her one and only customer at her diner. The Sea Hag and one of her Goons try to force Wimpy into eating a burger. Popeye rushes into the diner only to get tossed aside by the Goon. When Popeye hits the wall, his spinach can rolls on the floor. Popeye falls on the can, allowing the spinach to fly across the room and into Wimpy's mouth. Wimpy gains strength from eating the spinach and bops the Goon. The Sea Hag screams, "He's a madman," and takes off. At the conclusion of the cartoon, Wimpy is holding up Popeye and contentedly chomping on a plate of hamburgers. In "The Whiffle Bird's Revenge" (Paramount, 1961), Wimpy attempts to eat the magical Whiffle Bird. The bird casts a spell on Wimpy so that whenever he says the word "hamburger," he'll turn into a werewolf. Children got a chance to learn a little bit of the history of the werewolf in this amusing TV cartoon. In "Going, Boing, Gone" (Paramount, 1961), Wimpy butters up Brutus in hopes the brute will buy him a hamburger. Brutus becomes enraged and chases after Wimpy. Wimpy puts on some vanishing cream and becomes invisible. He then strolls into Rough House's diner and beats up on Brutus. He eats Brutus's hamburger, and Rough House believes that Brutus is trying to get away without paying. Wimpy gets even with Brutus but decides to keep the cream on and begins to eat Rough House's hamburgers.

In the Hanna-Barbera cartoons for "The All New Popeye Hour," Wimpy was again used mainly as an announcer and given a voice like W.C. Fields—an unfortunate step, since Wimpy was never meant to be a copy of W.C. Fields. He was truly a character in his own right.

In the "Popeye and Son" series, Wimpy owned his own eatery and had a little nephew who got involved with Popeye's son's adventures.

Swee'pea

Swee'pea first appeared in the "Thimble Theatre" comic strip in 1933. The tyke made his animated cartoon debut in the Fleischer-produced cartoon "Little Swee'pea" in 1936. In this cartoon, Popeye takes Swee'pea to the zoo only to have the lad become involved with the antics of the animals. Popeye gets bopped around by the various animals while trying to save Swee'pea from harm. When the pair get back to Olive's house, Popeye tries to amuse Swee'pea with a toy monkey on a string. Swee'pea screams in terror, and Olive beats Popeye over the head with her mop. Popeye sings at the cartoon's conclusion, "There's no ifs or maybes, I'll never have babies ... I'm Popeye the Sailor Man."

Swee'pea appeared in three cartoons in 1937. In "Lost and Foundry," Swee'-pea crawls into the factory where Popeye works and gets mixed up with the machinery. Popeye tries, in vain, to grab Swee'pea and is whacked by the machines in the process. It is Swee'pea who eats Popeye's spinach and ends up saving both the sailor and Olive from a giant press that would have squashed his elders. In "I Likes Babies and Infinks," Swee'pea won't stop crying, so a desperate Olive enlists Popeye's and Bluto's aid to soothe the crying child. The swabs try almost every trick to get the baby laughing, but nothing works. Bluto starts to beat up on Popeye by creating a "Pop-Pie" (by tossing Popeye in an oven) and a "Frosted-Pop" (by throwing Popeye into the freezer). Bluto slides Popeye against the kitchen wall and is pounding the sailor. Popeye sees a can of spinach on the cabinet and reaches for it, but grabs a can of onions by mistake. Bluto bursts open the can of onions, and soon Popeye, Bluto, and Olive begin crying. Swee'pea finds this situation extremely funny and bursts out laughing as the cartoon ends. In "The Football Toucher Downer," Swee'pea won't eat his spinach, so Popeye tells the lad a story from his childhood football days. After hearing the story, Swee'-pea eats the spinach—and clobbers Popeye!

In 1938's "The Jeep," Swee'pea has a habit of climbing on the window ledge and gets caught up in the window shade as Popeye uses Eugene the Jeep to locate the boy. "Never Sock a Baby" (1939) starts out with Popeye giving Swee'pea a spanking. Popeye says to the crying lad, "That'll teach ya not to be bad ... an' ya ain't getting yer supper." Swee'pea decides to run away, and Popeye goes in search of the boy. Popeye and Swee'pea end up on the edge of a cliff, where Popeye pulls out his spinach can only to discover that it's empty. Popeye and Swee'-pea fall from the cliff, but it turns out to be only a dream that Popeye is having. Popeye runs into Swee'pea's room, grabs Swee'pea, and kisses him. In 1940s "Doing Impossikible Stunts," Swee'pea follows Popeye to a director's studio, where the sailor hopes to be chosen as a stuntman. Popeye shows the director scenes from his previous cartoons. When the director sees the scene from "Lost and Foundry" where Swee'pea saves his elders from the press, Popeye doesn't become the new stuntman. The job goes to Swee'pea! In the last Fleischer-produced Popeye cartoon, "Baby Wants a Bottleship" (1942), Popeye babysits Swee'-pea on a huge battleship. Swee'pea crawls all around the ship while Popeye gets bopped and tossed about trying to grab him. Swee'pea ends up on a missile headed towards a room full of explosives. Olive grabs Popeye's spinach can and feeds the spinach to Popeye, who slowly chews it in a half-dazed state. When he sees Swee'pea moving closer to the room, Popeye chews up the spinach and gets Swee'pea off the missile and lifts up the explosive room so that the missile passes

Opposite, top: **"If ya spanks kids I betcha yer conscious will get ya says Popeye the Sailor Man" sings Popeye as he keeps a firm grip on Swee'pea from "Never Sock a Baby" (Fleischer, 1939). Swee'pea's visual design in the Fleischer films matched that of his comic strip counterpart.** *Opposite, bottom:* **Swee'pea is shocked to find spinach in his mouth! From "Baby Wants Spinach" (Famous Studios, 1950). In the few films Swee'pea appeared in for Famous Studios he looked like a generic tyke.**

King Blozo manages to catch Swee'pea, who was captured by Prof. O.G. Wotta-Snozzle to make Swee'pea Soup ... which, after Blozo eats it, will make the King every bit as sweet as Swee'pea. From "Swee'pea Soup" (King Features, 1960; produced by Gene Deitch and William Snyder).

safely underneath and goes off in the ocean. Popeye tries to give Swee'pea little sailboats to keep him happy, but he keeps crying. At the finish of the cartoon, we see Popeye dragging the huge vessel through the streets with Swee'pea at the ship's wheel ... steering.

Swee'pea looked very much like his comic strip counterpart in the Fleischer cartoons, but in the few Famous Studios cartoons he popped up in, he looked like an average baby. In 1950s "Baby Wants Spinach," Swee'pea, again, gets involved with zoo animals. When Popeye tries to save the baby from a fierce ape, the ape grabs Popeye and pounds him into the ground. Popeye's spinach can rolls out of his uniform, and the sailor attempts to grab it. Just when it looks as if Popeye will eat the spinach, the ape squashes the can with his big foot. The spinach lands in Swee'pea's big crying mouth, and the tyke punches the big ape into three tiny apes. In "Thrill of Fair" (1951), Popeye attempts to save Swee'pea from being injured while wandering through a livestock show and carnival. Swee'pea crawls into a balloon and lets the stopper out. The balloon sails through the air until Popeye eats his spinach, shoots after Swee'pea like a rocket, and brings the lad to safety. One of the best-paced Famous Studios cartoons was 1953's "Child

Sockology" where Swee'pea wanders on to a skyscraper with Bluto and Popeye in pursuit. Bluto gets Popeye caught in a girder and drills him into it further. Bluto grabs Swee'pea but falls onto some pipes and is screaming for help. In an unusual twist, Popeye eats his spinach to save not only Swee'pea but Bluto too! In "Nurse to Meet Ya" (1955), Nurse Olive is babysitting Swee'pea and Popeye and Bluto try to get the lad to stop bawling. In an amusing scene, Popeye pulls on his face, turning it into a dog's.

Swee'pea appeared frequently in the King Features television cartoons of 1960-61. In 1960s "Interrupted Lullaby" (Gene Deitch/William Snyder), Brutus tries to kidnap Swee'pea, who has inherited a million dollars from his late uncle. While Brutus beats on Popeye, Swee'pea finds a can of spinach and spells out "S-P-I-N-A-C-H ... Popeye," and pours the spinach into Popeye's mouth.

In "Swee'pea Soup" (Gene Deitch/William Snyder, 1960), Popeye, Olive, and Swee'pea visit King Blozo. The people under Blozo's rule fall in love with Swee'pea and want the lad to become their new king. King Blozo wants to find out what makes Swee'pea so sweet and has his mad scientist study Swee'pea. In 1960s "Baby Phase" (Gerald Ray), Swee'pea wants to become a world-famous juggler, but Popeye gets upset when he sees the lad juggling on top of the house. Popeye dreams that Swee'pea has run away and become a famous juggler, signing a 99-year contract with the circus.

In many of the Jack Kinney–produced Popeye TV cartoons for King Features, Popeye was seen telling Swee'pea fairy stories, including, "Lil' Olive Riding Hood" (1960), "Trojan Horse" (1960), "Westward Ho-Ho" (1960), "The Green Dancin' Shoes" (1960), "The Troll That Got Gruff" (1960), "Popeye the Ugly Ducklin'" (1960), "Old Salt Tale" (1960), "Jeep Tale" (1960), "The Golden Type Fleece" (1960), "Rip Van Popeye" (1960), "Popeye Revere" (1960—actually a Poopdeck Pappy tale), "Forever Ambergris" (1960) and "Uncivil War" (1960). In "Poppa Popeye" (Paramount, 1960) a man visits Popeye claiming to be Swee'pea's real father. Popeye sadly gives up the lad, but the man actually turns out to be a crooked circus performer who needs a baby for his tightrope act. Popeye becomes very ill until Swee'pea comes back home. The bogus father attempts to reclaim Swee'pea, but the lad stays with Popeye—because Popeye has nailed Swee'pea's clothes to the floor. What's interesting about this cartoon is that the plot was taken from an E.C. Segar Sunday sequence involving Swee'-pea's mother coming back to claim her son. The gag about clothes being nailed to the floor and the idea of Popeye becoming ill were also taken from Segar's strip. "The Baby Contest" (Paramount, 1960) had Popeye and Olive entering Swee'pea in a baby contest. Brutus enters a boy named Bully Boy (his son? Their relationship is never spelled out) in the contest. Brutus helps Bully Boy cheat to win a few events, but Swee'pea ends up the final winner. Brutus attempts to bribe the judge (Wimpy) with a tray of hamburgers, but Popeye butts in. Brutus punches Popeye into a tree and beats up on the trapped sailor. Popeye's spinach pops out of his pocket and rolls towards Swee'pea. The lad eats it and wallops Brutus, who lands in Bully Boy's crib. Swee'pea then pushes home his crib, containing Popeye and his trophy, as he sings, "I'm strong to the finich when I eats the spinach of Popeye the Sailor Man." In "Pop Goes the Whistle" (Paramount,

1961), Swee'pea keeps following the whistling sounds in the neighborhood, with Popeye getting whacked about while running after him. In "Popeye Thumb" (1961), the last Paramount-produced Popeye TV cartoon and the end of Paramount Pictures' long association with the one-eyed sailor, Swee'pea isn't allowed to play baseball with the other boys because they think he's too small. Popeye tells him the story of Popeye Thumb, who despite his size did a lot for his family. Swee'pea sticks his hand in Popeye's shirt and pulls out his spinach. The lad eats the spinach and runs off to play baseball, hitting a home run! The boys begin fighting over Swee'pea because each of them wants the lad to play on his team. Popeye sings: "Ya can be small as a mite but have plenty of height ... says Popeye the Sailor Man!"

In both the King Features TV cartoons and the Hanna-Barbera productions, Swee'pea's character design matched his comic strip counterpart, but in the Hanna-Barbera cartoons, Swee'pea's captain's hat was replaced by a sailor's hat. In Hanna-Barbera's "Popeye Goes Sightseeing" (1978) and "Swee'pea Plagues a Parade" (1978), the lad again wanders off with Popeye trying to catch him. In "Mother Goose Is on the Loose" (1978), Bluto and Popeye tell Swee'pea their own versions of Mother Goose fairy tales.

It might have been nice for confused audiences if just one of the animated films had clarified Swee'pea's origins, but none did. In the E.C. Segar strip, Swee'pea was Popeye's adopted son. Some cartoons carried on in this tradition, notably the aforementioned "Poppa Popeye," in which Popeye suffers greatly when a "real" father shows up claiming Swee'pea. In other cartoons, however, the infant is under Olive's care, including his debut appearance in "Little Swee'pea" (1936) and the 1940 cartoon "Nurse Mates." Still other films refer to him as "Cousin Swee'pea." Evidently the creators of the animated cartoons did not hesitate to rewrite Swee'pea's family history whenever the plot demanded.

Poopdeck Pappy

Poopdeck Pappy was created by Segar because sometime in the late 1930s, King Features Syndicate decided that Popeye was becoming too rough a character. Popeye would often punch an animal for no apparent reason, or swear under his breath. Segar was given orders to clean Popeye up because children were falling in love with the character's antics and the sailor was becoming a bad role model. Segar did soften Popeye up a bit, but to bring back the old spunk the sailor had, he created Popeye's father, Poopdeck Pappy. Pappy not only belted animals, but women too! Even Olive Oyl often found herself on the receiving end of one of Pappy's punches. Apparently it was perfectly acceptable for an old man to be seen beating up women and swearing. Segar would have Pappy do some pretty wacky things in the strip, and Popeye would have to bail his father out of trouble.

Pappy made his animation debut in the classic Fleischer-produced cartoon "Goonland" in 1938. The story dealt with Popeye searching for his long-lost father and locating him on "Goon Island." Popeye pleads with his father, who is

Poopdeck Pappy and Popeye from the 1936 "Thimble Theatre" story, "Mystery Melody" by E.C. Segar. This tale was effectively adapted into an animated cartoon by Paramount Cartoon Studios in 1961.

captured and holed up in a cave, to return with him. Pappy replies, "I don't like relatives!" Popeye is then captured by the hulking Goons and strapped to the ground with the Goons preparing to hurl a huge boulder on him. Pappy manages to get Popeye's spinach and saves his son. The two swabs beat up the tribe of Goons and go home together. The characterization of Poopdeck Pappy in his debut cartoon was extremely close to his comic strip counterpart.

Pappy returned in animated form in the 1940 cartoon "My Pop—My Pop." In this cartoon Pappy had his own theme song, which began, "Oh … I'm Popeye's Poopdeck Pappy … a sea-going son of a gun" and concluded with, "I'm ninety-nine and pretty tough … ahoy … ahoy … ahoy!" In this film, Popeye is building a boat, and Pappy wants to help. Popeye feels that Pappy is too old for boat building and tries to get the elder sailor to go home. Pappy claims he can build a boat, so the two decide to compete to see who can build the better side of the vessel. Naturally, while Popeye does a bang-up job, Pappy is an utter failure. While the old man sleeps, Popeye eats his spinach and rebuilds his father's side of the boat. Popeye then props up his Pappy so that when he awakens, he will think he produced the stunning boat. Pappy goes home happy, singing his theme song as he goes. This scene is typical of many of the Fleischer Popeye cartoons, which showed a strong bond between father and son.

Other cartoons showed Popeye trying to keep an eye on his father—and usually being outsmarted. "With Poopdeck Pappy" (1940) features Popeye's attempts to keep his father inside for the night. The old sailor sneaks out and ends up in a dance hall, where he steals a sailor's girlfriend. Popeye arrives on the scene and bails out his father, but the cartoon ends with Popeye trapped inside his bed while his father goes out on the town. The 1941 cartoon "Problem Pappy" dealt with Pappy taking on a job as a flagpole sitter. Popeye tries in vain to stop his father, but the old sailor stops his son at every turn. It isn't until a raging storm occurs that Pappy decides to quit his new position and allows Popeye to save him.

"Quiet Pleeze" (1941) had Pappy coping with a hangover. Popeye attempts to silence all the noise in the neighborhood so that his father can get some rest. When it looks like Pappy will be able to sleep very soundly, Popeye arrives back home to hear a party going on in another apartment. Popeye swings open the door and discovers that his Pappy is having a wild time at this function. The cartoon ends with Popeye falling into bed where his father spent most of the cartoon, with a hot water bottle topping his forehead.

The last Fleischer-produced cartoon to feature Pappy was 1941's "Pest Pilot." In this film, Popeye runs an airplane service, and Pappy begs his son to let him be a pilot. The two fight over Pappy being too old, so the elder sailor gets into an aircraft by himself and promptly loses control! The plane crashes, but Pappy survives. A panic-stricken Popeye tells his dad to "get the heck outa here." Pappy turns his back on his son and whimpers, "I only wanted to be an ace pilot like you, Son!" Popeye feels sorry for his dad and decides to let him pilot the lawnmower instead.

Pappy returned in Famous Studios' "Popeye's Pappy" (1952), which told a new version of how Popeye found his father. In this cartoon, Pappy is the king of an island of man-eating natives. Popeye tries to get his father to return home, not only to him but to his mother. It is only when the hungry natives decide to cook Popeye in a stewing pot that his father comes to his senses and eats a can of spinach to save his offspring. This film has not been viewed on television for the past few years because the figures of the black natives are reminiscent of certain racial stereotypes.

Pappy appeared in a few of the King Features TV cartoons of 1960-61. In 1961's "Tooth Be or Not Tooth Be" (Gene Deitch/William Snyder), Pappy tells Swee'pea the tale of when the Sea Hag captured him because she wanted his sparkling teeth. In the cute 1960 cartoon "Jeopardy Sheriff" (Gerald Ray), Pappy fills Swee'pea's head full of tales about his adventures as a famous sheriff. To defend himself against Popeye's charge that he is making it all up, Pappy attempts to capture a gang of bank robbers. The old man not only captures the crooks, but saves Popeye too. He sings at the finish of the cartoon, "I may tell a whopper, but I am the popper of Popeye the Sailor Man!" In 1960s "Me Quest for Poopdeck Pappy" (Paramount), Popeye once again goes in search of his Pappy on the island of "Goona." No Goons on this island, but a sailor-eating "monster of the sea" menaces Popeye until his father eats the spinach to rescue his son. This cartoon was based loosely on Segar's strip-version of how Popeye found his Pappy. Some of the lines are taken directly from Segar's strips. Another Paramount-produced King Features TV cartoon based on a Segar "Thimble Theatre" strip from the late 1930s was "Myskery Melody" (1961). In this cartoon, Pappy is under the spell of "Rose o' the Sea," who is actually the Sea Hag in disguise. As in Segar's strip, Popeye needs the aid of Eugene the magical Jeep to locate his father. Again, many of the lines used by the characters in this cartoon came from Segar's scripts. In all the King Features TV cartoons, Pappy wore a blue sailor's uniform with white pants.

Pappy was featured in a few of the Hanna-Barbera Popeye cartoons. In "Pappy Fails in Love" (1978), the old salt and Bluto compete for the love of a rich woman aboard a cruise ship. Popeye is hardly seen in this cartoon as his old man is the center of attention. At the conclusion of the film, neither Pappy nor Bluto ends up with the woman as she falls in love with Wimpy and his cooking skills.

"The Decathlon Dilemma" featured Pappy attempting to have his son work out with him for the decathlon. Popeye tells his father that he's too old, but with the help of Eugene the Jeep, Pappy comes off as a winner and Popeye the loser! In 1978's "Shark Treatment," Pappy and Popeye go in search of a nasty shark. At one point in this cartoon, Popeye pulls out his spinach, but the shark freezes him solid before he can eat any. Pappy uses his pipe (which was not seen in the majority of Pappy's appearances in the Hanna-Barbera cartoons) to melt the ice containing Popeye's spinach and chows it down. Pappy then takes care of the shark in typical Popeye fashion. Popeye sings at the end, "He's strong to the finish cause he ate me spinach … he's Poopdeck the Sailor Man!" Pappy popped up in one "Popeye and Son" cartoon where he visits his grandson and tells Junior's classmates stories of Junior's relatives. The classmates aren't impressed, and Pappy sadly leaves Junior's school. Later, Junior, Olive and his classmates get in an out-of-control bus. Pappy eats spinach and not only grapples with a grizzly bear but saves the bus from falling over a cliff.

It is a pleasure to note that some of the spunk Segar bestowed on Poopdeck Pappy is retained in the animated cartoons. It would be a shame if the character lost the very characteristics for which he was created.

The Sea Hag

Popeye's oldest enemy, the Sea Hag, made her debut in the "Thimble Theatre" strip in 1929 and has continued to bother Popeye and his pals. The witch made her animated cartoon debut starting with the King Features TV cartoons of 1960-61. She didn't look a lot like her comic strip counterpart, as her face was elongated and colored green; however, this visual design suited her characterization of an evil old witch.

In 1960s "Hag Way Robbery" (Gene Deitch/William Snyder), the Hag steals Eugene the Jeep and, to confuse Popeye, puts spinach labels on cans of food that do not contain spinach. In 1960s "Voice from the Deep" (Gene Deitch/William Snyder), the Sea Hag pretends to be an evil "voice" in a cave so that the natives will leave their land and the witch can turn it into a resort for criminals. "The Last Resort" (Gerald Ray, 1960) featured the Sea Hag and her sidekick, "Toar" (a character from Segar's strips, not as dumb as he is seen in this cartoon), cranking out phony money until Popeye stumbles onto their scheme! In the poorly animated "Sea Hagracy" (Jack Kinney, 1960), the Hag attempts to get Wimpy to bump off Popeye and then sends lightning bolts to finish the job. In "Lil' Olive Riding Hood" (Jack Kinney, 1960), the Sea Hag is after Olive's basket full of hamburgers. In "Jeep-Jeep" (Jack Kinney, 1960) the Hag and Brutus (with whom she was linked in some cartoons) kidnap the Jeep so that the animal will lead them to gold. In "Old Salt Tale" (Jack Kinney, 1960), the Hag steals a salt grinder (given to Popeye by the Goons) that grants wishes to its owner—but only if they asked politely. Naturally the Sea Hag doesn't ask politely and gets buried under mounds of salt by the cartoon's finish. In "Mobey Hick" (Paramount, 1960), the Sea Hag tricks Popeye into attempting to kill Mobey Hick, a cute whale that swallowed a treasure chest the Hag wants to get her bony hands on. In "Voo-Doo-to You Too" (Paramount, 1960), the Sea Hag puts Olive into a trance so the gal becomes her "zombie slave." She then takes a wax doll of Popeye and ties the doll's arms behind its back so the real Popeye won't be able to move his arms. She tosses the doll into a sea chest and orders her pet vulture to "take it out and lose it." With the aid of Eugene the Jeep, Popeye manages to break the spell over his arms and frees Olive from the zombie spell.

The Sea Hag made a holiday appearance in "Spinach Greetings" (Paramount, 1960). In this cartoon, the witch captures Santa Claus and holds him captive in her lair to stop everyone from becoming so happy during the holiday. Popeye finds Santa and, after a rousing battle with the Hag's vulture, frees Saint Nick. This is a delightful holiday cartoon, though Santa is seen driving a plane rather than a sleigh.

In "Gem Jam" (Paramount, 1960) the Sea Hag needs Olive to steal a jewel from the top of a cursed idol's crown because whoever steals the jewel becomes cursed! Popeye eats his spinach and grabs the Hag, but because he can't hit a woman, Olive eats the remainder of what's in the spinach can and beats her up. Popeye then tosses the jewel back onto the idol's crown. In "Aladdin's Lamp" (Paramount, 1960), the Sea Hag steals Aladdin's Lamp (which Olive just bought at an auction) because the lamp contains a genie. Popeye goes after the lamp, but the Sea Hag cries, "Quick, genie, before he can get the spinach from his blouse, shrink Popeye down to the size of a mouse!" The Sea Hag then chases the mouse-sized Popeye all over her ship until she throws a can on him. Of course, the can turns out to be Popeye's spinach can with some left in it. Popeye returns to normal size and finishes off the genie by sucking him into his pipe and then putting him in a bottle. He corks the bottle and tosses the genie into the sea. When

The Sea Hag prepares to kidnap Swee'pea from "A Mite of Trouble" (Paramount, 1961). By her side is her ever faithful vulture.

Popeye returns the lamp to Olive, she tells him to throw it away as she's found something better: a combination lamp and coffee grinder! In "The Leprechaun" (1961), the Sea Hag pretends to be a starving old woman to trick a leprechaun into revealing where his pot of gold is hidden. The Sea Hag and her vulture carry off the gold. Popeye stops them, but the Hag gives him her "evil-eye-whammy" ... that is, until Popeye eats his spinach and gives her whammy right back at her.

In "A Poil for Olive Oyl" (Paramount, 1961), Popeye invades the Sea Hag's pearl bed under the ocean when he wants to string a pearl necklace for Olive's birthday present. The Sea Hag sends her dogfish to attack Popeye, but Popeye calls upon a school of catfish. The Hag then sends more dangerous sea life to battle with Popeye until Olive sees what's going on, eats a can of spinach, and pile-drives the Sea Hag into the floor of the ocean. In "A Mite of Trouble" (Paramount, 1961), the Sea Hag hires a midget to impersonate Lil' Swee'pea so that she can locate Popeye's treasure map. The midget finds the map, but it's a fake. The real treasure map is written on Swee'pea's diaper.

The Sea Hag popped up in a few Hanna-Barbera cartoons from "The All New Popeye Hour." She appeared in the Treasure Hunt adventure "I Wants Me Mummy" (1978), as well as "Popeye Snags the Sea Hag" (1978). The character design of the witch in the Hanna-Barbera cartoons matched that of Segar's original design of the character, with a pushed-in face.

The Sea Hag appeared in two "Popeye and Son" cartoons. In the first, she wreaks havoc in getting a stolen mermaid statue back to her. In the second, Bluto and Popeye land on her island to fight off menaces and claim her for the prize. This second cartoon is the best cartoon from the "Popeye and Son" series because the "Son" appears only in the beginning. This is mainly a Popeye cartoon, unlike the bulk of the cartoons in the "Popeye and Son" series.

The Sea Hag also appeared in the CBS prime-time Valentine Day's special produced by Hanna-Barbera.

Bluto, the Big Guy Who Hates Popeye, Sonny Boy, Brutus

Popeye's bearded rival for the affections of Olive Oyl, Bluto, first appeared in the "Thimble Theatre" comic strip in 1932. He was not portrayed as the Bluto audiences know from the animated cartoons. Segar's Bluto was a bloodthirsty pirate with murder on his mind. Bluto was the sailor's first tough opponent. Many daily strips were taken up with the pair swinging blows at one another. Popeye's twisker punch finally did the trick in defeating the brute.

At the time Popeye was having this adventure with Bluto in the comic strip, the "Popeye" animated film series was getting underway and Fleischer Studios decided to pluck Bluto from the strip and make the character the permanent heavy for the films. In both Segar's strip and the Fleischer films from the 1930s, Bluto wore a captain's hat and short-sleeved black shirt with a button. Often his eyes were squinty and his buckteeth protruded from his heavy beard. In 1942,

Segar's Bluto from the "Thimble Theatre" comic strip from 1932 is pictured on the left as compared to Ralph Stein and Bill Zaboly's version on the right from a 1959 strip sequence.

starting with the film, "Kickin' the Conga Round" (Fleischer), Bluto lost his squint and started wearing a white sailor's uniform in an unflattering way. (His stomach hung out.) When Famous Studios took over production of the films, Bluto remained in the Navy uniform, with the exception of a few films. When the "Popeye" movie cartoons were released to television in September of 1956, the character was introduced to a new generation of children. It would seem natural for the bearded bully to appear alongside the rest of the Popeye cast in the comic books, games and toys which followed the success of the cartoon's exposure on the small screen. However, this was not to be an easy task. Although Bluto only appeared once in "Thimble Theatre," Bud Sagendorf wanted to

A pencil drawing of Bluto on bended knee as he appeared in "Nearlyweds" (Famous Studios, 1957).

revive the character for the "Popeye" comic book series he was writing and illustrating. Paramount Pictures, who financed the "Popeye" cartoons for both the Fleischer and Famous Studios were under the impression that the character, Bluto, was created by them for use in the films. King Features Syndicate failed to correct Paramount that the brute appeared in the comic strip first.

Due to the lack of research on the Syndicate's part, Sagendorf was allowed to use the image of the bully but not his name. A brute looking a lot like the guy Popeye was punching on the small screen appeared in "Popeye" #40, 1957. In the story, "The Mystery of the Magic Flute," the Sea Hag says to one of her evil spies, "Now bring in the big guy that hates Popeye." The big guy shows up, looking like Bluto but we never read his name in this story. In several comic book stories, this "big guy who hates Popeye" would be on the scene, referred to as "Olive's new boyfriend" or he would go unnamed.

Sagendorf obviously got tired of this no name business and finally settled on making him the son of the Sea Hag, with the nickname, "Sonny Boy." What is strange about this situation is that while this was going on in the comic books, Ralph Stein, who was writing the "Thimble Theatre" comic strip at this time, had Popeye do battle with Bluto! Toward the end of the 1950s, Popeye and his traveling companion, Sir Pomeroy, had encounters with Bluto the Pirate, who looked like the Famous Studios version though he wore what appeared to be a striped prison shirt and hat. The question remains, why was the name Bluto allowed to be used in the comic strip but not in the comic books? One can only

The Sea Hag says to her henchman, "Now bring in the big guy that hates Popeye" and in walks, for the first time in the comic books, a brute who looks a lot like Bluto, though he goes unnamed in this comic book story, "The Mystery of the Magic Flute" (Popeye #40, 1957). Panel courtesy of Donnie Pitchford.

speculate that whoever was reviewing the strips before they were approved, was not aware of the alleged copyright conflict. The name Bluto was also being used on Popeye products during the late 1950s, but this would change with the announcement of the new "Popeye" TV cartoon series (1960-61).

Al Brodax, head of the motion picture and film division of King Features Syndicate was required to change the name of the bully for this new series of TV productions. He chose the name "Brutus" based on the name of Julius Caesar's assassin. Brutus implied brutal, a characteristic well entrenched in his personality. For many years it was assumed that Walt Disney wanted the brute's name changed to Brutus as Bluto sounded too much like Pluto, Mickey Mouse's dog. I wrote to Jackson Beck, who was the voice of both versions of Popeye's foe, and he explained that to his recollection, Bluto was a late character in Popeye and owned by Fleischer or Paramount. When King Features Syndicate wanted to produce a new series of TV cartoons, they had to change the name.

Brutus, in these TV cartoons, wore a short sleeved, button down the front shirt, which hung over due to his large belly. Although the name Brutus was now being used on TV and in products, it took awhile for Bud Sagendorf to introduce

After being called "Sonny Boy" for several issues, the name Brutus was first used in the comic books beginning with the story, "Ghosk Mountain" (Popeye #67, 1963). Panel courtesy of Donnie Pitchford.

the name in the comic books. The first time the name "Brutus" is used was in "Popeye" #67 (1963). The name finally took hold in both the strip and comic books by 1963. When Hanna-Barbera decided to produce a new series of Popeye cartoons for Saturday mornings in 1978, the bully went back to being called Bluto, though he was still being called Brutus in the strip and on merchandise. In these new adventures for television, Bluto was back to wearing his captain's hat but now donned a short-sleeved striped shirt. His nose was tiny with a fuller beard around his mouth. The name, Bluto, remained for the 1980 Popeye feature film and the animated series, "Popeye and Son" (1987-88). In "Popeye and Son," Bluto looked as he appeared in the comic strip by Bud Sagendorf, with more of a rounded face, open eyes and a rounder shaped beard. He was usually seen in a loud business suit.

Around 1996, King Features Syndicate began using the Fleischer design of the brute on new merchandise. Though the version presented is clearly the Fleischer Studios design of Bluto, the syndicate had him named Brutus. Fortunately there are manufacturers who have given him his original name to match the look of the Fleischer Studios. Bluto and Popeye squared off right from the start in the animated cartoons. However, wooing Olive Oyl was not his only role in the "Popeye" film series. In "Let's You and Him Fight" (1934) he was a boxer, a role he would again have in "Spinach-Packin' Popeye" (1944) and "Out to Punch" (1956), a hypnotist in "The Hyp-Nut-Tist" (1935), and "The Fistic Mystic" (1947), a dancer in "The Dance Contest" (1934), a football player in "You Gotta Be a Football Hero" (1935) and "The Spinach Bowl" (1978) and a conductor in "The Spinach Overture (1935).

Popeye and Bluto were also not always at each other's throats. In 1940's "Fightin' Pals," they are what the title of the cartoon indicates, fighting pals. In this film, Bluto pulls out a can of spinach from his shirt pocket to revive Popeye. In "Seein' Red, White n' Blue" (1942) Bluto joins Popeye in a battle against the Japanese. "We're on Our Way to Rio" (1944) starts off with pair traveling together, similar to Bob Hope and Bing Crosby from one of their famous "Road" feature films.

Brutus uses Popeye's head as a bell ringer from "Bell Hop Hop Popeye" (Jack Kinney, 1960).

When Bluto was revived for TV cartoons seen in "The All New Popeye Hour," he could no longer be physically violent, but he had a bag of dirty tricks. Whether it was a road race, bicycle race, or competing for various business contracts, Bluto was constantly pulling dirty tricks in order to best Popeye. In "Popeye and Son," Bluto had settled down and married. He had a son named, Tank, who hated Popeye's boy, Junior. It was in this series that Bluto was most tame. He often ended up shouting at Popeye and let his son play the dirty tricks.

When Bluto became known as Brutus in the TV Popeye cartoon series (1960-61), he had a darker streak than Bluto. He would often just walk into Popeye and stomp over him. He would grab Olive Oyl and drag her to the ground. Brutus would also kidnap one of Popeye's pals and hold him for ransom. The brute would also team up with the Sea Hag on occasion. Brutus' more memorable plots in these TV cartoons included: "Childhood Daze" (Larry Harmon, 1960) when he turned Popeye into a little baby; "Popeye's Hypnotic Glance" (Jack Kinney, 1960) when he tried to hypnotize Olive into loving him; "Weight for Me" (Gene Deitch/William Snyder, 1960) when he attempted to keep Olive as plump as he was; "Scairdy Cat" (Paramount, 1961) when he made fear gas to keep Popeye frightened of him; and "Robot Popeye" (Paramount, 1961) when he built a robot of Popeye to create problems for the real sailor man.

In one of the Hanna-Barbera cartoons, "Close Encounters of the Third Spinach" (1978), Jack Mercer flubbed his line and called Darth Bluto, "Darth Brutus." Honestly, with all the confusion over the name and visual appearance of Popeye's bearded foe, it's amazing this only occurred in one cartoon!

The Whiffle Hen/Bird

Popeye initially gained his super-human strength and indestructibility, not from a steady diet of spinach in the "Thimble Theatre" comic strip, but by rubbing the head feathers of the Whiffle Hen. The hen was owned by Olive Oyl's brother, Castor Oyl. In the sailor's first adventure in print, he survived a hail of bullets fired at him by rubbing the head feathers of the creature. When the hen was dropped from the strip, spinach became the explanation for sustaining his strength. Of course, eating spinach became the plot device in the animated films for the sailor to jump into action.

The hen was largely forgotten until the character was revived in the television cartoons produced by King Features Syndicate. "Quick Change Ollie" (Paramount, 1960) featured the animation debut of the creature, now called the Whiffle Bird. Popeye rubs the bird's head feathers, which transport the sailor, the Whiffle Bird and Wimpy back to Ye Olden Days. In "Hamburgers Aweigh" (Paramount, 1961), Popeye rubs the bird's head feathers to make Wimpy hate hamburgers while he is guarding a hamburger cargo.

Olive suffers a case of "Giddy Gold" (Paramount, 1961) when the bird makes all of the fake treasure, seen during a boat ride at a carnival, become real. Wimpy gets the bird angry when the moocher tries to eat the creature in "The Whiffle Bird's Revenge" (Paramount, 1961). The bird casts a spell on Wimpy; every time he says "hamburger" he turns into a werewolf! Paramount Cartoon Studios, one of the studios producing these TV Popeyes, made it a point to research the old "Thimble Theatre" comic strips by E.C. Segar. They found the Whiffle Hen in

Popeye's original source of strength, pictured from the sailor's first comic strip adventure in 1929, was from rubbing the head of feathers of the Whiffle Hen.

"Popeye is finished cause I ate the spinach, for Popeye the Sailor Man," sings Olive's little niece, Deezil, at the conclusion of "Popeye's Junior Headache" (Gerald Ray, 1960).

the strips and adapted the character for the television films. Jack Mercer provided the voice of the Whiffle Bird.

Deezil

As Popeye's nephews were a creation of the animation studios, rather than the comic strip, so too was Olive Oyl's niece, Deezil. She was created for the TV Popeye cartoons and was animated by three different studios. Deezil was a pint-sized version of Olive Oyl, though she wore children's clothes. She debuted in "Popeye's Junior Headache" (Gerald Ray). Although I'm not fond of cartoons where Popeye gets physically punished, this cartoon featured a witty script. Olive calls a dead-tired Popeye so he can babysit her little niece. Deezil treats Popeye like a horse, rides on his back and brands him. When Popeye has had enough, he bounces toward the kitchen and eats what he thinks is a can of spinach. It turns out Deezil has changed all the labels of the cans and she has eaten the spinach. Deezil says to Popeye, "Unc ... Uncle Popeye, what do I do?" Popeye replies, "You'll find out, I mean, I'll find out." With that, Deezil rams into the sailor with her fists flying. Popeye ends up in the hospital, alone at last, until Olive arrives with Deezil. The brat shoots an arrow at the weight above Popeye's head, which falls and knocks him out. Deezil sings, "Popeye is finished 'cause I ate the spinach for Popeye the Sailor Man." She then shoots two arrows at Popeye's pipe, causing smoke to pop out. Deezil returns as Swee'pea's playmate in "Coach Popeye" (Jack Kinney, 1960). Deezil gets a bedtime story from Popeye in "The Mark of Zero" (Paramount, 1961). Mae Questel provided the voice for Deezil in all three cartoons, though in "Coach Popeye," Deezil was given a nasal twang.

Rough House

Rough House is like a character actor on television. You've seen him a lot, but don't quite remember his name. The rotund, bearded cook wearing the chef's hat first appeared in the "Thimble Theatre" comic strip in the early 1930s. He appeared in several Sunday comic strip pages by Segar and his successors, Tom Sims and Bela Zaboly. In the strip, Rough House was usually the fall guy to Wimpy's schemes to get free food.

Rough House was often seen on Popeye merchandise during the 1930s. He made his animation debut in the TV cartoon "Quick Change Ollie" (Paramount, 1960), seen cooking hamburgers for Wimpy and Popeye. He next appeared serving

Rough House thinks that Brutus is up to no good! From "Going, Boing, Gone" (Paramount, 1961).

milk to Popeye in "The Valley of the Goons" (Paramount, 1960). "Wimpy the Moocher" (Paramount, 1960) would feature Rough House's biggest role in a cartoon. Wimpy claims to have found a pearl in one of the oysters Rough House has served him. The cook gives Wimpy a huge plate full of hamburgers for the pearl. Rough House tries to pawn the pearl at Geezil's pawn shop. He discovers that Wimpy bought a fistful of phony pearls for ten cents a handful before entering Rough House's establishment. This cartoon was based on a 1930s "Thimble Theatre" Sunday page. Rough House next appeared in "The Whiffle Bird's Revenge" (Paramount, 1961), when the bird cast a spell on Wimpy because he tried to eat the creature. Rough House sees Wimpy turn into a werewolf!

His final outing, was in "Going, Boing, Gone"(Paramount, 1961) thinking Brutus has eaten two hamburgers without paying when actually it's Wimpy pulling tricks while invisible. Both Jackson Beck and Jack Mercer provided Rough House's voice.

Spinach

You may be thinking, spinach as a supporting character? Well, yes! The vegetable, which has given Popeye the strength to help him out of dire situations, has long been an important part of his life in print and film. Although Popeye originally received his super-abilities from rubbing the head feathers of the Whiffle

Bluto prepares to substitute Popeye's spinach with Mexican jumping beans. From "Toreadorable" (Famous Studios, 1953).

Brutus looks straight at the audience and says, "You didn't think I was going to play fair with that runt and take a chance against his spinach!" From "County Fair" (Paramount, 1961).

Hen in the "Thimble Theatre" comic strip, Segar soon had Popeye eating spinach to maintain his strength. Fleischer Studios actually deserves the credit for forever associating spinach with Popeye.

Popeye consumed the vegetable infrequently in Segar's strip in comparison to the numerous times he pulled a can out of his shirt pocket in the Fleischer films. On occasion, the spinach can would take on a life of its own. In the 1936 Fleischer film, "I Wanna Be a Lifeguard," a battered Popeye whistles for his can of spinach, which is in his locker room. Upon hearing the whistle, the can quivers, drops to the ground and rolls toward Popeye. In Famous Studios, "Friend or Phony" (1952), Bluto tricks Popeye into throwing away his can of spinach. The can lands on the back of a moving truck and yells, "You'll be sorry!" As Bluto uses construction equipment to pound Popeye into the ground, the sailor sends out an SOS via the smoke in his pipe. The spinach can sniffs the smoke, jumps off the back of the truck, hops toward Popeye, pops itself open and pours the spinach inside Popeye's mouth.

Popeye's bearded foe was also keenly aware of the results of eating spinach. In the Fleischer cartoon, "The Twisker Pitcher" (1937), Popeye drops his can of spinach and Bluto eats it after mumbling, "Oh boy, he dropped his spinach. What a break for me." In both "Rodeo Romeo" (Famous Studios, 1946) and "Tore-

By the time the 1960-61 TV Popeye cartoons were in production, the animators didn't find it necessary to spell out the entire name spinach on Popeye's can. In "Popeye's Double Trouble" (Paramount, 1961), the audience need only see the first three letters of the label to know what's inside the can.

adorable" (Famous Studios, 1953), Bluto dumps Popeye's spinach out of his can, knowing the strength it gives the sailor. In "Taxi Turvy" (Famous Studios, 1954) Bluto actually pulls the spinach can out of Popeye's pipe before the sailor can suck it through to his mouth, saying, "Oh no ... you ain't eating no spinach in this picture." An event similar to this occurred in the 1936 Fleischer cartoon, "A Clean Shaven Man," when Bluto, upon seeing Popeye pull out his can of spinach, grabs it and says, "Hey, none of that stuff!" The most telling example of Popeye's bearded foe knowing there is something special about Popeye's spinach occurred in the 1961 cartoon, "County Fair" (Paramount). Popeye and Brutus are competitors in a spinach eating contest and the test to "prove its strength." Brutus promises to keep this contest fair but, instead, tosses Popeye aside, looks right at the viewing audience and says, "You didn't think I was going to play fair with that runt and take a chance against his spinach." The key words being "his spinach."

Although Popeye achieved super strength by also eating it straight out of the garden, apparently his own stock packed more of a punch. By the time these TV Popeye cartoons were in production, the link between Popeye and his spinach was so firmly established that the animators often didn't write the name "spinach" on the can, or had the audience see only the first three letters, S-P-I.

The Goons

The Goons appeared in Segar's original comic strip during the 1930s. They were adapted to animation starting with the 1938 Fleischer-produced cartoon "Goonland." It was established in this cartoon that the Goons live on their own island and don't like humans.

When Segar originally created the Goons, children were having nightmares about them, and parents were telling their kids, "Be good or the Goon will get you." Segar was asked to soften the Goons, especially the Sea Hag's assistant in terror, Alice the Goon. Originally Alice was a hulking monster, but she later became Swee'pea's babysitter after falling for the little tyke.

Alice did not appear in any Famous Studios cartoons but did pop up in many King Features cartoons produced for television. She appeared in "Old Salt Tale" (Jack Kinney, 1960), "Hypnotic Glance" (Jack Kinney, 1960), "The Golden Touch" (Jack Kinney, 1960), and "Fashion Fotography" (Jack Kinney, 1960), but her biggest role was in 1960s "Frozen Feuds" (Jack Kinney). In this tale, Popeye is in Alaska and asked to search for the mysterious "Goon." Whoever sees Alice turns all white. While Popeye goes looking for Alice, the big Goon falls in love with the sailor man. She keeps trying to attract Popeye's attention and finally catches him. Popeye promises to give Alice a picture of himself if she'll give him a hat like hers for Olive Oyl. The picture of Popeye actually is a television set with the sailor man on screen. The cartoon ends with Alice, wearing a sailor's hat, singing the Popeye theme in her native talk, then tooting her pipe. Despite shaky animation, "Frozen Feuds" is a cute entry in the King Features series.

Various Goons appeared in "Popeye the Ugly Duckling" (Jack Kinney, 1960), "The Valley of the Goons" (Paramount, 1960), "Goon with the Wind" (Gene Deitch/William Snyder, 1960), "Which Is Witch" (Gene Deitch/William Snyder, 1960), and "The Cure" (Paramount, 1961).

In "Popeye the Ugly Duckling," young Popeye is so ugly that he runs away and lands on Goon Island. The Goons don't think he's so ugly and take him in. They bring little Popeye up and teach him their culture. Popeye reads books like "Alice in Goon-der Land" and "The Wizard of Goon." He plays sports like "Touch Goon," and he is fed spinach. When Popeye is ready to leave the island, the Goons give him his pipe and a song. Popeye heads back to the school house he ran away from and beats up bully Brutus. Brutus ends up on Goon Island, but the Goons have trouble educating the brute.

The Goons popped up in the Hanna-Barbera cartoons, including "A Goon Gone Gooney" (1978), in which Alice the Goon is portrayed as a mean queen who wants Popeye as her king. Olive eats Popeye's spinach and takes care of the Goon tribe. Bluto ends up being Alice's new king. In "Here Stew You" (1978), Popeye and Olive end up stranded on Goon Island, and Olive Oyl is captured. Olive is forced to cook stew for the Goons to keep them in line until Popeye arrives

Sgt. Blast calls "Oyl" and "Goon" to attention in a scene from a "Private Olive Oyl" cartoon segment from Hanna-Barbera's "The Popeye and Olive Comedy Show," 1980–83.

to save her. At the close of the cartoon, the Goons aid Popeye and Olive in rowing home … as long as Olive fixes them stew.

Alice the Goon became Olive Oyl's co-star in the "Private Olive Oyl" cartoons, which appeared as part of "The Popeye and Olive Comedy Show." In these cartoons, Alice speaks in her native Goon tongue, which drives Sgt. Blast crazy. The only other Popeye regulars to appear in the "Private Olive Oyl" cartoons were Swee'pea, Wimpy, and (in the last one) Eugene the Jeep.

Alice also appeared in a "Popeye and Son" cartoon. Junior's pal, Woody, had run away and landed on Goon Island, where Queen Alice wanted to make him a member of the Goon tribe.

Despite starting off as characters who gave little children nightmares, the Goons have become beloved members of Popeye's animated gang.

Eugene the Jeep

The Jeep appeared in Segar's "Thimble Theatre" comic strip in 1936 and quickly became a popular addition to the cast. The animal made his animation

Eugene the Jeep targets Olive Oyl and Popeye for love in this publicity photo for the Popeye Valentine Special, which aired on the CBS television network.

debut in the 1938 Fleischer-produced film, "The Jeep." In this cartoon, Popeye brings over the Jeep to visit with Swee'pea only to learn the child has run away. Popeye and the Jeep go in search of Swee'pea but finally discover he was rolled up in Olive's window shade all that time.

The Jeep made a brief cameo appearance in 1939's "Wotta Nitemare" and played a bigger role in 1940s "Popeye Presents Eugene the Jeep." In this amusing film, Olive gives Popeye the Jeep as a birthday present but advises him that he has to sleep outdoors at night. Popeye tries to keep the animal outside, but he keeps getting back in. At the film's conclusion, Popeye is sleeping in the Jeep's tiny bed outside, and we see the Jeep magically appearing on the snoring sailor's lap.

The Jeep did not appear in any of the Famous Studios cartoons but was in many of the King Features television cartoons of 1960-61. The Sea Hag captured the Jeep in "Hag Way Robbery" (Gene Deitch/William Snyder, 1960). The Jeep popped up in "Jeep-Jeep" (Jack Kinney, 1960), "Popeye's Museum Piece" (Jack Kinney, 1960), "Popeye and the Magic Hat" (Jack Kinney, 1960), "Popeye and the Spinach Stalk" (Jack Kinney, 1960), "Aztec Wreck" (Jack Kinney, 1960), "Jeep Tale" (Jack Kinney, 1960), "Swee'pea Through the Looking Glass" (Jack Kinney, 1960), "Popeye's Testimonial Dinner" (Jack Kinney, 1960), "Jeep Is Jeep" (Paramount, 1960), "Voo-Doo to You, Too" (Paramount, 1960), and "Myskery Melody" (Paramount, 1961).

The Jeep's powers included appearing and disappearing, shooting sparks from his tail, and walking through walls and other objects. His favorite food was orchids.

The Jeep also appeared in the Hanna-Barbera cartoons for "The All New Popeye Hour." In "Peask and Quiet" (Hanna-Barbera, 1978) Popeye tries to catch some peace and quiet and takes the Jeep along for company. In "The Decathlon Dilemma" (Hanna-Barbera, 1978) the Jeep uses his powers to help Pappy prove he can compete in the decathlon with Popeye.

The Jeep played a big role in the Treasure Hunt adventure "I Wants Me Mummy" (1978). In this adventure, the Jeep helps Popeye, Olive, and Bluto track down a mummy's treasure. The animal also does battle with the Sea Hag's magic wand ray.

The Jeep also made a guest star appearance in the last "Private Olive Oyl" cartoon, titled "Jeep Thrills" (1980). The Jeep pays Olive and Alice the Goon a visit and drives Sgt. Blast crazy as she tries to locate the animal. But by the cartoon's end, the general decides that the Jeep would be a perfect mascot for the base.

The Jeep also appeared in a few "Popeye and Son" cartoons. In one tale, the animal keeps stealing orchids from people. Popeye learns that it's because Eugene has a family to feed: his wife and baby Jeeps!

The Nephews

Popeye's nephews, created not by Segar but by the animators at Fleischer Studios, were first seen on film as the children of Popeye and Olive in the 1940

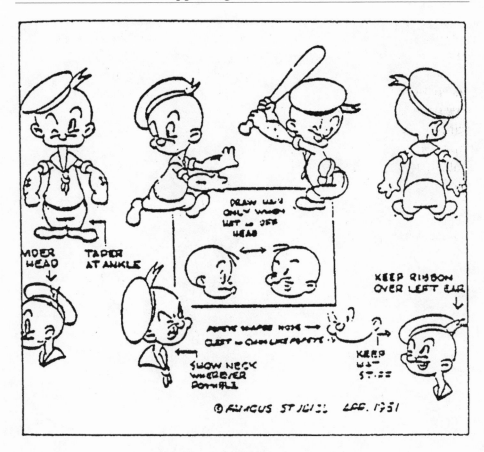

A 1951 model sheet of Popeye's look-alike, sound-alike nephews, who appeared on a regular basis in the Famous Studios cartoons.

cartoon "Wimmin Is a Myskery." Olive dreamed that she was married to Popeye and the lads (who all looked and sounded just like Popeye) were their children. The four kids turned out to be junior terrors and turned Olive's house upside down. In 1942, they returned to the screen as Popeye's nephews for the cartoon "Pip-eye-Pup-eye-Poop-eye and Peep-eye." In this cartoon, Popeye eats his spinach and performs various stunts to convince the lads to chow down their food. The nephews aren't impressed, so Popeye spanks them. When Popeye finishes spanking the tykes, they eat their spinach and gain strength. Then the nephews attack Popeye. The cartoon ends with a defeated Popeye landing on the sidewalk and his nephews walking over him to go fishing. The cartoon closes with a line spoken in the style that would become the nephews' trademark, each one speaking a word in turn: "But," "we," "don't," "like," "spinach!"

The nephews became a staple during the run of the Famous Studios cartoons, but as the years went on their ranks decreased. Popeye started with four nephews, then had three, and in 1957 (the last year of the Famous Studios cartoons) ended up with two.

Popeye gives his nephews a lift in this publicity photo from the early 1940s during the Famous Studios era.

The nephews appeared in the first color Popeye cartoon, "Her Honor the Mare" (1943). In this cartoon the lads bring home a horse and try to hide it from Uncle Popeye. They decide to keep the horse after she becomes a mother. In 1948's "Spinach vs. Hamburgers," Popeye and Olive try to convince the boys to eat their spinach, but they want to eat at Wimpy's Hamburger Heaven. Popeye shows the boys scenes from three of his cartoons to encourage the boys to eat the strengthening vegetable. The boys eat; then they use their strength to link a chain together, chain Popeye and Olive to a post, and walk over to eat hamburgers at Wimpy's Hamburger Heaven.

In "Popeye Makes a Movie" (1950), the nephews visit a movie set where Popeye is filming a picture. The lads cause problems, leading Popeye to shackle them. The boys, however, toss Popeye a can of spinach when he finds himself suspended over a pool of sharks. In "Riot in Rhythm" (1950), Popeye sends the boys to bed too early and they decide to make musical instruments out of household items and keep Popeye up all night! This cartoon was a color remake of an earlier Famous Studios film, "Me Musical Nephews" (1942). In "Lunch with a Punch" (1950), the boys don't want to eat their spinach lunch, until Bluto grabs Popeye from behind and uses his face as a punching bag. The boys pound on Bluto and sing, "We wins at the finish cause we eats our spinach, like Popeye the Sailor Man." In "Tots of Fun" (1952), Popeye tries to build a house, but once he closes the door the place falls in on him. In a sequence set to music, the nephews rebuild Popeye's house but knock the sailor man about in the process of rebuilding. In 1953's "Popeye's Mirthday," Olive tells the boys to keep Popeye out of her house until his birthday surprise party is ready. The lads hit Popeye with all they can think of to keep him out. They shoot a rocket off in the chimney when Popeye attempts to climb down it. The rocket gets caught in Popeye's shirt and the sailor goes off into space. The rocket explodes, and Popeye and his can of spinach get clipped to a clothes line. Popeye grabs his spinach (which looks like a damp towel), squeezes its contents into his mouth, and lifts up Olive's house—and discovers the party.

By 1955, Popeye was down to two nephews in "Gift of Gag." In this film, the two lads try to keep Popeye from learning what's in a big box the boys are carrying around. When the nephews haul the box on the roof, Popeye scoops the boys into his arms, causing the box to fall and break open. It contains a king-size can of spinach for Popeye's birthday! Popeye takes the boys in his hands and embraces them.

In the nephews' final appearance in a theatrical cartoon, "Patriotic Popeye" (1957), Popeye tries to show the two lads the danger of shooting off fireworks. The boys don't listen and attempt to shoot off an atomic sky rocket, which drills into the ground and comes up underneath the barrel the boys are hiding in, carrying them skyward. They scream for Uncle Popeye, who eats his spinach and travels upward in hot pursuit to rescue the boys. The cartoon concludes with the lads popping balloons which Popeye is blowing up for them in rapid succession.

Because the nephews had been created by Fleischer Studios, Paramount Pictures owned the copyright on the characters, which kept the boys from appearing in the King Features TV cartoons. They did reappear in the Hanna-Barbera cartoons, starting in 1978 with "The All New Popeye Hour." In "Bad Company" (1978), the lads go off with Uncle Bluto instead of Popeye and Olive for a day at the fair. They soon become upset with Bluto's dirty tricks and give spinach to a hog that Bluto is trying to catch. The spinach-fed hog turns into a wild boar and drags Bluto along the ground. In "A Seal with Appeal" (1978) the lads take home a seal but have to hide it from Popeye. When the seal manages to save one of Popeye's prized possessions (a ship in a bottle), the sailor man allows the boys to keep their pet. In "Old McPopeye Had a Farm" (1978), the boys help their Uncle Angus get his crops ready for market despite farmer Bluto's tricks. In "Unidentified Fighting Object" (1979) the boys tangle with neighbor Bluto and his dog, "Bullo," when Bluto tries to capture a visiting alien creature who is a friend of Popeye and Olive. In this cartoon, one of Popeye's four nephews is introduced as "Papeye."

In the Fleischer cartoons, Popeye's nephews wore a mini-version of Popeye's original comic strip attire, but when the sailor man switched to a white uniform, so did the boys. In the Hanna-Barbera cartoons they were back in the original Fleischer-style outfits.

Popeye's nephews appeared in many of the "Popeye Health and Safety Tips" featured in the "Popeye" series produced by Hanna-Barbera and aired on CBS Saturday mornings from 1978 to 1983.

Shorty

Popeye's little sailor buddy, Shorty, was a creation of Famous Studios. He always wanted to help Popeye, but caused more harm than good. In his debut cartoon, "Happy Birthdaze" (1943), Shorty and Olive help Popeye celebrate his birthday, but the one-eyed sailor ends up getting socked about thanks to Shorty's misguided efforts. At the finish of the cartoon, Popeye and Shorty end up in a furnace, and while Shorty sings, "Happy birthday to my pal … to my pal … happy birthday to my pal," Popeye shoots him! Of course the shooting occurs in darkness. Despite Popeye pulling the trigger, Shorty returned in 1943's "Marry-Go-Round." In this entertaining cartoon, Popeye wants to propose to Olive but lacks the nerve. Shorty tries to give Popeye some courage but ends up being the object of Olive's attraction. Olive

Shorty, voiced by both Jack Mercer and Arnold Stang, was a proverbial pain in the neck for Popeye. In the three animated cartoons he appeared in, Popeye was in for trouble!

puts on a frilly dress and goes after Popeye's pint-sized sailor buddy. When Olive kisses Popeye by accident, she promptly bops him over the hat with a baseball bat. Popeye decides to throw in the towel. He tosses Olive Oyl into a washing machine and walks off with Shorty in his hands. At the cartoon's finish, Popeye is nailing pictures of Dorothy Lamour over his bunk—pictures originally belonging to Shorty—while pictures of Olive hang over Shorty's bunk.

Shorty made his final appearance in 1944's "Moving Aweigh." In this cartoon, the two sailors help Olive move, but in the process, Popeye gets banged up. In one scene a policeman uses Popeye's head as a drum and pounds on it with his nightstick. Popeye manages to tie up Shorty, who has been causing all of Popeye's woes, but that still doesn't prevent a grand piano from landing on the policeman, who then sends Popeye, Shorty, and Olive Oyl to jail.

Supporting Cast Summary

Here is a summary of the supporting cast from "Popeye" as seen in each series:

Fleischer Series (1933–42)

Olive Oyl
Wimpy
Swee'pea
Poopdeck Pappy
The Goons
Bluto
Eugene the Jeep
Popeye's nephews
Geezil
Oscar

Famous Studios (1942–57)

Popeye
Olive Oyl
Bluto
Wimpy
Swee'pea
Poopdeck Pappy
Popeye's mother
Popeye's nephews

King Features TV Cartoons (1960-61)

Olive Oyl
Wimpy
Swee'pea
Brutus
Poopdeck Pappy
The Sea Hag
Eugene the Jeep
Rough House
Geezil
King Blozo
Prof. O.G. WottaSnozzle
Alice the Goon
The Whiffle Hen

Hanna-Barbera Cartoons: "The All New Popeye Hour" and "The Popeye and Olive Comedy Show" (1978–83)

Olive Oyl
Wimpy

Swee'pea

Popeye's nephews

Bluto

Alice the Goon

The Sea Hag

Eugene the Jeep

Poopdeck Pappy

"Popeye and Son" (1987-88)

Popeye

Olive Oyl

Wimpy

Bluto

Lizzie (Bluto's wife)

Junior (Popeye's son)

Tank (Bluto's son)

Eugene the Jeep

Dee-Dee

Woody

Francis (Wimpy's nephew)

The Sea Hag

Poopdeck Pappy

Alice the Goon

PART _____
SIX

Popeye Out and About

Popeye at the Parks

During the 1990s, both Popeye and Betty Boop were featured as part of the family attractions at the MGM Grand in Las Vegas. Popeye, Olive Oyl and Brutus would greet visitors at the MGM theme park. Hundreds of products bearing the likeness of the sailor man and his crew were sold, including clocks, candies, shirts, hats, pens, ceramic pieces and key chains. At this time, Popeye was also part of a theme park in New Jersey at Darien Lake. A huge portion of the park was devoted to children and called, "Popeye's Seaport." Cut-outs of Popeye and all of his crew decorated the grounds. There was also a live Popeye show which worked children into the performance. Darien Lake lost the rights to Popeye when they switched to using Warner Brothers' characters at the start of 2000. MGM decided to close down their family activities in favor of adult entertainment.

In 1999, Universal Studios in Florida opened "Universal's Islands of Adventure," featuring Popeye as one of the big attractions. Popeye and Bluto are featured in their own popular water ride, among other attractions related to the one-eyed sailor. The various stores at the park contain hundreds of Popeye items—everything from hats, beanie babies (Popeye, Olive, Swee'pea and Eugene the Jeep), tee shirts, notebooks, postcards, pens, straws and PVC figures, to drinking glasses, mugs, large foam spinach cans, magnets and pins. Popeye, Olive and Brutus also greet visitors at the park.

Dolly DeMeo is greeted by Brutus at Universal Studio's "Islands of Adventure" in 2001.

In 1999, at the annual "Popeye's Picnic" held in Chester, IL, birthplace of E.C. Segar, Universal Studio's president and CEO, Tom Williams, made the official announcement of Popeye's inclusion at the theme park. It was quite a thrill for me to see Popeye's face and muscle staring down from a huge billboard promoting his addition to the park in Cambridge, Massachusetts. As of 2003, Popeye remains a popular attraction at Universal Studios in Florida, and he is also seen at their theme park in California. Though not a theme park, the Barker Character Comic, Cartoon Museum and Art Gallery located in Cheshire, Connecticut, also has a strong Popeye presence. Herb and Gloria Barker, owners of the museum, created a haven for children to get exposed to collectibles. They hope this will inspire kids to begin collecting as an alternative to undesirable activities. Thousands of comic and cartoon character collectibles are on display to the public, free of charge. Popeye items from his origins to the present day are a featured attraction.

The art gallery sells animation cels by many famous artists. During the summer months, the "Cartoon Theatre" at the museum is open where the public is invited to see classic "Popeye" theatrical films on the movie screen. Herb Barker was born six days after Popeye in 1929 and the sailor is his favorite comic and cartoon character.

Popeye, the World Traveler

Popeye and his crew are not just known in the United States but all over the world. When American comic strips had to be banned from European newspapers during the war, public outcry demanded that "Thimble Theatre Starring Popeye" wasn't among them. In Germany, he is known as "Popeye der Spinatmatrose," and in Finnish he is called, "Kippari Kalle." For decades, Popeye has been featured in a number of digest-sized comic books in Italy. He is known there as either "Popeye" or "Braccio di Ferro" (Iron Arm). Popeye is very popular in Japan with many products bearing his image. Popeye items, which have been produced overseas, include:

Overalls, pants, shorts, jackets and dresses from Brazil
Chocolates, chewing gum and toffees from Chile
Soft drinks, juices, plain milk products and story books from Saudi Arabia
Keys, pillows, quilts and bath robes from Belgium
Optical frames, watches and PVC figures from France
Mirrors, dolls, crockery, laundry bags, music boxes, pendants from Japan
Comic books from Thailand
Caps and T-shirts from Australia

I first discovered Popeye's international fame in 1975 when my father and brother took a trip to Italy and returned home with many Popeye items. From the 1960 to the 1990s, various publishers in England printed "Popeye Annuals," which were hardback collections of original stories, American comic strips and comic book material. Popeye cartoons have also been syndicated to TV stations all over the world. Many of the public domain titles from both Fleischer and Famous Studios have been dubbed in different languages and sold on video and DVD. Cartoons from both the King Features Syndicate and Hanna-Barbera television produced episodes not available on video and DVD in the United States have been available in this format internationally.

Popeye the Cable Man

For decades, the various "Popeye" animated series appeared on hundreds of independent television stations across the United States. In Boston, Massachusetts, he was a fixture on channel 4, channel 9, channel 38, channel 25 and channel 56. By the mid–1990s, Popeye cartoons were disappearing from television stations. This had little to do with a decline in their popularity, but rather the disappearance of independent stations that aired them.

In their place, stations emerged, which were owned by the Disney Corporation, the UPN Network, the Fox Network or the WB (Warner Brothers) Network. Each network owns a huge catalog of motion pictures, television movies, television series and animated cartoons. It has made purchasing programming from a television syndicator unnecessary. Cartoon series, which once dominated the airwaves, everything from "Felix the Cat" to "Mr. Magoo" have been affected by this change.

Talk shows now dominate the morning and afternoon time periods once occupied by animated cartoon series. Infomercials have also replaced animated shows, as they are much more profitable to a television station than purchasing the rights to a cartoon series, which is not under their ownership.

During the 1980s, "Popeye" was having more of a presence on cable television. WTBS, the "Super Station" in Atlanta, GA, initially aired the King Features TV-cartoons and then later switched to the colorized Fleischer and Famous Studios package on their popular "Tom and Jerry's Fun House." Popeye remained a fixture on this program, along with "Bugs Bunny" and "The Three Stooges" for years.

The sailor was also seen daily and on Sunday mornings on the cable station, TNT, also based in Atlanta, GA. Though this was called "The Popeye Hour," mixed in with the sailor's films were MGM and Warner Brothers' cartoons, which did not feature central characters.

Popeye was also seen as part of the highly rated, "Bugs Bunny and Pals," which aired Saturday evenings on TNT.

The Family Channel bought the rights to the "All New Popeye" cartoon package from Hearst Entertainment and aired this 65 episode, half-hour series for five straight years. Unfortunately, the Family Channel was pulling episodes out of series and cartoon programs that they felt had objectionable content. The sailor's cartoons, mainly featuring the Sea Hag, were not seen on their broadcasts. "Popeye and Son" also appeared briefly on both the Family Channel and the USA Network.

Popeye cartoons (public domain theatricals and the TV cartoons) have been a staple of the award winning cable television series "Drawing with Fred" seen in New
England beginning in 1992. Pictured is the program's host, Fred Grandinetti (left),
and guest, singer Logan McCarty, from a 2001 episode.

In 1992, Popeye settled in for a long run as part of "Drawing with Fred,"
an award-winning cable children's series, seen in parts of New England. The series
is a throwback to the old "Uncle" hosted programs and features cartoon lessons,
special guests and safety tips.

Launched in November of 1996, was the cable channel, Locomotion, for the
Latin American population. The program lineup featured many series from King

Features Syndicate, as King's parent group, the Hearst Corporation, was co-owner of the channel. The TV Popeye cartoons became a popular attraction on Locomotion.

Popeye, along with many animated cartoon characters, moved over to the Cartoon Network when the cable channel was founded in the early 1990s. This has been more of a mixed blessing. In 1993, the Cartoon Network presented a week-long celebration honoring Popeye's 60th year as an animated character. From Monday, July 12 to Saturday, July 17 at 9:00 P.M., the network

Publicity art by Hy Eisman, who draws the Sunday Popeye strip of the sailor, and showing Dr. Domenic D'Amico, which was used to promote "The Italian Dentist" episode of the cable series "Drawing with Fred."

aired a "Popumentary"—Popeye films tied together with a similar theme. The week-long broadcast was later repeated on Sunday, July 18, in its entirety. Though the Network promoted this special on WTBS and TNT with a good amount of press coverage, the "Popumentary" failed to score with audiences. Why? This event was supposed to be of an historical nature, but the colorized Fleischer films were aired instead of the black and white originals.

On July 3, 1993, the network launched "The Popeye Show," a two-hour weekly series aired on Saturday mornings beginning at 6:00 A.M. The Popeye films were mixed with cartoons featuring singing flowers or dancing bears. If children tuned into this program, halfway into it, they would have no way of realizing that this was in fact "The Popeye Show." This series lasted for several months, but was later shifted to the wee hours of the morning.

Popeye then became a staple on the network's "Acme Hour" program, which featured "Tom and Jerry," "Bugs Bunny" and other cartoon characters. The Cartoon Network aired the black and white Popeyes as part of their "Late Nite Black and White" series, though the films themselves had their openings altered to eliminate the title slide which states, "Associated Artists Presents." This 30-to-60-minute program had yet to air earlier than 1:00 A.M., and also presented black and white cartoons from the Warner Brothers and MGM studios.

During the 1990s, the colorized Fleischer films and the Famous Studios cartoons were a rotating segment on the network's Saturday afternoon series, "Super Chunk," which featured trivia questions.

The colorized Popeyes, along with the Famous Studios cartoons, have been

The original opening title sequence to the black and white "Popeye the Sailor" cartoons, which were seen on the films of 1941 and 1942. This title sequence was never aired on television until November 2001 for "The Popeye Show" on Cartoon Network (courtesy of Jerry Beck).

The original opening title sequence to the black and white "Popeye the Sailor" cartoons, which were seen on the films of 1942 through 1943. This title sequence was never aired on television until November 2001 for "The Popeye Show" on the Cartoon Network (courtesy of Jerry Beck).

aired, on a rotating basis, on the Cartoon Network's sister channel, "Boomerang," in different time periods and as all-day marathons. However, "Boomerang" has yet to achieve the wide audience enjoyed by the Cartoon Network.

Cartoon Network announced they would be restoring the original openings and closings (with the Paramount Pictures mountain) to 39 Fleischer and Famous Studios films for a new "Popeye Show" planned to debut in October 2001. In the October 19 edition of *USA Today*, the newspaper stated: "Popeye, strong to the finish and still eating spinach, will make a triumphant return to TV in a form never seen since the 1930s and 40s. Starting Oct. 28, [actually this half-hour series did not make the airwaves until November] the Cartoon Network is giving the salty swab a weekly series, 'I'm Popeye.' [The show was later changed to "The Popeye Show."] Each half-hour episode will include three 'Popeye the

Sailor' cartoons that have been restored to their original theatrical state." Mike Lazzo, head of programming at the Cartoon Network, scheduled the show for Mondays at 1:00 A.M., due to the fact the majority of the films in the series are in black and white. The network offered this reason for the time period: "Children see black and white cartoons; they think old, and turn off." This reasoning is flawed because "The Popeye Show," like the network's "The Bob Clampett Show," "Toonheads" and "The Chuck Jones Show" are narrated and produced with the adult audience in mind. These programs contain historical information pertaining to the making of cartoons which a child probably wouldn't sit through, but an adult audience would certainly appreciate.

Furthermore, on "The Bob Clampett Show," the network had aired several black and white films starring Porky Pig during the 9:00 P.M.–10:00 P.M. time period. Black and white cartoons had also been aired on "Toonheads," which usually aired in a time period starting as early as 9:00 P.M.

In the January 29, 2002, edition of *The Boston Phoenix*, Laurie Goldberg, who is in the public relations department at the Cartoon Network, confirmed she has been "deluged" with requests to move "The Popeye Show" to an earlier time slot. "I've been getting e-mails daily from Popeye people to get it on earlier," she stated in the paper.

Decisions other than ratings have played a part in Popeye's erratic schedule. Who owns a cartoon character plays a part in determining its time slot. AOL/Time Warner owns the Cartoon Network; they also own the Fleischer/Famous Studios "Popeye" films. They do not, however, own the merchandising rights to the sailor and his crew. Any revenue that is gained on the production of Popeye items through his exposure on the Cartoon Network goes to the Hearst Corporation. AOL/Time Warner, by airing Popeye in an early time slot, would be giving exposure to a character they can't make money from licensing. Today, much of the success of a cartoon character is determined by whether it will be successful in the field of merchandising. AOL/Time Warner would rather give prime exposure to the cartoon characters that they own. A former Warner Brothers employee explained that running Popeye doesn't generate any revenue for Warner Brothers and it is licensing which rules the Warner Brothers' universe. It has little to do with what the audience actually wants to see.

It was welcome news when the Cartoon Network, due to changes in programming personnel and audiences' pleas, moved "The Popeye Show" to 9:30 P.M. Sundays as part of their lineup tailored for adults in September of 2002. The series was switched to an earlier time period at 7:30 P.M., Sunday evenings in January 2003. "The Popeye Show" gained critical acclaim and performed very well in the ratings during its 10-month broadcast in its more convenient time periods. Unfortunately, the licensing issue and management's personal preference for cartoon characters has since kept the series bouncing about the Cartoon Network's schedule. Audiences can either gather to watch Popeye or must set their VCRs for the more inconvenient time periods.

In the December 2002 edition of *Boston* magazine, Warner Brothers spokesman, Scott Rowe, stated that the studio hoped to commemorate the 70th anniversary of the Popeye cartoon series in 2003 in a special way. "It's too early to let the proverbial spinach out of the can," Rowe stated. Unfortunately, the lid to the spinach can was sealed tight as no special or mention was made of this milestone in animation history, which again demonstrated the Cartoon Network's indifference toward Popeye. On October 28, 2003, Joe Swaney from the Boomerang cable network stated, "The classic Popeye theatrical shorts will continue to run on Boomerang."

Popeye: For All Generations

During the summer of 2001, King Features Syndicate had licensed the rights for Popeye and his pals to be used for a product, which caused a minor media furor. Bally Gaming Inc. planned to introduce "Popeye" slot machines to the New Jersey area. The game, featuring scenes of Popeye fighting Brutus and Wimpy chomping hamburgers, allowed people the opportunity to win $100,000.

Popeye's association with products marketed to adults is hardly anything new. The sailor's image has been used on everything from kitchenware and mops to lighters, telephones and checkbooks. Segar's version of the sailor man was seen gambling on the docks, and the original movie cartoons were produced with the adult audience in mind. The idea of a vending machine brought the "slots for tots" issue to the floor where regulators have voted in the past to ban machines with figures that are well known to children. Deputy Attorney General Charles Kimmel told the Casino Control Commission, which reviews all slot-machine proposals and voted 5–0, to allow Popeye slots "Popeye is indeed mainly a nostalgia figure." Bally Gaming representatives told New Jersey Casino Control Commissioners that Popeye is fondly remembered by baby boomers and their elders, but not familiar to today's children. "By and large, Popeye is a nostalgic figure at this point, one that doesn't appeal to people under 20," lawyer Gilbert Brooks told regulators.

While it is true that in recent years Popeye has been marketed more to the adult audience rather than children, whether or not the character still appeals to the younger set in the United States is a subject of debate. Sold in toy stores throughout 2002, were a Popeye bendable, talking doll and row boat figure manufactured by Precious Kids. These items were marketed with the younger audience in mind and geared to ages four and up. The first set of "Popeye" action figures, as well as the 12-inch doll of the sailor man, produced by Mezco toys have been sold in both "Kaybee" and toy store locations whose primary audience is children.

The live action *Popeye* feature film is still sold in the children's section in video stores as are the public domain animated films and Hanna-Barbera television cartoons.

Perhaps the best example of Popeye's ability to still capture the hearts of children can be attributed to the efforts of the Watertown Free Public Library and its branch locations, located in Watertown, Massachusetts. Since February 1994, 16mm prints of "Popeye the Sailor" cartoons have continually been screened in the children's area. Cartooning workshops featuring the sailor man draw large crowds and are greeted with enthusiasm by the younger set, this often being their first introduction to Popeye. Watertown's libraries also circulate a

To Joyce and Joanna Daniels,
Sincerely

Willard G. Bowsky
2-10-37.

Artwork by Fleischer Studios animator Willard G. Bowsky, February 10, 1937.

number of "Popeye" books, videos and toys to the public inside and outside of Massachusetts through their interlibrary loan system. Many of these items are located in the children's area among the sea of books and videos featuring more contemporary characters. Ms. Elaine M. Garnache, children's librarian from Watertown said, "As adults, we sometimes forget Popeye has a timelessness that translates into something today's children respond to as well."

In Popeyed Conclusion

Popeye cartoons, whether bouncing about the Cartoon Network's schedule; airing on a rotating basis on the Cartoon Network's Boomerang channel; aired with other classic cartoons; shown on cable access channels; aired uncut, restored, edited, colorized, fully animated, with limited animation or placed on both high quality and low budget video and DVD collections; or heard in Italian, Greek, Spanish, Japanese and German, continue to be seen 70 years after Popeye, in his film debut, first danced the hula with Betty Boop in 1933.

Popeye has become one of the most popular and sought after character collectibles on the market today. Collectors are willing to pay more than $2,000 for items that have been produced not only in the United States but worldwide. With the continuing production of products, whether marketed for children or adults, Popeye continues to have strength in the collectible marketplace. Plans for the sailor include a new 3-D CGI animated special for television to be aired during the holiday season of 2004 in honor of the character's 75th birthday. It has been reported the special will remain true to the character's original form. The Empire State Building was lit green in honor of Popeye's favorite vegetable on the occasion of his 75th birthday on January 17, 2004.

Would E.C. Segar have thought when he created this sailor with a face like a shipwreck that he would still be embraced today? Perhaps he would utter a phrase which would sum up the situation nicely: "Well, Blow Me Down!"

EPISODE GUIDE

The Fleischer Studios (1933–1942)

Dave Fleischer is billed as the director of each film.
Whether he actually was or wasn't has been a subject of debate.

Popeye the Sailor (release date: 7/14/33). Animators: Willard Bowsky, George Germanetti and Orestes Calpini. This was actually an entry in the "Betty Boop" series where Popeye was featured to see if he was popular enough with audiences to warrant his own series. Popeye takes Olive Oyl to the carnival but Bluto follows along. The bully ties Olive to the railroad tracks and pounds on Popeye. The sailor calmly takes the beating and pulls out a can of spinach. He knocks Bluto into a coffin made out of a tree and saves Olive Oyl. He proclaims at the end, "I'm Popeye the Sailor Man." The film was a big success and the sailor's film career was launched.

I Yam What I Yam (release date: 9/29/33). Animators: Seymour Kneitel, William Henning. This cartoon features the first appearance of Wimpy, who uses one of his classic phrases, "Come on in for a duck dinner, you bring the ducks." Popeye battles Indians and despite Olive screeching for help, she knocks out quite a few of them. When Popeye eats his spinach, he consumes it can and all!

Blow Me Down (release date: 10/27/33). Animators: Willard Bowsky, William Sturm. Popeye travels to Mexico and watches Olive do a Mexican dance. Her feet get stuck in two pots, a scene pulled out of Segar's "Thimble Theatre" comic strip of the period.

I Eats My Spinach (release date: 11/17/33). Animators: Seymour Kneitel, Roland Crandall. Popeye takes Olive to a bullfight and gets involved with the actual bullfighting while Bluto pursues Olive Oyl. This is the first cartoon where you hear the recognizable fanfare when Popeye pulls out his can of spinach. It is also the first cartoon to feature Mae Questel's familiar Olive Oyl voice.

Seasin's Greetinks (release date: 12/17/33). Animators: Seymour Kneitel, Roland Crandall. Popeye teaches Olive how to ice skate in the first holiday-themed cartoon.

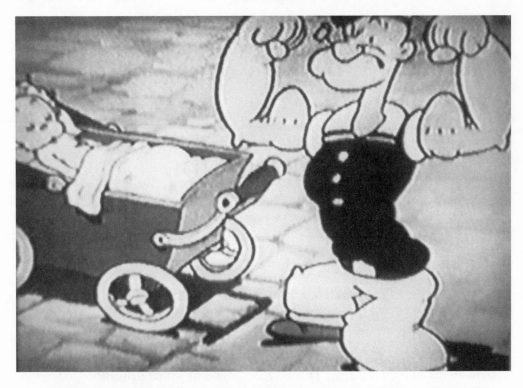

Popeye prepares to quiet several automobiles' honking horns! From "Sock-A-Bye Baby" (Fleischer, 1934).

Wild Elephinks (release date: 12/29/33). Animators: William Bowsky, Bill Sturm. Popeye and Olive are stranded in the jungle with wild beasts. Olive manages to pull a big can of spinach out of her shoe to feed the can's contents to Popeye.

Sock-a-Bye Baby (release date: 1/19/34). Animators: Seymour Kneitel, Roland Crandall. Popeye takes Betty Boop's baby brother out for a stroll and tries to keep the surroundings quiet so he won't start crying. Harpo Marx (in animated form) makes a cameo appearance.

Lets You and Him Fight (release date: 2/16/34). Animators: William Bowsky, William Sturm. Popeye has his first boxing match with Bluto.

The Man on the Flying Trapeze (release date: 3/16/34). Animators: William Bowsky, Dave Tendlar. Popeye goes after Olive Oyl who has joined a trapeze act. This is the only appearance of Olive Oyl's mother in a Fleischer film.

Can You Take It (release date: 4/27/34). Animators: Myron Waldman, Thomas Johnson. To join the Bruiser Boy's Club, Popeye is put through a series of punishing tests.

Shoein Hosses (release date: 6/1/34). Animators: Willard Bowsky, Dave Tendlar. Popeye and Bluto compete to see who will be hired as Olive's assistant in her blacksmith business.

Strong to the Finich (release date: 6/29/34). Animators: Seymour Kneitel, Roland

Wimpy tries to get a grip on some ghostly hamburgers. From "Shiver Me Timbers" (Fleischer, 1934).

Crandall. Popeye feeds spinach to a chicken, a tree and two cows to convince a group of children that eating it will make you healthy and strong.

Shiver Me Timbers (release date: 7/27/34). Animators: Willard Bowsky, Bill Sturm. Popeye, Olive and Wimpy end up on a haunted ship full of ghosts. Even the hamburgers Wimpy attempts to eat are ghostly images.

Axe Me Another (release date: 8/30/34). Animators: Seymour Kneitel, Roland Crandall. When Bluto tosses Olive Oyl into the ocean because "he didn't like my spinach," Popeye challenges the brute to see who can cut down trees the best way.

A Dream Walking (release date: 9/26/34). Animators: Seymour Kneitel, Roland Crandall. This has become a classic in the field of animation with its use of depth, movement and musical score. Olive ends up sleepwalking right onto a construction site with Popeye and Bluto in pursuit.

The Two Alarm Fire (release date: 10/26/34). Animators: Willard Bowsky, Nick Tafuri. Olive's house is on fire and firemen Popeye and Bluto compete to be the first one to put it out. Popeye saves Bluto from the fire but after he makes sure he is okay, he slugs him!

The Dance Contest (release date: 11/23/34). Animators: Willard Bowsky, Dave Tendlar. Popeye can't dance that well until spinach charges up his skills. This cartoon gives the illusion of real ballroom dancing.

We Aim to Please (release date: 12/28/34). Animators: Willard Bowsky, Dave Tendlar. Popeye and Olive open up an eatery. Wimpy and Bluto try to get free meals.

Beware of Barnacle Bill (release date: 1/25/35). Animators: Willard Bowsky, Harold Walker. Olive plans to marry Barnacle Bill the Sailor but when Popeye licks him, Olive wants her old beau back. Popeye promptly rejects her!

Be Kind to Aminals (release date: 2/22/35). Animators: Willard Bowsky, Charles Hastings. Popeye and Olive stop Bluto from mistreating a horse. It certainly doesn't sound like William Costello's voice as Popeye in this cartoon. The sailor sounds like he has a bad head cold!

Pleased to Meet Cha (release date: 3/22/35). Animators: Willard Bowsky, Harold Walker. Popeye and Bluto both visit Olive and whoever performs the best trick stays. This is the first cartoon where we hear Popeye sing, "I'm strong to the finich cause I eats me spinach, I'm Popeye the Sailor Man."

The Hyp-Nut-Tist (release date: 4/26/35). Animators: Seymour Kneitel, Roland Crandall. Popeye and Olive become part of Bluto the Hypnotist's act.

Choose Your Weppins (release date: 5/31/35). Animators: Dave Tendlar, George Germanetti, Sam Stimson, Nick Tafuri, William Sturm. Olive runs a pawnshop and comes across an escaped felon.

Dizzy Divers (release date: 6/26/35). Animators: Willard Bowsky, Harold Walker. Popeye and Bluto look for buried treasure in the sea, planning to split it 50-50. Bluto tries to take the whole treasure chest but even after Popeye defeats him, the sailor still gives the brute his share with a sock to go along with it.

For Better or Worser (release date: 6/28/35). Animators: Seymour Kneitel, Roland Crandall. Popeye and Bluto both want to marry the same woman, Olive Oyl, but neither has seen her face yet. This is the last cartoon featuring William Costello as the voice of Popeye.

You Gotta Be a Football Hero (release date: 8/30/35). Animators: Willard Bowsky, Nick Tafuri, George Germanetti, Harold Walker, Bill Sturm, Orestes Calpini. Popeye, not voiced by William Costello, plays football against Bluto and his team. This cartoon shows how fickle Olive Oyl can be. She starts off rooting for Bluto's team, using her body to spell out his name while cheerleading. When Popeye starts to trounce Bluto's team, she says, "I'm changing my mind. Hooray for Popeye."

King of the Mardi Gras (release date: 9/27/35). Animators: David Tendlar, William Sturm, Graham Place, Nick Tafuri, Harold Walker, Eli Brucker. Popeye and Bluto both run shows at the Mardi Gras, seeking Olive Oyl's attention. This is the first cartoon featuring Jack Mercer as the sailor's voice.

Adventures of Popeye (release date: 10/25/35). Animators: none credited, most of the cartoon is made up of stock footage. This cartoon mixes live action footage of a little boy being picked on by a bully and an animated Popeye, who jumps out of a storybook to show the tyke what he did to guys who thought they were tough. The boy eats spinach, though it looks like burnt leaves, and punches the bully through a window.

Spinach Overture (release date: 12/7/35). Animators: Seymour Kneitel, Roland Crandall. Popeye conducts an orchestra only to have Bluto take it over. Once Popeye eats his spinach, he takes back his band and conducts Bluto with several punches!

Vim, Vigor and Vitaliky (release date: 1/3/36). Animators: Seymour Kneitel, Roland Crandall. Bluto dresses up as a woman to become part of Popeye's fitness class for women.

A Clean Shaven Man (release date: 2/7/36). Animators: Seymour Kneitel, Roland Crandall. Olive sings, "I want a clean shaven man!" Popeye and Bluto decide to make each other over. This is the first time Bluto lets the audience know he realizes what will happen when Popeye eats his spinach. When the sailor pulls out his can, Bluto yells, "Hey, none of that stuff." He throws the can away, which hits a wall and rolls back to Popeye. Geezil, a character from Segar's "Thimble Theatre" comic strip, makes a cameo at the end of the film.

Brotherly Love (release date: 3/6/36). Animators: Seymour Kneitel, Roland Crandall. Olive wants Popeye to preach brotherly love.

I Ski–Love Ski–You Ski (release date: 4/3/36). Animators: Willard Bowsky, George Germanetti. Popeye takes Olive mountain climbing but Bluto secretly tags along.

Bridge Ahoy (release date: 5/1/36). Animators: Seymour Kneitel, Roland Crandall. Popeye, Olive and Wimpy decide to build a bridge when Bluto's Ferry Service charges too much.

What No Spinach (release date: 5/7/36). Animators: Seymour Kneitel, Roland Crandall. "There's nothing in the world that can compare with a hamburger juicy and rare," Wimpy sings at the start of this cartoon. The moocher tries to steal free food at the diner where he works. It won't be easy because Bluto's the owner!

I Wanna Be a Lifeguard (release date: 6/26/36). Animators: David Tendlar, William Sturm, Joe Oriolo, Eli Brucker, Nick Tafuri, Graham Place. Written by Edward Watkins, Joe Ward and Joe Stultz. Popeye and Bluto compete for a lifeguard job. Popeye's spinach can takes a life of its own when it comes to the sailor after he whistles for it!

Let's Get Movin' (release date: 7/24/36). Animators: Willard Bowsky, Orestes Calpini. Written by Joe Stultz and Bill Turner. It's moving day for Olive Oyl and Popeye is jealous over Bluto the moving man.

Never Kick a Woman (release date: 8/28/36). Animators: Seymour Kneitel, Roland Crandall. Popeye instructs Olive in the art of self-defense while a Mae West type instructor falls for the sailor. This is the first and only Fleischer film where Olive eats the spinach to fight the flirt.

Little Swee'pea (release date: 9/25/36). Animators: Seymour Kneitel, William Henning. Popeye takes Swee'pea, in his animated film debut, to the zoo and gets bopped about, trying to rescue the lad from the animals.

Hold the Wire (release date: 10/23/26). Animators: Willard Bowsky, Orestes Calpini. Bluto bugs Olive's phone line and impersonates Popeye's voice; "Yer homely, skinny and thin. You looks like something the cat dragged in." Popeye sings at the end of the film; "Romance will be brighter when you have a fighter like Popeye the Sailor Man!"

The Spinach Roadster (release date: 11/26/36). Animators: Willard Bowsky, George Germanetti. Popeye takes Olive for a ride in his car which Bluto tries to wreck!

Popeye the Sailor Meets Sindbad the Sailor (release date: 11/27/36). Animators: Willard Bowsky, George Germanetti, Ed Nolan (Academy Award nominee, 1936). The first of three, two-reel color Popeye specials. Sindbad the Sailor captures Olive, and Popeye must rescue her. This cartoon features dazzling colors and 3-D backgrounds. A classic in the field of animation.

I'm in the Army Now (release date: 12/25/36). Animators: None credited. Popeye and Bluto try to enlist but there is only room for one soldier and he has to be good! They show the recruiting officer scenes from previous films so he can choose between the two.

Paneless Window Washer (release date: 1/22/37). Animators: Willard Bowsky, Orestes Calpini. This cartoon has become a fan favorite. Bluto tries to take over Popeye's window cleaning business.

Organ Grinder's Swing (release date: 2/19/37). Animators: Dave Tendlar, Bill Sturm. Wimpy is an organ grinder but, while Popeye and Olive love his music, Bluto can't stand it.

My Artistical Temperature (release date: 3/19/37). Animators: Seymour Kneitel, Abner Matthews. Popeye wants to create a statue of Olive while Bluto wants to create a painting. This cartoon has a scene which is sometimes cut out when aired on television. Popeye squirts some black paint on Bluto's picture. The paint lands on the sun, which gains eyes and a mouth and says, "Mammy"!

Hospitaliky (release date: 4/16/37). Animators: Seymour Kneitel, William Henning. To land in the hospital to be tended by nurse Olive, Popeye and Bluto attempt to get injured. Popeye feeds Bluto his spinach so he will get severely beaten up and land in the hospital.

The Twisker Pitcher (release date: 5/21/37). Animators: Seymour Kneitel, Abner Matthews. Popeye's baseball team doesn't fare too well against Bluto's, especially after the brute eats Popeye's spinach. When he notices the can on the ground, Bluto mumbles, "Oh boy, he dropped his spinach. What a break for me." This proves that Bluto isn't that stupid when it comes to knowing what spinach can do for you.

Morning, Noon and Nightclub (release date: 6/18/37). Animators: Willard Bowsky, George Germanetti. Olive and Popeye have a nightclub act which Bluto tries to ruin.

Lost and Foundry (release date: 7/16/37). Animators: Seymour Kneitel, Abner Matthews. Swee'pea wanders into the factory where Popeye works. Popeye gets bopped around, trying to rescue the tyke. Swee'pea ends up eating the spinach to save both Popeye and Olive from being squashed by a giant press.

I Never Changes My Altitude (release date: 8/20/37). Animators: Willard Bowsky, Orestes Calpini. Olive goes off with Bluto the aviator but soon regrets it. Popeye goes after her and it takes feeding a duck half of his spinach to help rescue her.

I Likes Babies and Infinks (release date: 9/18/37). Animators: Seymour Kneitel, Graham Place. Swee'pea won't stop crying. Bluto and Popeye perform stunts to get the lad to laugh. This cartoon features the well-remembered scene of Popeye trying to grab a can of spinach but gets a can of onions by mistake. When the can gets opened, onion gas makes Olive, Popeye and Bluto bawl. Seeing the adults crying is very funny to Swee'pea, who begins laughing.

The Football Toucher Downer (release date: 10/15/37). Animators: Seymour Kneitel, Graham Place. Popeye tells Swee'pea a story of how he needed his spinach to help him win a football game when Bluto's team was cheating.

Proteck the Weakerest (release date: 11/19/37). Animators: Seymour Kneitel, William Henning. Olive forces Popeye to take her "sissy dorg" out for a walk. They run into Bluto and his bulldog, who beat up the pair. Olive's dog mimics Popeye eating

Olive Oyl's dog, Fluffy, toots Popeye's pipe at the conclusion of "Proteck the Weakerest" (Fleischer, 1937).

his spinach and beats up Bluto's bulldog. Popeye sings at the end," Now jus' cause yer taller, don't hit someone smaller says Popeye the Sailor Man!"

Popeye Meets Ali Baba's Forty Thieves (release date: 11/26/37). Animators: Willard Bowsky, George Germanetti, Orestes Calpini. The second of three two-reel color specials. Popeye battles Abdul Hassan (Bluto). This cartoon features dazzling 3-D background effects. Popeye sings at the end, "I may be a shorty but I licked the forty. I'm Popeye the Sailor Man!"

Fowl Play (release date: 12/17/37). Animators: Dave Tendlar, William Sturm. Olive gets a gift from Popeye. It is a talking parrot to keep her company when he goes to sea. Bluto would like to see the bird buried! Popeye literally beats the paint off of Bluto in the fight scene.

Let's Celebrake (release date: 1/21/38). Animators: Seymour Kneitel, William Henning. This cartoon demonstrates how Popeye is a multi-dimensional character. He feels terrible that Olive Oyl's grandmother will be staying home alone on New Year's Eve, so he takes her to a party. Grandma gets fed some spinach and she and Popeye win a dancing contest. Throughout this film, Bluto and Popeye are pals, willing to share their time with Olive Oyl.

Bound by Indians, Popeye is happy to see his old friend pop out of his shirt pocket. From "Big Chief-Ugh-Amugh-Ugh" (Fleischer, 1938).

Learn Polikness (release date: 2/18/38). Animators: Dave Tendlar, Nicolas Tafuri. This cartoon, where Popeye is instructed on the art of being a gentlemen, features Jack Mercer's under-the-breath mumblings. When Bluto, as the instructor, escorts Olive and Popeye inside, he says, "entree," to which Popeye mumbles, "I already et young feller."

The House Builder Upper (release date: 3/18/38). Animators: Seymour Kneitel, Abner Matthews, William Henning. Olive's house burns down because she washed her dress with a gallon of gasoline. Popeye and Wimpy try to build her a new one. This amusing entry in the series again proves how the Fleischer Studios tried to stray from using the Popeye-Olive-Bluto triangle as the focal point of the films. Popeye and Wimpy make a good comedy team.

Big Chief Ugh-Amugh-Ugh (release date: 4/25/38). Animators: William Bowsky, George Germanetti. Olive almost becomes an Indian chief's squaw. When it looks as though Popeye won't be able to eat his spinach, he says, "There goes my vitality!"

I Yam Love Sick (release date: 5/29/38). Animators: Seymour Kneitel, William Henning. When Olive ignores Popeye, he fakes sick in order to win her back. When Popeye collapses, Olive pokes her head into the movie audience and asks if there is a doctor in the house! After this film, Bluto is absent for quite a while.

Plumbing Is a Pipe (release date: 6/17/38). Animators: Willard Bowsky, Orestes Calpini. Olive's plumbing goes haywire and, while waiting for Wimpy the plumber to show up, Popeye tries to fix it himself.

The Jeep (release date: 7/15/38). Animators: Seymour Kneitel, Graham Place. Popeye brings Eugene the Jeep to Olive Oyl's apartment to play with Swee'pea. Eugene is a magical dog and can disappear, among other tricks. When Swee'pea is discovered missing, Popeye and the Jeep try to track him down. This cartoon marks the first appearance of Eugene the Jeep, who we learned in the "Thimble Theatre" strip is from the fourth dimension, in animated form.

Bulldozing the Bull (release date: 8/19/38). Animators: Willard Bowsky, George Germanetti. Popeye is thought to be a bullfighter but refuses to fight or kill a bull. This is the first cartoon where Popeye uses his pipe to suck up his spinach. Popeye sings at the end, "Don't be noble fighter, cause kindness is righter, says Popeye the Sailor Man."

Mutiny Ain't Nice (release date: 9/23/38). Animators: Dave Tendlar, William Sturm. Popeye won't allow Olive to sail with him because women are considered to be a jinx aboard a boat. She accidentally stows away and the crew is after her.

Goonland (release date: 10/21/38). Animators: Seymour Kneitel, Abner Matthews. Popeye finds his long lost father, Poopdeck Pappy, who has been held captive for 30 years on Goon Island. This film has become a classic and features the first appearance of Poopdeck Pappy and the Goons in animated form. Popeye and Pappy wage such a fierce battle with the Goons, that the film snaps and two human hands have to repair it with a safety pin.

A Date to Skate (release date: 11/18/38). Animators: Willard Bowsky, Orestes Calpini. Popeye tries to teach Olive how to skate and looks to the movie audience for a can of spinach when he leaves his at home. This would be the last cartoon for the Fleischers in which Mae Questel provides Olive Oyl's voice. According to published sources, Questel only provided Olive's voice in six out of the ten cartoons the character appeared in 1938.

Cops Is Always Right (release date: 12/29/38). Animators: Seymour Kneitel, William Henning. Popeye causes trouble for a policeman while trying to help Olive with her spring cleaning. While she probably handled Olive's voice during Mae Questel's absence in 1938, Margie Hines takes on her voice on a regular basis starting with this cartoon.

Customers Wanted (release date: 1/27/39). Animators: Seymour Kneitel, William Henning. Both Popeye and Bluto want Wimpy as a customer for their penny movie machines. The movies are scenes from previous Fleischer films. One of Bluto's is titled, "Never Kick a Woman," a cartoon he didn't appear in.

Aladdin and His Wonderful Lamp (release date: 4/7/39). Animators: Dave Tendlar, Nick Tafuri, Bill Sturm, Reuben Grossman. The final of the three, 2-reel color features. Olive writes a script for "SURPRISE PICTURES," featuring Popeye as Aladdin and herself as a princess. When Popeye prepares to kiss the princess, he turns beet red and says to the audience, "I've never made love in Technicolor before!"

Leave Well Enough Alone (release date: 4/28/39). Animators: Seymour Kneitel, Abner Matthews. Popeye feels bad about the pets cooped up in Olive's pet store. He buys all the animals and frees them. All the animals leave except a parrot that sings to Popeye, "Leave Well Enough Alone."

Wotta Nitemare (release date: 5/19/39). Animators: Willard Bowsky, George Germanetti. Popeye dreams that he is living in the clouds with Olive, who is an angel, and

Bluto, who is a hairy beast! Wimpy, Swee'pea and Eugene the Jeep make brief cameos. This is a very surreal cartoon. The thought has been that both Jack Mercer and Pinto Colvig alternated as the voice of Bluto about this time. Popeye has trouble with his spinach in this film, as he pulls out cans of other vegetables instead. This cartoon and the three which follow do not feature the ship door opening.

Ghosks Is the Bunk (release date: 6/14/39). Animators: William Henning, Abner Matthews. Bluto lures Popeye and Olive to a haunted house and tries to scare them. This cartoon, along with "Customers Wanted," features a strange voice for Bluto. It is certainly not Jack Mercer's version.

Hello, How Am I (release date: 7/14/39). Animators: William Henning, Abner Matthews. Another Fleischer cartoon which twists the Popeye formula. To get a hamburger dinner from Olive, Wimpy dresses up as Popeye. The spinach scene is played out unusually long, as you see Popeye pull out his can, Wimpy's frightened reaction to it, the sailor eating it and tossing the empty can towards the movie audience. Popeye sings at the end, "I am me and just me and there's no other me cause I'm Popeye the Sailor Man."

It's the Natural Thing to Do (release date: 7/30/39). Animators: Thomas Johnson, Lod Rossner. Olive receives a letter from "The Popeye Fan Club" who ask the trio to knock off the rough stuff and try acting more refined. Bluto says, "Gentleman, eh, must be a character part!" Popeye replies, "I can act rough, but what's roughfined?" They do their best but by this delightful film's end, they're all brawling.

Never Sock a Baby (release date: 11/3/39). Animators: William Henning, Abner Matthews. Popeye spanks Swee'pea for being bad and then has a horrible nightmare that the tyke has run away. For the sake of the plot, Swee'pea has been portrayed as being in Popeye's care or Olive's. This cartoon marks the return of the ship door opening.

Shakespearian Spinach (release date: 1/19/40). Written by George Manuell. Animators: Roland Crandall, Ben Solomon. Popeye and Olive perform Romeo and Juliet. Bluto wants to play Romeo so he plots to get rid of Popeye. Writing credits are now given on each film.

Females Is Fickle (release date: 3/8/40). Written by Joe Stultz. Animators: Dave Tendlar, William Sturm. Popeye dives into the ocean to rescue Olive's goldfish. Starting with this film, the animation looks brighter, reflected due to the move of the Fleischer Studios from New York to Florida.

Stealin' Ain't Honest (release date: 3/22/40). Written by George Manuell. Animators: Tom Johnson, Frank Endres. Olive Oyl has a secret goldmine, which doesn't remain a secret when Bluto finds out about it. This is the first pairing of animators Tom Johnson and Frank Endres, who would work often as a team until the last theatrical Popeye film was released in 1957.

Me Feelin's Is Hurt (release date: 4/12/40). Written by Bill Turner. Animators: Robert Leffingwell and Orestes Calpini. Olive has run off with Bluto the Cowboy and Popeye tries to prove he's the better man. Olive sings, "I don't want a cowboy I'll take you en-how boy, my Popeye the Sailor Man."

Onion Pacific (release date: 5/24/40). Written by Joe Stultz. Animators: Willard Bowsky, Jim Davis. Popeye and Bluto compete in a train race. The winner gets to kiss Olive Oyl. The last Fleischer cartoon to feature Wimpy.

Wimmin Is a Myskery (release date: 6/7/40). Written by Ted Pierce. Animators: Willard Bowsky, Joe DiIgalo. Olive dreams she is married to Popeye and they have four bratty children, who would later become Popeye's look-a-like, sound-a-like nephews in the series.

Nurse Mates (release date: 6/20/40). Written by George Manuell. Animators: Graham Place, Lou Zukor. Bluto and Popeye baby-sit lil' Swee'pea. When Olive says to the boys, "now just follow this chart," Jack Mercer (as Popeye) mutters, "Where's the chart going?"

Fightin' Pals (release date: 7/12/40). Written by Joe Stultz. Animators: Willard Bowsky, Robert Bentley. Popeye goes in search of his good friend, Dr. Bluto, who is lost in Africa. It is Dr. Bluto who pulls a can of spinach out of his shirt pocket to revive a weakened Popeye.

Doing Impossikible Stunts (release date: 8/2/40). Written by Jack Ward. Animators: Thomas Johnson, Frank Endres. Popeye shows a movie director scenes from his previous films to become a stuntman. Swee'pea wants to be hired too, so he switches a reel on Popeye. The director watches his heroic scene from "Lost and Foundry" and hires the tyke.

Wimmin Hadn't Oughta Drive (release date: 8/16/40). Written by George Manuell. Animators: Orestes Calpini, Rueben Grossman. Olive says to Popeye, "Learn me how to drive" and the trouble begins!

Puttin' on the Act (release date: 8/30/40). Written by Bill Turner. Animators: Dave Tendlar, Thomas Golden. Popeye and Olive think vaudeville is coming back and rehearse their old act. Popeye stretches his face to impersonate Jimmy Durante, Groucho Marx and Stan Laurel.

Popeye Meets William Tell (release date: 9/20/40). Written by Dan Gordon. Animators: Al Eugster, James Culhane. Popeye takes on the role of William Tell's son. Groucho Marx makes a cameo appearance.

My Pop, My Pop (release date: 10/18/40). Written by Bill Turner. Animators: Arnold Gillespie, Abner Kneitel. Poopdeck Pappy, who is 99 years old, wants to help his son build a boat. Another example of Popeye's warm nature is shown when he lets his father think he has finished building the boat.

With Poopdeck Pappy (release date: 11/15/40). Written by George Manuell. Animators: Bill Nolan, Winfield Hoskins. Poopdeck Pappy causes problems in a saloon with his son in pursuit.

Popeye Presents Eugene the Jeep (release date: 12/13/40). Written by Joe Stultz. Animators: Grim Natwick, Irving Spector. Popeye gets Eugene the Jeep as a birthday present from Olive but the animal must sleep outdoors at night. This isn't easy as the animal keeps reappearing inside the house. The animation of Popeye, in certain scenes, harkens back to the New York era Fleischer Studios.

Problem Pappy (release date: 1/10/41). Written by Ted Pierce. Animators: Myron Waldman, Sidney Pillet. To help balance his budget, Pappy entertains by sitting on top of a flagpole, juggling.

Quiet! Pleeze (release date: 2/7/41). Written by Milford Davis. Animators: Willard Bowsky, Lod Rossner. Poopdeck Pappy is recovering from a hangover so Popeye tries to keep things quiet. Footage of Popeye socking a radio to silence a singer and knocking down girders is pulled from an early Fleischer film, "Sock-A-Bye Baby."

Olive's Sweepstake Ticket (release date: 3/7/41). Written by Ted Pierce. Animators: Dave Tendlar, Tom Golden. Olive's winning sweepstake ticket blows out the window and Popeye runs around trying to catch it. The prize turns out to be an ugly bird.

Flies Ain't Human (release date: 4/4/41). Written by Eric St. Clair. Animators: Thomas Johnson, George Germanetti. Popeye tries to get some sleep but a fly eats his spinach and prevents his slumber. This is the first cartoon where one of nature's creatures beats up on the sailor. While this is a cute cartoon in isolation, the repeated theme of Popeye, who does not initially put these creatures in peril, getting beaten up by them gets disturbing as the plot is repeated.

Popeye Meets Rip Van Winkle (release date: 5/9/41). Written by Dan Gordon. Animators: Myron Waldman, Sidney Pillet. Rip Van Winkle is kicked out of his home so kindhearted Popeye takes him in. The ol' man begins sleepwalking and Popeye has to rescue him.

Olive's Boithday Presink (release date: 6/13/41). Written by Joseph Stultz. Animators: Arnold Gillespie, Abner Kneitel. Popeye goes hunting for a bearskin coat for Olive but his tender heart stops him from shooting a bear. Geezil, a character from the comic strip, appears in this cartoon.

Child Psykolojiky (release date: 7/11/41). Written by George Manuell. Animators: Bill Nolan, Joe Oriolo. Pappy tries to make a he-man out of Swee'pea but almost ends up destroying the house. This is the last cartoon to feature the ship door opening.

Pest Pilot (release date: 8/8/41). Written by George Manuell. Animators: Dave Tendlar, Tom Baron. Poopdeck Pappy takes to the skies in this first cartoon featuring a different opening sequence and the last film appearance of Poopdeck Pappy in a Fleischer Studios production.

I'll Never Crow Again (release date: 9/19/41). Written by Cal Howard. Animators: Orestes Calpini, Reuben Grossman. Popeye tries to get rid of the crows in Olive's garden but has trouble. Olive's laughing doesn't help the sailor's efforts so he ends up using her as a scarecrow. This cartoon is the first to feature Popeye's pipe and face in the title sequence.

The Mighty Navy (release date: 11/14/41). Written by Bill Turner and Ted Pierce. Animators: Seymour Kneitel, Abner Matthews. Popeye joins the Navy and has trouble adjusting his methods with theirs. This is the first cartoon where Popeye wears his white sailor's uniform. This is also the first film with gives a hint of what's happening in the real world, the possibility of a war. Popeye eats his spinach and, with one blow of his fist, destroys an enemy's battleship. He is then told that his picture, wearing his black shirt and captain's hat, will be the official insignia of the Navy's bombing squadron.

Nix on Hypnotricks (release date: 12/19/41). Written by Bill Turner and Cal Howard. Animators: Dave Tendlar, John Walworth. Popeye has to rescue Olive Oyl, who is under the spell of a hypnotist. While munching on his spinach, the "S" from the can, falls on the sailor's chest helping to make a costume similar to that of Superman!

Kickin' the Conga Round (release date: 1/17/42). Written by Bill Turner and Ted Pierce. Animators: Tom Johnson, George Germanetti. Bluto, wearing for the first time a white sailor's uniform, goes after Popeye's date. Popeye, Olive and Bluto all dance to the Conga in this energetic cartoon.

Popeye bops a Japanese spy from "Blunder Below" (Fleischer, 1942). Due to the stereotypical character design of the spy, this scene, though not in every airing, has been edited out of the cartoon.

Blunder Below (release date: 2/13/42). Written by Bill Turner and Ted Pierce. Animators: Dave Tendlar, Harold Walker. Popeye just can't seem to adjust to the Navy's more traditional way of doing things but when the Japanese attack, it's his spinach-powered muscles that get the job done. The first "Popeye" cartoon to show the Japanese as the enemy.

Fleets of Stren'th (release date: 3/13/42). Written by Dan Gordon and Jack Mercer. Animators: Alfred Eugster, Tom Golden. Popeye is reading a "Superman" comic book when the enemy attacks. While Jack Mercer, Popeye's voice, had always contributed to the series, this is the first cartoon where he gets screen credit as a writer.

Pip-eye-Pup-eye-Poop-eye and Peep-eye (release date: 4/10/42). Written by Seymour Kneitel. Animators: Seymour Kneitel, George Germanetti. Popeye tries to get his four nephews to eat spinach. After he spanks them, they consume it and turn on their uncle. This is the last theatrical "Popeye" to feature Popeye in his comic strip attire for a while.

Olive Oyl and Water Don't Mix (release date: 5/8/42). Written by Jack Mercer and Jack Ward. Animators: Dave Tendlar, Abner Kneitel. Olive Oyl wants a tour of a boat. Popeye and Bluto compete to determine who will give it to her.

Many Tanks (release date: 5/15/42). Written by Carl Meyer and Bill Turner. Animators: Tom Johnson, Frank Endres. Bluto trades his army uniform for Popeye's sailor suit so he can go on a date with Olive. Popeye is stuck in Bluto's army! When

Though this scene never occurred in the actual cartoon, it is a publicity still from the Fleischer Studios, color, two-reel classic "Popeye the Sailor Meets Sindbad the Sailor" (1936).

Popeye's can of spinach gets flattened by a tank, he looks at the audience and says, "Tha's all any self-respecting sailor can stand."

Baby Wants a Bottleship (release date: 7/13/42). Written by Jack Mercer and Jack Ward. Animators: Alfred Eugster, Joe Oriolo. Swee'pea wanders onto a battleship and Popeye tries to save him from danger. This is Swee'pea's last appearance in a Fleischer cartoon and the final entry released by this studio.

Popeye, using footage from the Betty Boop film, "Popeye the Sailor," also appeared in "Sing Along with Popeye," a four-minute follow-the-bouncing-ball cartoon from the Fleischer Studios.

The Three 20-Minute Fleischer Popeye Specials

Popeye the Sailor Meets Sindbad the Sailor (1936). Popeye, Olive Oyl, and Wimpy land on Sindbad's Island, where the brute's huge vulture captures Olive! While Wimpy hunts food, Popeye intends to prove to Sindbad that he's the better sailor. A fierce battle takes place, and after Popeye eats his spinach, he knocks the stuffing out of Sindbad. This was the first color Popeye cartoon, and the Fleischers did an outstanding job with the 3-D backgrounds. This cartoon proved to be very popular during its original run and remains a classic in the field of animation today.

Popeye, known in this color two-reeler from the Fleischer Studios as "Aladdin," prepares to swing his spinach can over to his mouth. From "Aladdin and His Wonderful Lamp" (1939).

Popeye the Sailor Meets Ali Baba's Forty Thieves (1937). Hot on the success of "Sindbad," the Fleischers produced another Popeye cartoon with 3-D backgrounds. Popeye and his fellow travelers, Olive Oyl and Wimpy, battle Ali Baba (Bluto). Popeye licks all 40 criminals and sings at the end, "I may be a shorty but I licked the forty, I'm Popeye the Sailor Man!"

Aladdin and His Wonderful Lamp (1939). Olive Oyl writes a script for Surprise Pictures in which Popeye plays Aladdin and she the princess. When the script is completed, Olive receives a letter from the studio: "Your story is being thrown out and so are you," signed "SURPRISE Pictures." Margie Hines provided the vocals for Olive Oyl, and Jack Mercer sang a cute little song in the cartoon, "What Can I Do for You."

Famous Studios

You're a Sap, Mr. Jap (release date: 8/7/42). Written by Jim Tyler and Carl Meyer. Animators: Jim Tyler, George Germanetti. Directed by Dan Gordon. Popeye is out at sea looking for "Mr. Jap," thus the lyrics to the film's theme song "You're a Sap, Mr. Jap, You Make the Yankees Crazy." He runs across a whole boat full of Japs but, thanks to his spinach, does Uncle Sam proud. At the conclusion of the cartoon, the Jap boat sinks into the ocean as you hear the sound of a toilet flushing in the background. Needless to say, this cartoon vanished from television screens by the 1980s.

Alona on the Sarong Sea (release date: 9/4/42). Written by Jack Ward and Jack Mercer. Animators: Dave Tendlar, Abner Kneitel. Directed by Isadore Sparber. Popeye dreams of an island adventure, with Bluto and his dream girl, the Princess Alona (a dark-skinned Olive Oyl). This cartoon and the previous entry credit the film as being produced by Max Fleischer, though they're both by Famous Studios.

A Hull of a Mess (release date: 10/16/42). Written by Jack Ward and Jack Mercer. Animators: Al Eugster, Joe Oriolo. Directed by Isadore Sparber. Bluto and Popeye compete for a contract to build ships for the Navy. This is the last black and white film to feature Popeye wearing his captain's hat. Bluto is particularly nasty in this film, blowing up Popeye's ship. Popeye's spinach-strength helps him win the contract and he sings at the end, "Me ships I did finish, cause I ate me spinach, I'm Popeye the Sailor Man!"

Scrap the Japs (release date: 11/20/42). Written by Carl Meyer. Animators: Tom Johnson, Ben Solomon. Directed by Seymour Kneitel. Popeye tangles with the Japanese in the sky and on land in this patriotic film.

Me Musical Nephews (release date: 12/25/42). Written by Jack Ward and Jack Mercer. Animators: Tom Johnson, George Germanetti. Directed by Seymour Kneitel. Popeye's nephews won't go to sleep; instead they create their own musical instruments, which keep their uncle up all night. Popeye literally jumps out of the picture (motion picture screen) at the conclusion of the film. The nephews also pray in this cartoon: "Bless Olive Oyl and Wimpy and Swee'pea and Bluto and Popeye!"

Spinach fer Britain (release date: 1/22/43). Written by Carl Meyer. Animators: Jim Tyler, Abner Kneitel. Directed by Dan Gordon. Popeye sails a cargo of spinach to Britain and deals with the Nazis along the way.

Seein' Red, White n' Blue (release date: 2/19/43). Written by Joe Stultz. Animators: Jim Tyler, Ben Solomon. Directed by Dan Gordon. Bluto gets a draft notice but tries to injure himself so he won't have to serve. When Popeye is beaten up by several Japanese spies disguised as war orphans, Bluto comes to his rescue. Popeye feeds spinach to himself and Bluto so they can mop up the floor with the spies. A cleverly written and funny film, filled with patriotism.

Too Weak to Work (release date: 3/19/43). Written by Joe Stultz. Animators: Jim Tyler, Abner Kneitel. Directed by Isadore Sparber. Bluto feels he needs "a complete rest." He fakes an illness and checks himself into a hospital. When Popeye finds out he's faking, he dresses up as Bluto's nurse to teach him a lesson. Bluto is fed spinach through a tube to get the bearded sailor back to full strength.

A Jolly Good Furlough (release date: 4/23/43). Written by Joe Stultz. Animators: Joe Oriolo, John Walworth. Directed by Dan Gordon. Poor Popeye is victimized by his nephews home defense inventions when he takes a leave from the Navy to visit home.

Ration fer the Duration (release date: 5/28/43). Written by Jack Mercer and Jack Ward. Animators: Tom Golden, Dave Tendlar. Directed by Seymour Kneitel. Popeye visits a giant who is hoarding rubber and sugar needed for "Uncle Sam."

The Hungry Goat (release date: 6/25/43). Written by Carl Meyer. Animators: Joe Oriolo, John Walworth. Directed by Dan Gordon. A goat is starving and starts eating the boat Popeye is on. This is a wild, gag-filled, fast paced cartoon in the style of the "Looney Tunes" or Tex Avery animated films. While watching Popeye chase the goat on the movie screen, a boy in the audience says, "Aw why don't Popeye eat his spinach and sock him one." By this time the writers and directors were coming up with plots that didn't involve spinach and in which Popeye took a lot of punishment for the sake of humor.

Happy Birthdaze (release date: 7/16/43). Written by Carl Meyer. Animators: Abner Kneitel, Graham Place. Directed by Dan Gordon. Popeye's pint-sized buddy, Shorty, creates headaches for Popeye on his birthday. Popeye actually shoots Shorty at the end of this cartoon, with the credit reading, "The Bitter End." Some of Popeye's strangest animated films were produced during this period by Famous Studios.

Wood-Peckin' (release date: 8/6/43). Written by Joe Stultz. Animators: Nick Tafuri, Tom Golden. Directed by Isadore Sparber. This is another film where Popeye is subjected to a lot of punishment, this time from a woodpecker who doesn't want the sailor to cut down his tree for a mast. By the end of the cartoon, Popeye and the woodpecker make peace, but it is still a bit disturbing to see him outmatched by a bird.

Cartoons Ain't Human (release date: 9/3/43). Written by Jack Mercer and Jack Ward. Animators: Orestes Calpini, Otto Feuer. Directed by Seymour Kneitel. Popeye makes his own animated cartoon—stick figures with cartoon heads! The spinach returns in this cartoon, which is the final cartoon filmed in black and white. Robert Connavale, Anton Loeb, Robert Owen, Robert Little, Joe Dommergue and John Zago provided the scenes for the Famous Studios color cartoons.

Her Honor the Mare (release date: 11/26/43). Written by Jack Mercer and Jack Ward. Animators: Jim Tyler, Ben Solomon. Directed by Isadore Sparber. This is the first color "Popeye the Sailor" short, featuring the sailor decked out in a blue uniform. Popeye's nephews try to hide a horse from their uncle. When they haul the horse up to their room, the tykes pass him off as a painter by drawing Hitler's face on his behind.

The Marry Go Round (release date: 12/31/43). Written by Joe Stultz. Animators: Graham Place, Abner Kneitel. Directed by Seymour Kneitel. Apparently Popeye's bullet missed Shorty at the conclusion of "Happy Birthdaze" because the pint-sized sailor returns to cause Popeye more grief when he tries to marry him off to Olive Oyl. A fun cartoon! This is the final film featuring Margie Hines' voice as Olive Oyl.

We're on Our Way to Rio (release date: 4/21/44). Written by Jack Mercer and Jack Ward. Animators: Jim Tyler, Ben Solomon. Directed by Isadore Sparber. Popeye and Bluto are traveling buddies, inspired by Paramount Picture's "Road" movies. The pair end up in Rio, and both fall in love with Olive Oyl, who dances the Samba. Bluto excels in it but Popeye needs his spinach to get him up to speed. An excellent musical cartoon.

Anvil Chorus Girl (release date: 5/26/44). Written by Bill Turner and Jack Ward. Animators: Dave Tendar, Morey Reden. Directed by Isadore Sparber. Popeye and Bluto compete to be Olive's blacksmith. Bluto wins the job but it's Popeye who ends up with Olive Oyl as they both take a carriage ride into the moonlight at the end of the film. This cartoon would mark the return of Mae Questel as Olive's voice and the debut film for Jackson Beck providing Bluto's vocals.

Popeye accepts Shorty's offer to help him move Olive Oyl's furniture. Big mistake, Popeye! From "Moving Aweigh" (Famous Studios, 1944).

Spinach-Packin' Popeye (release date: 7/21/44). Written by Bill Turner and Jack Ward. Animators: Dave Tendlar, Joe Oriolo. Directed by Isadore Sparber. Popeye donates a gallon of blood and dreams that he loses a boxing match to Bluto and Olive walks out on him. This film contains scenes from "Sindbad" and "Ali Baba."

Puppet Love (release date: 8/11/44). Written by Joe Stultz. Animators: William Henning, Jim Tyler. Directed by Seymour Kneitel. A clever cartoon where Bluto constructs a Popeye marionette to ruin Popeye's date with Olive Oyl.

Pitchin Woo at the Zoo (release date: 9/1/44). Written by Bill Turner and Jack Ward. Animators: Nick Tafuri, Tom Golden. Directed by Isadore Sparber. Bluto the zookeeper makes his move on Olive Oyl.

Moving Aweigh (release date: 9/22/44). Written by Carl Meyer. Animators: Jim Tyler, Ben Solomon. No director credited. Popeye and Shorty help Olive move her furniture. With Shorty along, Popeye ends up taking a lot of physical abuse. This is Shorty's last appearance, though the character has remained memorable.

She-Sick Sailors (release date: 12/8/44). Written by Bill Turner and Otto Messmer. Animators: Jim Tyler, Ben Solomon. Directed by Seymour Kneitel. Bluto pretends he is Superman by pulling off phony stunts because Olive is in love with The Man of Steel. A great cartoon!

Pop-Pie a La Mode (release date: 1/26/45). Written by Dave Tendlar. Animators: Morey Reden, Joe Oriolo. Directed by Isadore Sparber. Popeye lands on an island full of cannibals who want him for supper. As the head cannibal puts it, "He is da specialty of da house." This film aired on television for years but was pulled in the 1980s due to its racial stereotypes.

Tops in the Big Top (release date: 3/16/45). Written by Joe Stultz. Animators: Nick Tafuri, Tom Golden. Directed by Isadore Sparber. Popeye and Olive have a circus act which Bluto tries to wreck to become Olive's new partner. Bluto actually kisses Olive several times in this film.

Shape Ahoy (release date: 4/27/45). Written by Jack Ward and Irving Dressler. Animators: Jim Tyler, Ben Solomon. Directed by Isadore Sparber. Popeye and Bluto enjoy life without dames while living on an island until Olive Oyl arrives on a raft. Frank Sinatra makes a cameo, in animated form, at the end of the film. Jack Mercer does not voice Popeye; it sounds like this may be one of the cartoons Mae Questel filled in.

For Better or Nurse (release date: 6/8/45). Written by Irving Dressler and Joe Stultz. Animators: Dave Tendlar, John Gentilella. Directed by Isadore Sparber. Popeye and Bluto fake illness in order to be near Nurse Olive, who they later find out works at an animal hospital.

Mess Production (release date: 8/24/45). Written by Bill Turner and Otto Messmer. Animators: Graham Place, Lou Zukor. Directed by Seymour Kneitel. Popeye and Olive compete for Olive's attentions while on the job. This is the first cartoon where Famous Studios attempts to redesign Ms. Oyl. She now sports a clump of hair at the top of her forehead and has (gasp!!) a bust.

House Tricks (release date: 3/15/46). Written by Jack Ward and Carl Meyer. Animators: Martin Taras, Graham Place. Directed by Seymour Kneitel. Popeye and Bluto brawl over who will build Olive's house. Bluto just won't stay down after Popeye's punches during the battle scene.

Service with a Guile (release date: 4/19/46). Written by Carl Meyer and Jack Ward. Animators: Jim Tyler, Ben Solomon. Directed by Bill Tylta. Popeye and Bluto help Olive run her gasoline station but end up fighting. Olive is wearing her new hairdo, with the clump of hair at her forehead, on the title slide of the cartoon. In the film itself, she is wearing it in its original style.

Klondike Casanova (release date: 5/31/46). Written by Izzy Klein and George Hill. Animators: Dave Tendlar, John Gentilella. Directed by Isadore Sparber. Dangerous Dan McBluto visits the saloon Popeye and Olive work at. He kidnaps Olive Oyl, with Popeye in pursuit. Popeye wears a blue sailor's uniform in this cartoon.

Peep in the Deep (release date: 6/7/46). Written by Bill Turner and Otto Messmer. Animators: Jim Tyler, William Henning. Directed by Seymour Kneitel. A Fleischer Studios–style Bluto goes after a sunken treasure that Popeye and Olive are also looking for. The treasure turns out to be a photo of Frank Sinatra.

Rocket to Mars (release date: 8/9/46). Written by Bill Turner and Otto Messmer. Animators: Jim Tyler, John Gentilella. Directed by Bill Tylta. In the previous four consecutive films, Popeye was not voiced by Jack Mercer. Mercer voices Popeye in this film until the ruler of Mars starts swinging something that looks like an axe at him, then we hear Harry Foster Welch's Popeye voice. In this cartoon, Popeye stops Mars men from invading Earth. An exciting film! Popeye sings at the finish, "Now they're peaceful and happy no more to be scrappy says Popeye the Sailor Man."

Rodeo Romeo (release date: 8/16/46). Written by Izzy Klein and Joe Stultz. Animation: Martin Taras, Dave Tendlar. Directed by Isadore Sparber. Popeye and Olive watch Bluto perform at the rodeo. Popeye says, "I'll show that cut-rate drugstore cowboy" and pulls a large can of spinach out of his shirt pocket. He out-performs Bluto, who stuffs Popeye's spinach can with locoweed. Popeye falls in love with a bull he mistakes for a woman. Bluto swallows the spinach can stuffed with locoweed and thinks Olive is a calf that needs branding. A wild cartoon! This would be the last theatrical to feature Olive Oyl's original look from the Fleischer period.

The Fistic Mystic (release date: 11/29/46). Written by Izzy Klein and Jack Ward. Animators: Graham Place, Nick Tafuri. Directed by Seymour Kneitel. As a mystic, Bluto makes a play for Olive and turns Popeye into a parrot. Olive's new look remains a fixture starting with this film.

The Island Fling (release date: 12/27/46). Written by Woody Gelman and Larry Riley. Animators: George Germanetti, John Gentilella. Directed by Bill Tylta. Olive Oyl and Popeye end up on the Island of Robinson Caruso (Bluto). This cartoon features scenes with black natives, which were edited out during the 1980s.

Abusement Park (release date: 4/25/47). Written by Joe Stultz and Carl Meyer. Animators: Dave Tendlar, Tom Golden. Directed by Isadore Sparber. A wild cartoon featuring a lunatic roller coaster ride with Popeye, Bluto and Olive Oyl.

I'll Be Skiing Ya (release date: 6/13/47). Written by Larry Riley and Bill Turner. Animators: Tom Johnson, George Germanetti. Directed by Isadore Sparber. Popeye fails to teach Olive how to skate so Bluto takes over. Of course, he has more on his mind than just skating. Jack Mercer returns as the voice of Popeye and never leaves the role for the remainder of the theatrical cartoons.

Popeye and the Pirates (release date: 9/12/47). Written by Jack Ward and Izzy Klein. Animators: Dave Tendlar, Martin Taras. Directed by Seymour Kneitel. Popeye battles cutthroat pirates to save Olive Oyl. Trapped at the bottom of the ocean and wrapped in chains, Popeye seems doomed until a fish swims by, reading a Popeye comic book. On the cover is Popeye holding a can of spinach, which the fish removes from the book's cover, and pours it into the sailor's mouth.

The Royal Four Flusher (release date: 9/12/47). Written by Joe Stultz and Carl Meyer. Animators: Tom Johnson, Frank Endres. Directed by Seymour Kneitel. Olive falls for a Count (Bluto), who ends up trapping her into a straightjacket.

Wotta Knight (release date: 10/24/47). Written by Carl Meyer and Izzy Klein. Animators: Tom Johnson, John Gentilella. Directed by Isadore Sparber. Knights, Popeye and Bluto duel for Sleeping Beauty, a blonde Olive Oyl! Scenes featuring a little black Sambo character were cut from this film in the 1980s.

Safari So Good (release date: 11/7/47). Written by Larz Bourne. Animators: Tom Johnson, Morey Reden. Directed by Isadore Sparber. Popeye and Olive discover Bluto the jungle man!

All's Fair at the Fair (release date: 12/19/47). Written by Izzy Klein and Jack Ward. Animators: Dave Tendlar, Martin Taras. Directed by Seymour Kneitel. Bluto the Strongman makes Popeye look foolish in order to steal away Olive Oyl.

Olive Oyl for President (release date: 1/30/48). Written by Joe Stultz and Larry Riley. Animators: Tom Johnson, John Gentilella. Directed by Isadore Sparber. Lyrics to "If I Were President" by Buddy Kaye. A musical fun-fest starring Olive Oyl, who Popeye dreams runs for president. "Little Audrey," another Famous Studios animated character makes a cameo appearance.

Wigwam Whoopee (release date: 2/27/48). Written by Izzy Klein and Jack Mercer. Animators: Tom Johnson, William Henning. Directed by Isadore Sparber. Pilgrim Popeye falls for Olive Oyl, an Indian maid, but the big chief has something to say about this union!

Pre-Hysterical Man (release date: 3/26/48). Written by Carl Meyer and Jack Mercer. Animators: Dave Tendlar, Morey Reden. Directed by Seymour Kneitel. Popeye and Olive encounter a cave man and his dinosaur.

Popeye Meets Hercules (release date: 6/18/48). Written by Izzy Klein. Animators: Tom Moore, George Germanetti. Directed by Bill Tytla. When Xena gets out of control, Hercules teams up with Popeye to stop... whoops, no, actually this film takes place in Greece. Popeye dukes it out with Hercules (Bluto).

Wolf in Sheik's Clothing (release date: 7/30/48). Written by Larry Riley and Izzy Klein. Animators: Tom Johnson, George Rufle. Directed by Isadore Sparber. A sheik lures Olive Oyl into his tent and when he kisses her, makes with the goose pimples.

Spinach vs. Hamburgers (release date: 8/27/48). Written by Bill Turner and Larz Bourne. Animators: Tom Moore, Al Eugster. Directed by Seymour Kneitel. Popeye's nephews don't want to eat the "Spinach Spanish Omelets" chef Popeye offers at his eatery. They would rather eat hamburgers at Wimpy's joint. Popeye, by explaining how spinach helped him in the past, tries to get the lads to eat the vegetable. He fails, and the nephews, while eating hamburgers, sing to Wimpy at the film's finish, "Four more and not to skimpy, with lots of mustard and onions Wimpy."

Snow Place Like Home (release date: 9/3/48). Written by Carl Meyer and Jack Mercer. Animators: Dave Tendlar, Martin Taras. Directed by Seymour Kneitel. Popeye and Olive run into problems in Alaska. A frisky, burly storeowner has eyes for Olive Oyl while a seal falls in love with Popeye.

Robin Hood Winked (release date: 11/12/48). Written by Larz Bourne and Tom Golden. Animators: Tom Johnson, Frank Endres. Directed by Seymour Kneitel. Popeye is Robin Hood battling Bluto the tax collector for maid Olive Oyl.

Symphony in Spinach (release date: 12/31/48). Written by Bill Turner and Larry Riley. Animators: Tom Johnson, John Gentilella. Directed by Seymour Kneitel. Popeye and Bluto are reading *Variety* and learn that Ms. Olive is looking for musicians. This is a fun filled musical outing.

Popeye's Premiere (release date: 3/25/49). Written by Izzy Klein and Bill Turner. Animators: Dave Tendar, John Gentilella. No director credited. A successful mixing of old footage from 1939's two-reeler "Aladdin and His Wonderful Lamp" and new scenes. Popeye and Olive go to the movies to watch the premiere of his new film.

Lumberjack and Jill (release date: 5/27/49). Written by Carl Meyer and Jack Mercer. Animators: Tom Johnson, George Rufle. Directed by Seymour Kneitel. This cartoon has an exciting "Olive in peril" scene with Popeye and Bluto in pursuit.

Hot Air Aces (release date: 6/24/49). Written by Izzy Klein. Animators: Bill Hudson, Al Eugster. Directed by Isadore Sparber. Popeye and Bluto compete in a plane race. Popeye uses cans of spinach to energize his plane after Bluto throws out the engine.

The Balmy Swami (release date: 7/22/49). Written by Carl Meyer and Jack Mercer. Animators: Tom Johnson, George Rufle. Directed by Isadore Sparber. Bluto, in a different voice, puts Olive in a trance and she ends up on a construction site. An exciting "chase" cartoon.

Tar with a Star (release date: 8/12/49). Written by Carl Meyer and Jack Mercer. Animators: George Germanetti, Steve Muffatti. Directed by Bill Tytla. Popeye becomes sheriff of a Texas town and deals with Wild Bill Bluto (Bluto with no beard but a mustache).

Silly Hillbilly (release date: 9/9/49). Written by Izzy Klein. Animators: Tom Johnson, Frank Endres. Directed by Isadore Sparber. Popeye is a traveling salesman who ends up in hillbilly country selling his goods and courting Olive Oyl.

Barking Dogs Don't Fite (release date: 10/28/49). Written by Carl Meyer and Jack Mercer. Animators: Tom Johnson, John Gentilella. Directed by Isadore Sparber. A remake of Fleischer's "Proteck the Weakerest," with Popeye taking Olive's French poodle for a walk only to run into "Bluto and the Beast." Popeye wears a blue Navy uniform in this fast paced cartoon.

The Fly's Last Flight (release date: 12/23/49). Written by Larz Bourne. Animators: Tom Johnson, Frank Endres. Directed by Seymour Kneitel. I have a vivid memory of my brother watching this cartoon on a Saturday morning and laughing because a fly was beating up Popeye! This pointless remake of Fleischer's "Flies Ain't Human" again has a fly (who actually starts the trouble), eating spinach and beating up Popeye.

How Green Is My Spinach (release date: 1/27/50). Written by Izzy Klein. Animators: Tom Johnson, William Henning. Directed by Seymour Kneitel. Bluto finally gets smart and tries to destroy all the spinach! A little boy, sitting in a movie theatre watching Bluto stomp Popeye on screen, tosses the sailor a can of spinach to save the day. The scenes with the little boy are live action, mixing in cleverly with the animation.

Gym Jam (release date: 3/17/50). Written by Carl Meyer and Jack Mercer. Animators: Tom Johnson, John Gentilella. Directed by Isadore Sparber. Bluto, disguised as a blonde woman, attends Popeye's gym class.

Beach Peach (release date: 5/12/50). Written by Larry Riley and Larz Bourne. Animators: Tom Johnson, Frank Endres. Directed by Seymour Kneitel. A lifeguard makes a play for Olive Oyl while trying to leave Popeye high and dry.

Jitterbug Drive (release date: 6/23/50). Written by Carl Meyer and Jack Mercer. Animators: George Germanetti, Harvey Patterson. Directed by Bill Tytla. Olive throws a swinging party but Popeye's parlor games are too dated. Although Olive sings at the start of the cartoon, "Popeye and Bluto Will Soon Arrive," it's a fellow named "Skate" who causes the sailor grief.

Popeye Makes a Movie (release date: 8/11/50). Written by Izzy Klein. Animators: Tom Johnson, George Rufle. Directed by Seymour Kneitel. Popeye's nephews visit Paramount Pictures to watch their uncle make a movie. Featuring footage from the "Ali Baba" two-reeler, this is the first appearance of Wimpy in a Famous Studios cartoon. Popeye wears his original comic strip attire in this film.

Baby Wants Spinach (release date: 9/29/50). Written by Carl Meyer and Jack Mercer. Animators: Al Eugster, William B. Pattengill. Directed by Seymour Kneitel. "Cousin Swee'pea" wanders away from Popeye's care and into the zoo. This is the first appearance of Famous Studios' version of Swee'pea.

Quick on the Vigor (release date: 10/6/50). Written by Carl Meyer and Jack Mercer. Animators: Tom Johnson, John Gentilella. Directed by Seymour Kneitel. This is without a doubt the "Popeye" cartoon I have watched the most. This film also features the typical Famous Studios plot around this period: Olive starts off her date with Pop-eye, sees Bluto, goes off with him until he asks for a kiss. Olive yells for help and Pop-eye saves the day.

Riot in Rhythm (release date: 11/10/50). Written by Seymour Kneitel. Animators: Tom Johnson, William Henning. Directed by Seymour Kneitel. Popeye's nephews keep their uncle up all night playing music. A color remake of "Me Musical Nephews" with slight variations.

Farmer and the Belle (release date: 12/1/50). Written by Joe Stultz. Animators: Tom Johnson, Frank Endres. Directed by Seymour Kneitel. Popeye and Bluto compete to be Olive's ranch hand. Popeye feeds a hen a bit of spinach to increase her egg production.

Vacation with Play (release date: 1/19/51). Written by Carl Meyer and Jack Mercer. Animators: Tom Johnson, John Gentilella. Directed by Seymour Kneitel. Popeye and Olive spend their vacation at Lake Narrowhead. Instructor Bluto makes a play for Olive Oyl while Popeye naps.

Thrill of Fair (release date: 4/20/51). Written by Carl Meyer and Jack Mercer. Animators: Tom Johnson, John Gentilella. Directed by Seymour Kneitel. Popeye watches over Swee'pea at the fair and the lad wanders off.

Alpine for You (release date: 5/18/51). Written by Carl Meyer and Jack Mercer. Animators: Steve Muffatti, George Germanetti. Directed by Isadore Sparber. Pop-eye and Olive go mountain climbing and run into Bluto, who wants to take his own private tour with Olive. Popeye punches Bluto into a mountain, and the impact is so hard that stars form around it. The mountain turns into the Paramount Pictures logo. This scene, which occurs at the conclusion of the film, was cut for the A.A.P. prints. Even as a child I noticed there was something edited out when the A.A.P. jumped in as soon as Bluto smashed into the mountain.

Double Cross Country Race (release date: 6/15/51). Written by Larz Bourne. Animators: Tom Johnson, Bill Hudson. Directed by Seymour Kneitel. Popeye and a tricky Count compete in a cross-country race. Popeye feeds his racing car spinach—"Spinach will put the sparks in yer plugs!"

Pilgrim Popeye (release date: 7/13/51). Written by Carl Meyer and Jack Mercer. Animators: Al Eugster, George Germanetti. Directed by Isadore Sparber. Popeye tells his nephews a phony story of how a turkey saved his life from a tribe of wild Indians when he was a pilgrim.

Let's Stalk Spinach (release date: 10/19/51). Written by Izzy Klein. Animators: Steve Muffatti, George Germanetti. Directed by Seymour Kneitel. Popeye tells his nephews that as a boy, he too hated spinach until he met up with a giant!

Punch and Judo (release date: 11/16/51). Written by Irving Spector. Animators: Tom Johnson, Frank Endres. Directed by Isadore Sparber. Popeye donates a televi-sion set to an orphan's home, and the little boys who live there help him win a box-ing match. A scene where Popeye's opponent is being spiffed up has been edited out because a little black Sambo character is seen polishing his shoes. Popeye, donating items to orphans, is a character trait that has stayed with each print and animated variation of the sailor.

Popeye's Pappy (release date: 1/25/52). Written by Larz Bourne. Animators: Tom Johnson, Frank Endres. Directed by Isadore Sparber. Popeye discovers his long-lost Pappy on an island where he is king. The natives of the island decide to cook Popeye until his father comes to his rescue. Rarely seen on television any longer due to the racial stereotypes of the natives.

Lunch with a Punch (release date: 3/14/52). Written by Carl Meyer and Jack Mercer. Animators: Al Eugster, George Germanetti. Directed by Isadore Sparber. Popeye, yet again, tries to get his nephews to eat spinach by telling them a story of himself, Olive and Bluto as kiddies. Bluto grabs Popeye and snarls, "Now I've got ya without yer spinach!" The nephews eat it and give Bluto a walloping!

Swimmer Take All (release date: 5/16/52). Written by Carl Meyer and Jack Mercer. Animators: Tom Johnson, John Gentilella. Directed by Seymour Kneitel. Popeye and Bluto compete in a swimming race. We see Popeye's pipe act like a mouth, chew and swallow the spinach. Winston Sharples, as usual, provides a delightful musical score.

Friend or Phony (release date: 6/30/52). Written by Irving Spector. Animators: Al Eugster, George Germanetti. Directed by Isadore Sparber. Bluto pretends he's dying to get Popeye to "throw away" his spinach. The sailor does, Bluto thrashes him, but the can comes alive and feeds itself to Popeye!

Tots of Fun (release date: 8/15/52). Written by Larz Bourne. Animators: Tom Johnson, Frank Endres. Directed by Seymour Kneitel. Popeye's nephews build their uncle's house while listening to music.

Popalong Popeye (release date: 8/29/52). Written by Carl Meyer and Jack Mercer. Animators: Tom Johnson, John Gentiella. Directed by Seymour Kneitel. Popeye tells his nephews about his days as a cowboy.

Shuteye Popeye (release date: 10/3/52). Written by Irving Spector. Animators: Al Eugster, George Germanetti. Directed by Isadore Sparber. A mouse can't sleep due to Popeye's snoring. This is another example of a small creature besting Popeye, which is not a popular theme among fans of the sailor.

Big Bad Sindbad (release date: 12/12/52). Written by Izzy Klein. Animators: Tom Johnson, William Henning. Directed by Seymour Kneitel. The musical score by Winston Sharples keeps this cartoon lively. The scores in this cartoon would be used for several later theatrical and television animated films. Popeye, wearing his original comic strip outfit, tells his nephews how he beat up Sindbad the Sailor. Footage from the Fleischer Studio's "Sindbad" two-reeler is used in this cartoon.

Ancient Fistory (release date: 1/30/53). Written by Irving Spector. Animators: Al Eugster, William B. Pattengill. Directed by Seymour Kneitel. Popeye does the Cinderella bit, with Bluto playing the mean stepmother... er, step-brute role! Actually he's Popeye's boss. Olive is the princess who is out to win Popeye's heart. An excellent musical score by Winston Sharples.

Child Sockology (release date: 3/27/53). Written by Carl Meyer and Jack Mercer. Animators: Tom Johnson, Frank Endres. Directed by Isadore Sparber. An excellent chase film! Swee'pea wanders onto a construction site with Popeye and Bluto in pursuit. Popeye not only has to save Swee'pea but Bluto as well. Winston Sharples' outstanding musical score keeps the action exciting.

Popeye's Mirthday (release date: 5/22/53). Written by Carl Meyer and Jack Mercer. Animators: Tom Johnson, Frank Endres. Directed by Seymour Kneitel. Olive and the nephews try to keep Popeye out of her house while she prepares his surprise birthday party.

A very pop-eyed Popeye looks at Olive Oyl's family album. From "Baby Wants a Battle" (Famous Studios, 1953).

Toreadorable (release date: 6/12/53). Written by Carl Meyer and Jack Mercer. Animators: Tom Johnson, John Gentilella. Directed by Seymour Kneitel. Popeye and Olive attend a bullfight, watching Bluto as the matador. Popeye eats his spinach and bests Bluto, until the bully puts jumping beans in his can!

Baby Wants a Battle (release date: 7/24/53). Written by Carl Meyer and Jack Mercer. Animators: Al Eugster, George Germanetti. Directed by Seymour Kneitel. Olive pulls out the family album and Popeye tells the story of how Bluto gave him his first black eye.

Fireman's Brawl (release date: 8/21/53). Written by Carl Meyer and Jack Mercer. Animators: Tom Johnson, Frank Endres. Directed by Isadore Sparber. Firemen Popeye and Bluto compete to see who will save Olive from her burning house. Actually, Olive, by eating Popeye's spinach, saves herself and makes the boys' firestation her new home.

Popeye, the Ace of Space (release date: 10/2/53). Written by Carl Meyer and Jack Mercer. Animators: Al Eugster, George Germanetti, William B. Pattengill. Directed by Seymour Kneitel. A film originally shot in 3-D. Popeye is brought to an alien planet and the space creatures test their weapons of destruction on him. The original ending to this cartoon, with Popeye's pipe smoke forming the Paramount Pictures mountain, first aired on television in 2001 on the Cartoon Network's "The Popeye Show."

Shaving Muggs (release date: 10/9/53). Written by Larz Bourne. Animators: Tom Johnson, Frank Endres. Directed by Seymour Kneitel. A color reworking of Fleischer's "A Clean Shaving Man." Bluto and Popeye decide to get shaves and haircuts. Actually, Bluto looks quite handsome without his beard in this film.

Floor Flusher (release date: 1/1/54). Written by Carl Meyer and Jack Mercer. Animators: Tom Golden, Bill Hudson. Directed by Isadore Sparber. Olive's plumbing goes haywire thanks to Bluto's tricks. Popeye sings "By a waterfall, I'm calling you-Who-who, we can share it all beneath a ceiling of blue."

Popeye's Twentieth Anniversary (release date: 4/2/54). Written by Izzy Klein. Animators: Al Eugster, George Germanetti. Directed by Isadore Sparber. Bob Hope, Bing Crosby, Dean Martin, Jerry Lewis and Jimmy Durante appear at a ceremony honoring Popeye's film anniversary. Alas, this cartoon is not a true retrospective as most of it is filled with scenes from two previous cartoons, "Tops in the Big Top" and "Rodeo Romeo."

Taxi-Turvy (release date: 6/4/54). Written by Irving Spector. Animators: Tom Johnson, Frank Endres. Directed by Seymour Kneitel. Bluto and Popeye compete as taxi drivers. In this film, Popeye is trying to suck his can of spinach with his pipe but Bluto drives by and says, "Oh no you ain't eatin' no spinach in dis' picture." A very memorable line, though Popeye does manage to eat his spinach and bop Bluto.

Bride and Gloom (release date: 7/2/54). Written by Larz Bourne. Animators: Tom Johnson, John Gentilella. Directed by Isadore Sparber. As she did in Fleischer's "Wimmin Is a Myskery," Olive dreams of what life would be like married to Popeye.

Greek Mirthology (release date: 8/13/54). Written by Izzy Klein. Animators: Tom Golden, William B. Pattengill. Directed by Seymour Kneitel. Popeye's nephews won't eat their spinach (hey, I would have given up by now!!) so the sailor tells them about their great, great, great, great Uncle Hercules. It seems Hercules discovered the power of spinach when sniffing garlic failed him.

Fright to the Finish (release date: 8/27/54). Written by Jack Mercer. Animators: Al Eugster, William B. Pattengill. Directed by Seymour Kneitel. Bluto scares the wits out of Olive Oyl on Halloween and puts the blame on Popeye. Without the aid of spinach, the sailor outwits the bearded bully.

Private Eye Popeye (release date: 11/12/54). Written by Izzy Klein. Animators: Tom Johnson, Frank Endres. Directed by Seymour Kneitel. Popeye is a private eye on the trail of a thief who has stolen a precious green stone from Olive Oyl.

Gopher Spinach (release date: 12/10/54). Written by Carl Meyer. Animators: Tom Johnson, John Gentilella. Directed by Seymour Kneitel. Popeye is bested by a gopher, who actually ends up saving the sailor's life from a raging bull. As expected, this cartoon does not rate too high for many.

Cookin' with Gags (release date: 1/14/55). Written by Carl Meyer. Animators: Tom Johnson, William Henning. Directed by Isadore Sparber. Bluto keeps pulling April Fools' gags on Popeye. The sailor gets his revenge without relying on his spinach.

Nurse to Meet Ya (release date: 2/11/55). Written by Jack Mercer. Animators: Al Eugster, William B. Pattengill. Directed by Isadore Sparber. Bluto and Popeye try to stop a baby from crying to please Nurse Olive Oyl.

Penny Antics (release date: 3/11/55). Written by Izzy Klein. Animators: Tom Johnson, Frank Endres. Directed by Seymour Kneitel. A color remake of Fleischer's "Customer's Wanted" with Bluto and Popeye both wanting Wimpy's business for their penny arcade machines.

Beaus Will Be Beaus (release date: 5/20/55). Written by Izzy Klein. Animators: Tom Johnson, John Gentilella. Directed by Isadore Sparber. Olive makes Popeye and Bluto promise to stop fighting. Bluto goads Popeye into breaking his word. Popeye

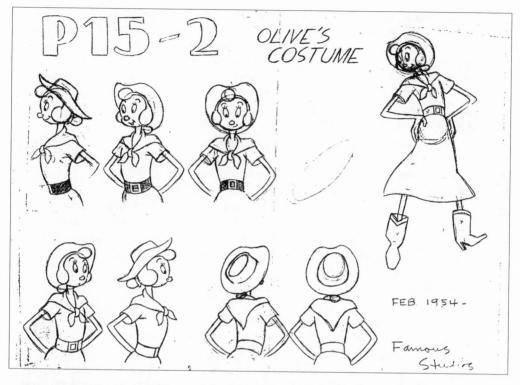

Famous Studios model sheet of Olive Oyl from "A Job for a Gob" (1955). Courtesy of William Janocha.

feeds spinach to Bluto who can't control his own strength and beats up the sailor. Olive, watching the battle, bops Bluto!

Gift of Gag (release date: 5/27/55). Written by Izzy Klein. Animators: Tom Johnson, Frank Endres. Directed by Seymour Kneitel. Popeye's nephews attempt to hide their uncle's birthday present.

Car-Razy Drivers (release date: 7/22/55). Written by Larz Bourne. Animators: Tom Johnson, John Gentilella. Directed by Seymour Kneitel. As he did in Fleischer's "Wimmin Hadn't Oughta Drive," Popeye teaches Olive how to use a car.

Mister and Mistletoe (release date: 9/30/55). Written by Jack Mercer. Animators: Al Eugster, William P. Pattengill. Directed by Isadore Sparber. Bluto dresses up as Santa Claus to woo Olive. This is a delightful holiday cartoon. It is the first cartoon shown on television without the A.A.P. opening and closing graphics.

Cops Is Tops (release date: 11/4/55). Written by Carl Meyer. Animators: Tom Johnson, Frank Endres. Directed by Isadore Sparber. Olive joins the police force and does quite well for herself until she meets a masher. Then, Popeye comes to her aid. This is a good story, excellent animation and great musical score by Winston Sharples.

A Job for a Gob (release date: 12/9/55). Written by Larz Bourne. Animators: Al Eugster, George Germanetti. Directed by Seymour Kneitel. Bluto and Popeye compete to be Cowgirl Olive Oyl's ranch hand. Popeye wins and Bluto goes loco trying to burn down the ranch.

Hill-billing and Cooing (release date: 1/13/56). Written by Jack Mercer. Animators: Tom Johnson, John Gentilella. Directed by Seymour Kneitel. A huge hillbilly woman makes a play for Popeye, and Olive has to consume his spinach to save the day. Olive sings at the end, "I'll knock the dame sky high, who tries to take my guy, Popeye the Sailor Man!" A good change of situation cartoon.

Popeye for President (release date: 3/30/56). Written by Jack Mercer. Animators: Tom Johnson, Frank Endres. Directed by Seymour Kneitel. Popeye and Bluto are running for president. Olive Oyl has the deciding vote.

Out to Punch (release date: 6/8/56). Written by Carl Meyer. Animators: Tom Johnson, John Gentilella. Directed by Seymour Kneitel. Bluto tries to slow Popeye down so he'll win the boxing match he has against the sailor.

Assault and Flattery (release date: 7/6/56). Written by Izzy Klein. Animators: Al Eugster, William B. Pattengill. Directed by Isadore Sparber. Judge Wimpy hears the case of Bluto vs. Popeye the Sailor. The bully is suing the sailor for assault and battery.

Insect to Injury (release date: 8/10/56). Written by Izzy Klein. Animators: Morey Reden, Tom Moore. Directed by Dave Tendlar. Popeye battles termites that are intent on eating him out of house and home. Popeye eats his spinach and defeats the insects. At last, Popeye wins against one of nature's creatures.

Parlez-Vouz-Woo (release date: 9/12/56). Written by Izzy Klein. Animators: Al Eugster, William B. Pattengill. Directed by Isadore Sparber. Bluto disguises himself as television star, "The International," to woo Olive. The brute actually stabs Popeye with a sword in this film. Popeye's spinach can is jabbed instead.

I Don't Scare (release date: 11/16/56). Written by Jack Mercer. Animators: Tom Johnson, Frank Endres. Directed by Isadore Sparber. Olive won't go out with Popeye on Friday the 13th because she thinks it will bring bad luck. Bluto provides Olive with the bad luck.

A Haul in One (release date: 12/14/56). Written by Larz Bourne. Animators: Al Eugster, William B. Pattengill. Directed by Isadore Sparber. Popeye and Bluto compete to see who will move Olive's belongings.

Nearlyweds (release date: 2/8/57). Written by Izzy Klein. Animators: Tom Johnson, Frank Endres. Directed by Seymour Kneitel. Popeye and Olive plan to wed but Bluto has other ideas. No spinach is needed for Popeye to stop Bluto from marrying Ms. Oyl. Disguised as a justice of the peace, Popeye gives Bluto a singsong rundown of what married life will be like and the brute runs off!

The Crystal Brawl (release date: 4/5/57). Written by Carl Meyer. Animators: Al Eugster, William B. Pattengill. Directed by Seymour Kneitel. Bluto takes Olive to a fortuneteller, who is actually Popeye in disguise. Olive doesn't like the future she sees (actually scenes from previous Famous Studios cartoons). The scene of Popeye using his foot to ring the bell at the start of this cartoon is from "Cops Is Tops" and the animation in this film is a bit limited for a theatrical release.

Patriotic Popeye (release date: 5/10/57). Written by Carl Meyer. Animators: Tom Johnson, Frank Endres. Directed by Isadore Sparber. Popeye's two nephews (who have been depleting in rank as the years have rolled on), want to use fireworks for their Fourth of July celebration. Uncle Popeye thinks it's too dangerous. The spinach theme music used in this cartoon would later be used in the "Popeye" television cartoons produced by Paramount Cartoon Studios.

Spree Lunch (release date: 6/21/57). Written by Jack Mercer. Animators: Tom Johnson, Frank Endres. Directed by Seymour Kneitel. Bluto and Popeye own diners and compete for Wimpy's business, but since when does Wimpy have money to spend on food? This is the last time the name "Bluto" is used for animation purposes for quite a long while.

Spooky Swabs (release date: 8/9/57). Written by Larz Bourne. Animators: Tom Johnson, Frank Endres. Directed by Isadore Sparber. Olive Oyl and Popeye end up on a ghost ship. The spirits who live there try to get rid of them before they return to civilization. Olive and Popeye sing at the finish—Olive: "The ghosts you did finish cause you ate your spinach." Popeye: "I'm Popeye the Sailor Man." The boat sails off into the sunset as does Popeye's theatrical career.

King Features Syndicate Cartoons (1960–1961)

(On a few of the television cartoons the copyright date is 1962)

Produced by Larry Harmon Studios

PRODUCER: Larry Harmon; DIRECTOR: Paul Fennell; ARTISTS: Tom Baron, C.L. Hartman, Z.T. Jablecki, Lou Schemer, Ervin Kaplan, George Rowley, Jean Blanchard, Hal Sutherland, Cal Dalton and Frank Onaitis; WRITER: Charles Shows; MUSIC: Gordon Zahler; EDITOR: Dan Milner.

Muskels Shmuskels. Popeye has to deal with Brutus the Strongman after he makes a play for Olive Oyl. Brutus may be strong, but the animation is weak, to say the least.

Hoppy Jalopy. Popeye and Brutus are in a car race.

Dead-Eye Popeye. Popeye is a sheriff and has to battle with the McBride Boys.

Mueleer's Mad Monster. Popeye and Olive invade the lair of a mad scientist and his monster creation.

Caveman Capers. An amusing cartoon in which Popeye explains to Olive Oyl why he loves spinach so much. It all started with "Popeye the Caveman."

Bullfighter Bully. Popeye versus Brutus the bullfighter.

Ace of Space. An alien captures Olive, and Popeye saves her with his "spinach rays."

College of Hard Knocks. Brutus tries to give Popeye an education … with bruises.

Abominable Snowman. Olive and her uncle try to find the abominable snowman, who befriends Popeye.

Ski Jump Chump. Brutus the skier competes with Popeye.

Irate Pirate. Popeye battles Brutus the pirate, but the ship Brutus mans blows up by cartoon's end, leaving Olive to say, "Oh, Popeye, let's go ashore; sailing is so boring."

Foola-Foola Bird. Popeye and Olive are searching for the rare foola-foola bird (but so is Brutus).

Uranium on the Cranium. Popeye and Brutus search for uranium and battle a gorilla.

Two-Faced Paleface. Popeye versus Brutus, disguised as an Indian.

Popeye twirls his pipe in anger over the "Irate Pirate" (Larry Harmon, 1960)

Childhood Daze. Popeye gets turned into a child, and Brutus has fun playing with baby Popeye. (His fun includes using the tyke as a basketball.) This is a cute cartoon.

Sheepich Sheepherder. Poopdeck Pappy sends for Popeye to help stop Brutus the sheep-stealer. Pappy shaves his beard and looks just like Popeye, which totally confuses Brutus.

Track Meet Cheat. Popeye and Brutus compete in a track meet.

Crystal Ball Brawl. Popeye inherits a crystal ball that makes Wimpy rich. Brutus wants the ball for himself. This is the last Larry Harmon–produced TV cartoon.

Produced by Gene Deitch/William Snyder/ Halas and Batchelor

Interrupted Lullaby. Brutus attempts to kidnap Swee'pea, who has inherited a million dollars.

Sea No Evil. Popeye and Olive go sailing, but Brutus keeps stealing items off Popeye's boat and then selling them back to the sailor. Jack Mercer provided the voice for Brutus.

From Way Out. Popeye and Olive deal with space aliens in this strangely animated cartoon.

Seeing Double. Crooks build a Popeye robot to commit crimes for them.

Swee'pea becomes a millionaire in "Interrupted Lullaby" (Gene Deitch/William Snyder, 1960)

Swee'pea Soup. King Blozo wants to learn what makes Swee'pea so sweet when the people of his kingdom want the baby to govern them.

Hag Way Robbery. In this poorly animated cartoon, the Sea Hag (in her first animated appearance) captures Eugene the Jeep and puts phony spinach labels on cans of different food to confuse Popeye. Watch for the scene where Olive is holding Swee'pea; the child has no arms. Popeye's closed eye has a nasty habit of disappearing when he's talking to Wimpy.

The Lost City of Bubble-On. Popeye visits the city of Bubble-On under the ocean and does battle with Brutus, who wants to steal the creature's treasure. A good entry in the series.

There's No Space Like Home. Brutus and Popeye go to Olive's costume party, but aliens crash the party. Believe it or not, Brutus feeds Popeye his spinach to battle the alien creatures.

Potent Lotion. Popeye wears a lotion that causes people to punch him. This cartoon is among the best of the King Features cartoons, with good animation by Halas and Batchelor.

Astronut. Popeye is cooped up in a space capsule while Brutus keeps time with Olive in this strangely animated cartoon.

Goon with the Wind. The Goons want Olive for their queen.

Insultin' the Sultan. Popeye and Olive fight, and the sailor joins the foreign legion. Popeye ends up saving Olive from becoming a bride for a fat sheik. By the cartoon's finish they're fighting again over who started the original battle.

Dog-Gone Dog-Catcher. Brutus the dog-catcher snares Olive's dog, and Popeye dresses up as a four-legged creature to rescue Olive's pet. Popeye's closing song: "I saved Olive's poodle, 'cause I used me noodle, I'm Popeye the Sailor Man."

Voice from the Deep. The Sea Hag pretends to be an evil "voice" in a cave to scare natives off their island home.

Matinee Idol Popeye. Director Brutus uses actor Popeye for a movie but wants to bump him off.

Beaver or Not. Two beavers cause havoc for Popeye while he vacations in a cabin. Among the best of the King Features cartoons.

The Billionaire. Popeye is a billionaire and gives his friends a million dollars to see if they spend it wisely. Olive builds a beauty salon to make herself beautiful so Popeye will marry her. Popeye laughs at Olive's makeover and says, "Don't cry, Olive … I likes ya ugly." One of the best of the King Features cartoons.

Model Muddle. Popeye tries to become an artist. This is a clever cartoon and well animated.

Which Is Witch. The Sea Hag creates an Olive Oyl robot to capture Popeye. A well animated cartoon.

Disguise the Limit. Popeye is a detective and tries to solve a case at the zoo.

Spoil Sport. Brutus takes Olive for a ride in his new sports car, which Popeye feels is too dangerous. In the end, Popeye sings to Olive: "There's nothin' as cuter than you on me scooter, says Popeye the Sailor Man."

Have Time Will Travel. Popeye and Olive travel back through time and meet cavemen and a friendly dinosaur.

Intellectual Interlude. In a well-animated cartoon, Popeye dreams he's a genius.

Partial Post. An alien mailbox causes havoc for Popeye and Olive Oyl.

Weight for Me. In this clever and well-animated cartoon, Olive gets fat, and while Popeye wants her to reduce, Brutus wants to keep her queen-size.

Canine Caprice. Roger the Talking Dog creates problems for Popeye and Olive.

Roger. The talking dog creates further headaches and gets involved with bank robbers.

Tooth Be or Not Tooth Be. Poopdeck Pappy tells Swee'pea the story of how the Sea Hag tried to steal his sparkling teeth. This is the last Popeye cartoon produced by the team of Gene Deitch/William Snyder, whose entries included some animation by Halas and Batchelor.

Produced by Gerald Ray

PRODUCER: Gerald Ray; DIRECTOR: Bob Bemiller; LAYOUT: Henry Lee; BACKGROUND: Dave Weidman; EDITOR: Norm Vizents; ANIMATORS: Izzy Ellis, Sam Kai, Casey Onaitus, Ray Young, Bill Higgins, Barney Posner, John Garling and Bud Partch.

Where There's a Will. Popeye and Brutus are required to be in attendance at the reading of a will.

Take It Easel. In this well-animated cartoon, artist Popeye competes with artist Brutus for a trophy for best painting.

I Bin Sculped. Olive needs a "pooped" model, so Popeye and Brutus try to look beat-up to get the job. An unusual closing song from Popeye: "I'm weak to the finish, I gave Brutus me spinach, I'm Poop-eye the Sailor Man."

Fleas a Crowd. Olive and Brutus watch Popeye's show with his singing fleas. Brutus causes the fleas to escape, and Popeye runs after them.

Popeye's Junior Headache. Deezil, Olive's bratty niece, needs a babysitter, and Popeye gets drafted. The little brat beats the living daylights out of Popeye and sings at the end, "Popeye is finished 'cause I ate the spinach for Popeye the Sailor Man." Among the best of the King Features cartoons.

Americom's 8mm Home Movies of "Popeye" featured box art taken from scenes in the TV Popeyes. Popeye and Olive, chained together, was taken from "The Last Resort" (Gerald Ray, 1960).

Egypt Us. Popeye must save Olive from becoming a human sacrifice.

The Big Sneeze. Popeye, Olive, Swee'pea, and their dog, Bernie, go skiing in the snow-filled mountains and meet a human echo.

The Last Resort. The Sea Hag and her partner, Toar, plot to make phony money. Popeye's closing: "At home or vacation, spinach is me salvation, says Popeye the Sailor Man."

Jeopardy Sheriff. This is a fun cartoon where Poopdeck Pappy tries to prove he's a famous sheriff.

Baby Phase. This entertaining cartoon begins with Swee'pea taking up juggling and nearly falling off the roof. Popeye punishes him and later dreams that Swee'pea has become a world-famous juggler and run off to join the circus. It is one of King Features' best entries.

Produced by Jack Kinney

CHECKING: Christine Decker, Molly McColley, Evelyn Sherwood, Barbara Ruiz, Pat Helmuth, Paul Marron and Jane Philippi; FILM EDITORS: Joe Siracusa, Cliff Mill-

Olive, hanging upside down, eats some spinach to get herself out of this awkward position. From "Popeye's Pep-Up Emporium" (Jack Kinney, 1960)

sap and Roger Donley; CAMERA: Jack Eckes, Bill Kotler and Jack Buehre; INK AND PAINT: Vera McKinney; SOUND: Ryder Sound Services and Marne Falls; BACKGROUNDS: Raymond Jacobs, Boris Gorelick, Vern Jorgensen, Jules Engel, Connie Matthews and Rosemary O'Connor; MUSIC: Ken Lowman; LAYOUTS: Raymond Jacobs, Noel Tucker, Ken Hultgren, Robert Givens and Bruce Bughman; STORIES: Raymond Jacobs, Jack Kinney, Jack Miller, Nick George, Ed Nofziger, Carol Beers and Ruben Apodaca; ANIMATION DIRECTORS: Harvey Toombs, Hugh Frasier, Rudy Larriva, Ed Friedman, Volus Jones, Eddie Rehberg, Ken Hultgren and Alan Zaslove

My apologies for anyone I have left out and for the generic descriptions to some of the following episodes. These are cartoons I didn't have access to.

Battery Up. Popeye plays a rough game of baseball.

Deserted Desert. Popeye gets lost in the hot desert but later comes across a gold mine.

Skinned Divers. Popeye and Brutus go skin diving.

Popeye's Service Station. Popeye pumps some gas.

Coffee House. Havoc ensues at the local coffee house when Olive and Brutus become Beatniks.

Popeye's Pep-Up Emporium. A good cartoon in which Popeye tries to teach Olive and Wimpy some exercise but runs into trouble when he drops a heavy weight and it lands on Brutus.

Bird Watcher Popeye. Olive tries to teach Popeye about our feathered friends.

Time Marches Backwards. A terrible cartoon, with shoddy animation. Popeye goes back in time and fights caveman Brutus. All Olive does is scream, which gets quite annoying.

Popeye's Pet Store. Brutus steals Popeye's pals' pets.

Ballet De Spinach. Olive talks Popeye into being in her ballet, and the one-eyed sailor man wears a tutu.

Sea Hagracy. The Sea Hag wants Popeye bumped off so the waters will be free for pirate crimes. She tries to use Wimpy to get rid of Popeye, but nothing gets rid of the lousy animation in this mess of a cartoon. It is among King Features' worst.

Spinach Shortage. Brutus controls all the spinach stock, leaving Popeye helpless.

Popeye and the Dragon. Popeye the Knight battles a fire-breathing dragon.

Popeye the Fireman. Popeye tries to save Olive from a burning building. Help! Someone put out the terrible animation in this cartoon!

Popeye's Pizza Palace. I'll take one spinach pizza to go, with better animation ... please!

Down the Hatch. Popeye tells Swee'pea how his ancestor battled Brutus the Pirate.

Lighthouse Keeping. Olive visits the lighthouse where Popeye works. Trouble ensues when Brutus shows up.

Popeye and the Phantom. A ghost ruins Popeye and Olive's evening at home.

Popeye's Picnic. Olive goes butterfly hunting, but a bull and some terrible animation spoil Popeye and Olive's afternoon.

Out of This World. This cartoon offers a peek into the future with Popeye, Olive, and Swee'pea.

Madame Salami. Brutus disguises himself as a fortuneteller and says Olive must marry him.

Timber Toppers. Popeye is a lumberjack. Watch out ... "timber" ... some terrible animation is heading your way if you watch this ghastly cartoon.

Skyscraper Capers. Popeye, Wimpy, and Brutus get involved with skyscraper troubles. A well-animated cartoon.

Private-Eye Popeye. Popeye, Olive, and the Jeep search for diamond smugglers Brutus and the Sea Hag. Exciting story with great animation.

Lil' Olive Riding Hood. Popeye tells Swee'pea about Lil' Olive Riding Hood and her basket of hamburgers.

Popeye's Hypnotic Glance. A cute entry, one of the best of the King Features cartoons. Brutus hypnotizes Olive, causing her to love him instead of Popeye. He then hypnotizes Alice the Goon into falling in love with Popeye.

Trojan Horse. The story of the Trojan horse ... Popeye style.

Frozen Feuds. Alice the Goon menaces Alaska.

Popeye's Corn-Certo. Popeye and Brutus compete in a talent showcase.

Westward Ho-Ho. Poopdeck Pappy out west.

Popeye's Cool Pool. A fun cartoon in which Popeye must dig a pool to keep Olive and Swee'pea happy.

Jeep-Jeep. The Jeep enters Popeye and Swee'pea's life.

Popeye's Museum Piece. Brutus attempts to steal a painting while Popeye's on guard.

Golf Brawl. Popeye, Olive, Wimpy, and Brutus play golf.

Wimpy's Lunch Wagon. Jukebox king Brutus causes problems for Popeye and Olive Oyl while Popeye minds Wimpy's store.

Weather Watchers. Popeye the Weatherman is a flop, thanks to Brutus's weather tricks.

Popeye and the Magic Hat. Popeye gets upstaged by Brutus and his magic hat.

Popeye and the Giant. Brutus turns Wimpy into a giant, intending to sell him to a circus. Popeye, Wimpy, Brutus, and the Sea Hag are all featured in this cartoon, but even their group effort fails to overcome the god-awful animation. This film features stock footage from previous Jack Kinney–produced Popeye cartoons, including a clip of Brutus laughing at a window that was originally a scene in "Ballet De Spinach."

Hill Billy Dilly. Popeye and Olive encounter two clans who resemble Brutus.

Pest of the Pecos. Popeye deals with a western criminal: Brutus!

The Blubbering Whaler. A whale helps Popeye out of trouble.

Popeye and the Spinach Stalk. Popeye goes after Brutus the Giant, who has captured Olive Oyl and the Jeep.

Shoot the Chutes. Popeye and Brutus compete in a sky diving contest.

Tiger Burger. Popeye and Wimpy go tiger hunting.

Bottom Gun. Popeye and Olive deal with Brutus in a western town.

Olive Drab and the Seven Swee'peas. A reworking of "Snow White and the Seven Dwarfs." A well-animated cartoon featuring Olive's father.

Blinkin' Beacon. Popeye and Swee'pea face problems from the Sea Hag!

Aztec Wreck. Popeye, Olive, and the Jeep search for Aztec treasure but encounter Brutus the Mexican bandit.

The Green Dancin' Shoes. Olive Oyl feels like dancing so the Sea Hag gives her a pair of green dancing shoes that won't stop dancing. A reworking of the classic tale "The Red Shoes."

Spare Dat Tree. Popeye as a forest ranger protecting the trees.

The Glad Gladiator. Popeye versus Brutus the gladiator.

The Golden Touch. The King Midas legend, Popeye style: King Popeye's touch turns everything and everyone into gold.

Hamburger Fishing. Wimpy goes in search of hamburgers and meets an enchanted cow.

Popeye the Popular Mechanic. Popeye builds his own robot servant, which Brutus turns against him. One of the worst of the King Features films. Footage of Brutus laughing at a window, originally seen in "Ballet De Spinach," is jarringly incorporated. The animation is terrible throughout. Popeye's pipe disappears, then reappears several times.

Popeye's Folly. Popeye and his Pappy build a steamboat and compete in a race against Brutus and the Sea Hag!

Popeye's Used Car. Popeye buys a used car from Wimpy but smashes into Brutus' new automobile.

Spinachonare. An interesting cartoon dealing with Japanese culture.

Popeye and the Polite Dragon. Popeye befriends a polite dragon and allows the creature to live with him.

Popeye the Ugly Ducklin'. The Goons befriend little Popeye when everyone else feels he's too ugly to be around. This is a cute cartoon featuring the Goons of Goon Island.

Popeye's Tea Party. Tea gets tossed overboard in this cartoon, and so should the rotten animation! A terrible entry.

The Troll That Got Gruff. Brutus the troll won't let anyone cross a bridge unless they pay him toll.

Popeye the Lifeguard. Popeye is a lifeguard and says to Olive, "I don't want pretty girls ... only you, Olive!"

Popeye in the Woods. Popeye and Wimpy go camping, and the moocher almost burns the forest down in his quest for food.

After the Ball Went Over. The script for this cartoon is entertaining and clever, with an unusual ending: Popeye loses, even though he tells Olive, "Ya knows I always win in these stories!" Unfortunately, the weak animation and repeated scenes make the cartoon very difficult to watch, despite the good script.

Popeye and Buddy Brutus. A well-animated undersea romp for Popeye and Brutus. Popeye saves Brutus when he gets the bends.

Popeye's Car Wash. Popeye and Brutus own competing car wash companies.

Camel-Ears. Popeye saves Olive from Brutus in the desert sands.

Plumber's Pipe Dream. Popeye tries to stop Olive's drip but soon has to stop the city from becoming covered in water.

Popeye and the Herring Snatcher. Brutus the Herring Snatcher causes problems for Popeye.

Invisible Popeye. Too bad the bad animation in this cartoon couldn't stay invisible.

The Square Egg. A well-animated cartoon about the discovery of a square egg, with which Brutus plans to make $$$$.

Old Salt Tale. Popeye tells Swee'pea a story about how the sea became salty. Perhaps he could also explain how he can be wearing a bathing suit in one shot and his white sailor's uniform in the next. A terrible, poorly-animated cartoon.

Jeep Tale. Popeye lives next door to a family of Jeeps, but so does nasty ol' Brutus.

The Super Duper Market. Popeye, Olive, and Wimpy go shopping in Brutus's market.

The Golden Type Fleece. Popeye goes in search of the golden fleece.

Popeye the White Collar Man. Popeye tries his hand at selling insurance to Brutus the stuntman.

Swee'pea Through the Looking Glass. Swee'pea and the Jeep walk right through a mirror and end up on the other side.

The Black Knight. Popeye tangles with Brutus the Black Knight.

Jingle Jangle Jungle. Also known as repeated animated scenes, repeated animated scenes, repeated animated scenes. Popeye, Olive, and Brutus go tiger hunting.

The Day Silky Went Blozo. King Blozo gets involved with a polite dragon and lousy animation.

Rip Van Popeye. A dreary cartoon incorporating the Rip Van Winkle legend. If you can stand the animation, watch closely for a scene in which Popeye drinks from a mug. The foam on the mug disappears, then reappears.

Mississippi Sissy. Riverboat problems for Popeye.

Double-Cross Country Feet Race. Brutus and Popeye compete in a foot race, but they'd better hurry, because that bad ol' animation is coming after them ... and gaining!

Fashion Fotography. Olive Oyl wants her picture taken for a fashion magazine.

I Yam Wot Yamnesia. Popeye, Swee'pea, Wimpy, and Olive get mixed-up personalities.

Paper Pasting Pandemonium. A well-animated cartoon, complete with a Popeye comic strip hanging on the wall.

Coach Popeye. Popeye tries to teach good sportsmanship to Deezil and Swee'pea.

Popeyed Columbus. Popeye as the famous explorer fighting off rebels and weak animation.

Popeye Revere. Poopdeck Pappy rides again.

Popeye in Haweye. Popeye and Brutus as tour guides compete for Olive's business.

Forever Ambergris. Popeye, Wimpy, and Brutus go in search for Ambergris.

Popeye DeLeon. Popeye discovers the fountain of youth but fails to locate any good animation.

Popeyed Fisherman. Swee'pea catches the big fish while Popeye fights a huge whale.

Popeye in the Grand Steeplechase. Popeye and a race horse deal with nasty Brutus and his nag.

Uncivil War. Popeye explains about bad drivers to Swee'pea.

Popeye the Piano Mover. Popeye and Brutus attempt to move Olive's piano.

Popeye's Testimonial Dinner. Popeye is honored by his pals for all his good deeds in previous Jack Kinney cartoons.

Round the World in 80 Days. Brutus and Popeye compete in a race that would win them a big cash prize.

Popeye's Fixit Shop. Popeye and Brutus try to clean some big clocks but end up fighting.

Bell Hop Hop Popeye. Brutus takes over Popeye's bellhop job to be near the Princess Olive.

Barbecue for Two. This was the pilot cartoon for the Jack Kinney–produced cartoon series, and the best. Popeye and Olive try to have a barbecue just for two, but Wimpy, Swee'pea, and a bearded neighbor Brutus all butt in. Popeye and the cast

Opposite page: Publicity used to illustrate how quickly independent stations picked up the television cartoons upon their release.

look like their comic strip counterparts, the only time this visual design was used in the King Features TV cartoons. The style of this fast-paced cartoon is somewhat reminiscent of the "Rocky and Bullwinkle" films.

Produced by Paramount Cartoon Studios

STORY: Seymour Kneitel, Carl Meyer and Jack Mercer; SCENICS: Anton Loeb and Robert Owen; MUSIC: Winston Sharples; ANIMATORS: WM B. Pattengill, I. Klein, Jim Logan, George Germanetti, Morey Reden, Dante Barbetta, John Gentilella, Dick Hall, Gerry Dvorak, Jack Ehret, Irving Dressler, Nick Tafuri, Sam Stimson and Al Pross; DIRECTOR: Seymour Kneitel. My apologies to anyone I may have left out.

Hits and Missiles. The pilot for the Popeye television cartoons produced by Paramount Pictures. Olive wears her old Famous Studios cartoon attire. In this cartoon, Popeye, Wimpy, and Olive travel to the moon and meet cheesemen.

The Ghost Host. Popeye and Olive are trapped in a haunted house.

Strikes, Spares an' Spinach. Brutus tries to wreck the bowling lessons Popeye is giving to Olive.

Jeep Is Jeep. Popeye babysits Swee'pea, but the Jeep arrives and Swee'pea wanders off.

The Spinach Scholar. A cute cartoon. Popeye has to go back to school and get an education or Olive will never see him again. Popeye flunks the sixth, fifth, fourth, third, second, and first grades. He lands in kindergarten and, with the aid of his spinach, correctly spells "cat" and passes. He tells Olive that he went through the whole school in one day.

Psychiatricks. Brutus and Olive try to stop Popeye's fighting outbursts.

Rags to Riches to Rags. Wimpy inherits a million dollars from his late uncle and bets it all on Kid Nitro, who is battling Popeye in a boxing match. Wimpy fixes the match so Kid Nitro will win, but at the last second, Wimpy gives Popeye spinach so the sailor can triumph. At the end of the cartoon, Wimpy is back to his hamburger-mooching ways. A well-animated cartoon, one of the best in the King Features series.

Hair Cut-ups. Popeye tells Swee'pea the story of Sampson and the hair that made him strong.

Poppa Popeye. A story based on a Segar "Thimble Theatre" comic strip from the 1930s where a phony claims to be Swee'pea's father and comes to claim the child.

Quick Change Ollie. Brutus the magician bedevils Popeye in this trip back to ye olden days, courtesy of the Magical Whiffle Bird.

The Valley of the Goons. In a well-animated and rousing adventure, Popeye tries to save the captive Goons from a band of pirates.

Me Quest for Poopdeck Pappy. Popeye travels to the island of Goona in search of Poopdeck Pappy. Based on Segar's "Thimble Theatre" strip.

Mobey Hick. The Sea Hag wants Popeye to knock off a cute whale because it has swallowed a treasure. Popeye closes the cartoon with, "When I eat my spinach, there's a whale of a finish, says Popeye the Sailor Man."

Mirror Magic. A magic mirror tells Brutus that he's not the strongest in the land while Popeye is around. A cute cartoon in the series.

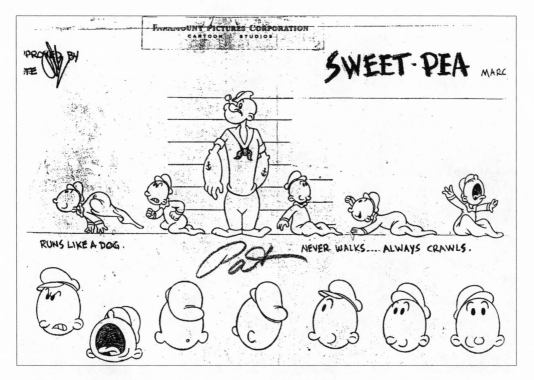

The standard model sheet for Swee'pea (spelled "Sweet-pea" on the sheet) given to all of the studios producing the TV Popeyes for consistency in the animation.

It Only Hurts When They Laugh. Another cartoon based on a Sunday Segar strip. Olive tells Brutus and Popeye to start laughing so she'll know they're not fighting.

Wimpy the Moocher. Wimpy passes a phony pearl as the real thing to get hamburgers. Based on a 1930s Sunday strip.

Voo-Doo to You, Too. The Sea Hag puts Olive in a trance and she becomes the Hag's zombie slave. Exciting story with excellent animation.

Popeye Goes Sale-ing. Olive takes Popeye shopping and Popeye ends up with a headache. A well-animated cartoon.

Popeye's Travels. Popeye does the Gulliver bit.

Incident at Missile City. An evil army of rockets wants to start a war with King Blozo. A well-animated cartoon.

Dog Catcher Popeye. A little pup falls in love with Popeye, but they both have to watch out for dog catcher Brutus.

What's News. Based on a Segar comic strip of the 1930s. Popeye starts his own newspaper, but the bruiser boys want to make sure it folds.

Spinach Greetings. The Sea Hag kidnaps Santa to stop people from being happy at Christmas. Popeye saves the day with the aid of his spinach. A fun, holiday-themed cartoon, one of King Features' best.

The Baby Contest. Popeye and Olive enter Swee'pea in a baby contest. Brutus likewise enters a baby ... his? A well-animated cartoon.

The Sea Hag creates a wax doll of Popeye and puts him under a voodoo spell from "Voo-Doo to You, Too" (Paramount Cartoon Studios, 1960)

Oil's Well That Ends Well. Olive buys a phony oil well and Brutus tries to steal her money.

Motor Knocks. Popeye and Olive end up at Brutus's gas station. Brutus pumps up Olive's ego and lets the air out of Popeye.

Amusement Park. Brutus steals Swee'pea to be the baby midget in his circus act. A well-animated cartoon with an exciting background score.

Duel to the Finish. Wimpy pretends he's in love with Olive to get more of her hamburgers, but Popeye thinks he's making a play for his girl. Wimpy suggests they have an "eating duel."

Gem Jam. The Sea Hag plans to steal a jewel from a cursed idol's crown.

The Bathing Beasts. Popeye and Brutus compete in a Mr. America contest to be able to drive in Olive's new car but she's never driven before.

The Rain Breaker. Popeye takes a trip over the rainbow to help a princess against an evil wizard.

Messin' Up the Mississippi. Brutus tries to grab the spotlight and tries to ruin Popeye's riverboat show.

Love Birds. Olive buys a love bird, but it runs away after an argument with its mate.

Sea Serpent. Olive is a reporter on the trail of a hot story about a monster.

Bordering on Trouble. Popeye and Brutus divide their hotel in half and try to show Olive who has the better side. Brutus is into great entertainment, but Popeye suggests fine food.

Aladdin's Lamp. Popeye is shrunk to mouse size thanks to the Sea Hag's genie.

Butler Up. Popeye pretends to be Olive's butler to impress Olive's old school chum Brutus!

The Leprechaun. The Sea Hag plots to steal a leprechaun's pot of gold. Popeye's closing song provides the moral: "A friend I am told is worth more than pure gold, says Popeye the Leprechaun."

County Fair. Popeye and Brutus compete in several events at a county fair including a spinach-eating contest along with the "test to prove its strength." Popeye closes with the observation that "Brutus was beaten, because he was cheatin', says Popeye the Farmer Man." A well-animated cartoon, among the best in King Features' series.

Hamburgers Aweigh. The Sea Hag wants to steal the hamburger cargo on Popeye's boat. She turns Wimpy into her partner in crime.

Popeye's Double Trouble. The Sea Hag finds that her vulture has mistakenly given her good luck coin to Popeye. She impersonates Olive Oyl to shake the coin out of the sailor.

Kiddie Kapers. The Sea Hag makes Brutus young again so the swab is able to win Olive's heart.

The Mark of Zero. Popeye tells Deezil a bedtime story about Zero the Hero.

Myskery Melody. Based on a Segar comic strip of the 1930s. The Sea Hag kidnaps Poopdeck Pappy for jilting her so many years ago.

Scairdy Cat. A good entry. Brutus uses a potion to make Popeye frightened of him.

Operation Ice-Tickle. Popeye and Brutus compete to bring back the North Pole.

The Cure. Popeye tries to get Wimpy to give up hamburgers ... forever! Fat chance!

William Won't Tell. Popeye is a sharpshooter who gets in trouble with the queen's husband.

Pop Goes the Whistle. Swee'pea is off in search of anything that "toots."

Autographically Yours. A little boy visits a movie set where Popeye and Brutus are filming a movie. He wants Popeye's autograph. Brutus tries to prove that he's a bigger star, better at movie stunts. At the conclusion, Brutus realizes that Popeye is the true hero ... an interesting switch.

A Poil for Olive Oyl. Popeye tries to make Olive a pearl necklace for her birthday but runs into trouble when he encounters the Sea Hag. A well-animated cartoon.

My Fair Olive. Popeye and Brutus compete for the hand of fair Olive.

Giddy Gold. Olive's greed takes over when she goes searching for treasure in a spooky cave.

Seering Is Believing. Thanks to wearing a ring which can foretell the future, Olive sees images in her head in this fun cartoon. Check out Mae Questel's interpretation of Wimpy's voice.

Strange Things Are Happening. Popeye wonders what's going on when his friends try to kidnap him. It turns out that Popeye is being honored on the show "This Is Your Day."

The Medicine Man. Brutus tries to ruin Popeye's sideshow business when the sailor pushes his Spinach Health Juice. Excellent animation.

A Mite of Trouble. The last King Features TV cartoon with the Sea Hag. The witch gets a midget to impersonate Swee'pea to search for Popeye's treasure map.

Who's Kidding Zoo. Brutus and Popeye compete for a job as Olive's zoo assistant.

Robot Popeye. Brutus constructs a robot of Popeye to spoil Olive's dinner with the sailor man.

Sneaking Peeking. Olive tells Swee'pea a story about the dangers of "sneaking peeking."

The Whiffle Bird's Revenge. The Whiffle Bird (an early Segar creation) casts a spell on Wimpy so that when he says the word "hamburger," he'll turn into a wolf.

Going Boing Gone. Wimpy uses vanishing cream to become invisible so he can get away from Brutus. Later he causes havoc in Rough House's diner. Last King Features TV cartoon to feature Brutus and Rough House.

Popeye Thumb. A nice way to finish! Popeye tells Swee'pea the story of Popeye Thumb who, though small, was big in brains. One of the best of the King Features cartoons.

The Popeye King Features TV cartoons were sold to television stations, already having success with the theatrical films. The TV Cartoons made King Features Syndicate three million dollars upon their initial release.

"The ABC Saturday Superstar Movie" (1972)

Popeye made his network television debut in the hour-long special, "The Man Who Hated Laughter" (also known as "Popeye Meets the Man Who Hated Laughter") in 1972. Several King Features comic strip characters appeared in this animated production which aired as part of "The ABC Saturday Superstar Movie" and was rebroadcast during the 1973-74 television season.

Hanna-Barbera's "All New Popeye Hour" (1978-79 and 1979-80)

"The Adventures of Popeye" cartoons

EXECUTIVE PRODUCERS: William Hanna and Joseph Barbera; PRODUCER: Art Scott; DIRECTOR: Chris Cuddington; STORY EDITOR: Larz Bourne; CHARACTER DESIGN: Bob Singer, Marty Murphy, Toby; INK AND PAINT SUPERVISION: Colin Dawes, Narelle Derrick; MUSICAL DIRECTOR: Hoyt Curtin; ANIMATORS INCLUDED: Peter Gardiner, Gerry Grabner, Greg Ingram, Paul Maron, Susan Beak, Ty Bosco, Astrid Brennan, Marion Brooks, Dick Dunn, Rodney D'Silva, Peter Eastment, John Eyley, Don Ezard, Arthur Filloy, Nicholas Harding, Athol Henry, Cynthia Leech, Henry Neville, Ray Nowland, Pamela Lofts, Philip Pepper, Viven Rey and Kaye Watts. My apologies to any one who was left out and for the generic descriptions to some episodes for which I didn't have access.

Many of the early Famous Studios cartoons featured Popeye aboard ship as seen in this publicity still.

Merry Madness at the Mardi Gras. Popeye, Olive, and Bluto attend the Mardi Gras. Olive sings, "When I look in your eyes, I know I won the prize, my Popeye, my sailor man."

Ships That Pass in the Fright. Bluto rescues both Olive and Popeye from a deserted island. He then tries to get rid of Popeye!

Peask and Quiet. Popeye tries to get some rest with the Jeep in the woods, but Olive's cry for help isn't far behind.

Popeye's Self Defense. Olive wants Popeye to learn self-defense so he doesn't have to rely on a can of spinach every time he gets in a jam. An enjoyable cartoon.

Popeye's Perilous Pursuit of a Pearl. Popeye goes on the hunt for a precious pearl, which the Sea Hag also wants.

Olive Goes Dallas. Bluto disguises himself as a judge so Olive will fumble and not become a Dallas cheerleader.

Sparing Partners. Popeye and Bluto compete for the job of Olive's health spa assistant.

Abject Flying Object. A space creature visits Popeye and Olive Oyl.

Top Kick in Boot Camp. Olive wants to join the Army, but Bluto has other plans.

Pappy Fails in Love. Pappy and Bluto compete for the favor of a rich woman aboard a cruise ship. She ends up falling for Wimpy because of his cooking skills. One of the better cartoons in the series.

The Umpire Strikes Back. Bluto and Popeye compete in a baseball game.

W.O.I.L. More trouble for Olive Oyl when she owns her own radio station and Bluto, also a station owner, wants to eliminate the competition.

Tough Sledding. Granny Oyl needs Popeye's help to save her ski lodge.

Getting Popeye's Goat. Popeye is assigned to take care of a goat that eats everything in sight. A cute cartoon in the series.

Close Encounters of the Third Spinach. A spoof on *Star Wars*, with Olive as Princess Olive-Pit, Poopdeck Pappy as Alta-Poppa and Bluto as Darth Bluto. Popeye calls Darth Bluto "Darth Brutus" in one scene. Probably the only cartoon in which the bully is called by both names, but one of the best in the series nevertheless.

Popeye's Finest Hour. Popeye is back in the Navy along with Bluto's nephew.

Popeye and the Pest. A pesty mosquito ruins Popeye's fishing plans after it eats his spinach. The pair call a truce by cartoon's finish.

Popeye Meets the Blutostein Monster. A monster resembling Bluto looks for a mate ... Olive Oyl!

Ship Ahoy. Popeye teaches his nephews how to run a ship, but Bluto causes problems at sea.

Here Stew You. Olive must keep cooking stew for a bunch of Goons to keep them happy when she and Popeye are stuck on Goon Island. An enjoyable cartoon.

Popeye and the Pirates. Popeye tangles with Bluto and his band of pirates.

Popeye Goes Hollywood. Popeye and Bluto compete for a job as a stuntman.

Popeye's Roots. Poopdeck Pappy tells Popeye's nephews stories featuring Popeye's ancestors.

Popeye Snags the Sea Hag. Popeye goes after Madame "No-No," alias the Sea Hag. Popeye sings, "The Madame's defeated, me job is completed, says Popeye the Sailor Man."

The Three Ring Ding-a-Lings. Popeye, Olive, and Bluto cause problems at the circus. Wimpy is the ringmaster.

Unidentified Fighting Object. Popeye's nephews meet a space creature and battle Bluto and his bulldog.

I Wouldn't Take That Mare to the Fair on a Dare. Swee'pea wants to enter his old horse in a pulling contest. Everyone laughs at the lad, until spinach turns the horse into a power-house.

Popeye of Sherwood Forest. Popeye Hood and Little Wimpy versus Bluto the evil sheriff.

Bad Company. Popeye's nephews go off with Bluto (much to Popeye's displeasure) but soon discover that "Uncle Bluto" is a cheater. A very good entry in the series.

A Goon Gone Gooney. Alice the Goon wants Popeye for her king and almost gets him, thanks to Bluto's help. But Olive eats the spinach and saves Popeye, who then takes care of Bluto. One of the better cartoons in this series.

Popeye of the Jungle. Popeye tells lil' Swee'pea the story of his jungle relative and mate, jungle Olive Oyl.

Alpine for You. Popeye and Olive enjoy living in the Alps, but Bluto horns in.

Tour Each His Own. Popeye and Bluto run sightseeing operations and compete for Olive's business.

Popierre the Musketeer. Musketeer Popeye's misadventures.

The Great Speckled Whale. Popeye tries to save a whale's hide from Bluto's harpoon.

Popeye the Carpenter. The first Popeye cartoon aired on "The All New Popeye Hour" in September of 1978. Popeye tries to fix Olive's house, but Bluto causes problems.

The Ski's the Limit. Popeye gives skiing instructions but learns a thing or two himself.

Popeye and the Beanstalk. Popeye climbs a beanstalk to rescue Olive Oyl from Bluto the Giant.

A Day at the Rodeo. Rodeo troubles plague Popeye.

The Decathlon Dilemma. Poopdeck Pappy works out for the decathlon, but Popeye feels his father is too old. A good cartoon in the series.

Chips Off the Old Ice Block. Popeye teaches Swee'pea how to skate, but Bluto butts in.

Popeye of the Klondike. Popeye goes in search of gold to help saloon gal Olive Oyl.

Popeye Goes Sightseeing. While Olive goes shopping, Popeye chases after Swee'pea, who has wandered off.

Shark Treatment. Poopdeck Pappy and Popeye go shark hunting.

Mother Goose Is on the Loose. Bluto and Popeye tell their own versions of famous nursery rhymes to lil' Swee'pea.

Bluto's Bike Bullies. Bluto wrecks Popeye and Olive's ride with his gang of bikers. In a change-of-pace ending, Bluto reforms by cartoon's end.

Steeple Chase at Ups and Downs. Olive inherits a race horse and enters the animal in a big race.

A Camping We Will Go. A camping trip creates excitement for Popeye, Olive and Popeye's nephews.

Eugene the Jeep lets Popeye know he will watch over his Pappy! From "The Decathlon Dilemma" (Hanna Barbera, 1978)

Take Me Out to the Brawl Game. Olive wants to play baseball alongside the men. Popeye's game but Bluto tries to stop her.

Popeye Versus Machine. Popeye uses his muscles and Bluto uses machines to build a new highway.

The Spinach Bowl. Football players Popeye and Bluto brawl.

Ballet Hooey. Popeye and Bluto get mixed up chasing the sailor's basketball and wind up on stage during Olive's ballet performance. Olive eats the spinach to stop the two from ruining her show. One of the best cartoons in this series.

The Big Wheel. Amusement park problems. The Hanna-Barbera cartoons featured fine animation with excellent story structure.

Popeye the Sleepwalker. Popeye, after a long sea voyage, begins sleepwalking. Olive tries to rescue him.

A Whale of a Tale. Popeye tells his nephews a story about one of his ancestor's tangles with sea king Bluto.

Olive's Shining Hour. Olive, Popeye, and Bluto get mixed up in tennis hijinks. Bluto has his own girlfriend in this cartoon: "Blutesa."

A Bad Knight for Popeye. Popeye tries to rescue Princess Olive from a mean dragon. Olive's singing is so awful it breaks the television set viewers are watching her on. A cute finish.

Popeye Goes Sale-ing. Bluto interrupts Olive's date with Popeye in this early Hanna-Barbera effort. Popeye sings, "I sent Bluto out whaling so we could go sailing, I'm Popeye the Sailor Man."

A Seal with Appeal. Popeye's nephews bring a pet seal home but have to keep it hidden from their Uncle Popeye. One of the better cartoons of this series.

The Crunch for Lunch Bunch. Cavemen Popeye and Bluto search for prehistoric food for Olive's diner.

A Day at Muscle Beach. Muscle-bound beachcomber Bluto makes a play for Olive.

Wilder Than Usual Blue Yonder. Popeye takes to the skies.

Popeye Out West. Popeye is sheriff of a town with Bluto as the number one outlaw.

Popeye the Plumber. Popeye and Swee'pea try to fix Olive's leaky pipes.

Spinach Fever. A disco take-off. Popeye and Olive meet Bluto, Mr. Disco.

Heir Brained Popeye. Popeye must locate a will which has made him an heir.

Popeye and Bigfoot. Bluto disguises himself as Bigfoot to ruin Popeye's plans with Olive Oyl.

Popeye's Engine Company. Popeye and Bluto are firemen trying to save Olive's apartment ... but it's only her cooking that's burning.

Olive's Bugged House Blues. Popeye's present to Olive, a cricket, causes problems for her when she tries to get some sleep.

Boo Who. Popeye, Olive and Bluto encounter spooks.

The Game. Bluto the game hunter is after two new creatures: Popeye and Olive Oyl.

Free Hauling Brawl. Popeye and Bluto get involved in a cross-country truck race.

Wotsa Matterhorn. The Matterhorn is the setting for Popeye's latest adventure.

Pedal Powered Popeye. Popeye enters a bike race with Olive and Bluto.

Popeye's Aqua Circus. Popeye's aqua circus is plagued by Bluto's tricks.

Take It or Lump It. Bluto pretends to be the host of a game show and gives grief to Popeye and Olive Oyl.

Popeye's Poodle Problem. Popeye takes Olive's poodle to a dog show, but Bluto wants to stop him so his own dog will have a better chance of winning.

Westward Ho-Ho. Popeye tells his nephews how he created the Grand Canyon.

Bad Day at the Bakery. While trying to pave the street, Popeye and Bluto almost ruin Olive's new bakery business.

Popeye the Painter. Popeye and Bluto compete for a painting contract.

Bully Dozer. By mistake Popeye eats red hot peppers, thinking it's spinach, in his efforts to awaken Princess Olive.

Popeye the Robot. On "National Popeye Day," Bluto uses a robot Popeye to tarnish the sailor's image. A particularly good cartoon in the series.

Swee'pea Plagues a Parade. Swee'pea wanders off and into more trouble.

Paddle Wheel Popeye. Popeye and Olive compete with Bluto in a boat race to New Orleans.

Yukon County Mountie. Popeye and Bluto tangle with a French criminal who is after Olive's payroll. Olive falls for the criminal, causing Popeye to sing, "We both look downhearted 'cause we've been outsmarted, says Popeye the Sailor Man."

Bluto dances with Olive while Sheriff Popeye prepares to eat his spinach! This is a publicity photo from the Hanna-Barbera cartoon "Popeye Out West" (1978) seen in "The All New Popeye Hour."

At last it happens! Olive slips out of Bluto's grasp and handles the bully herself! From "The Loneliness of the Long Distance Popeye" (Hanna-Barbera, 1979).

Queen of the Load. Trucker Olive Oyl gets help from Popeye against trucker Bluto.

Love on the Rocks. To show Olive how much he loves her, Popeye tries to create a statue of her in the Rocky Mountains, but Bluto makes a mess of his plans.

Popeye the Lone Legionnaire. Popeye gets help from Olive the Legionnaire to battle Bluto.

Roller Rink-a-Dink. Popeye and Bluto compete on roller skates.

Old McPopeye Had a Farm. Uncle Angus needs the help of Popeye and his nephews to harvest his crops.

Polly Wants Some Spinach. Popeye goes after Olive's parrot whom he thinks has run away.

The Loneliness of the Long Distance Popeye. Popeye, Olive, and Bluto compete in a road race. When Bluto puts the squeeze on Olive, she tosses the bully over her shoulder ... it's about time!

Popeye's High School Daze. Popeye and Olive recall their days as teenagers during the 1950s.

On Mule-itary Detail. Popeye takes charge of an Army mule but ends up regretting it.

Building Blockheads. Popeye, Olive, and Bluto create problems at a construction site, trying to build the world's tallest building.

"Popeye's Treasure Hunt" cartoons

Dublin or Nothin'
Around the World in 80 Hours
Hail, Hail the Gang's All Here
Beyond the Spinach Brick Road
In a Little Spinach Town
Forum or Against 'Em
I Wants Me Mummy
The Terrifyink Transylvanian Treasure
  Trek
Sword of Fitzwilling
Play It Again, Popeye
Captain Meno's Sunken Treasure
The Delmonica Diamond

The Treasure of Howe's Beyou
Spring Daze in Paris
Coldfinger
A Horse of a Flying Color
Mask of Gorgonzola
I Left My Spinach in San Francisco
A Trio in Rio
Popeye at the Center of the Earth
Boola-Boola Hula
Treasure of Werner Schnitzel
Plunder Down Under
The Reel Hollywood Treasure Hunt

"Popeye's Sports Parade" cartoons
(aired in 1979-80 season only)

King of the Rodeo
Sky High Fly Try
The Great Decathlon Championship

Popeye in Wonderland
Fantastic Gymnastics
Water Ya Doin'?

"Popeye's Health and Safety Tips": Subjects

Exercise
Junk Food
Skateboard Safety
Drugs
Immunization
Importance of Breakfast
Prescription Medicine
Smoking
Tooth Care
Bicycle Safety
Don't Overeat
Eat Balanced Meals
Sleep
Alcohol
Household Cleaners
Electricity
Bathroom Safety
Don't Open Doors to Strangers
Don't Play with Matches
Crossing the Street
Home Safety Toys
Clean Hands

Sharp Utensils
Don't Accept Rides from Strangers
Off Road Mini-Bike Safety
Roller Skates
Swimming Pools
Aerosol Sprays
Sunburn
Bike Signaling
Sportsmanship
A Friendly Attitude
City Sled Safety
Seat Belts
Boating Safety
Don't Eat Houseplants
Playground Safety
Bike Control
Ski Safety
Swimming
School Bus
Indoor Insecticides
Hiking
Buying Safe Toys

Toy Safety
Railroad Trestles
Waterfront Safety
Kites
Bad Company
Parked Cars
Ice-Skating
House Fires
Amusement Park Safety
Bike Brakes
Safe Use of Ladders
Construction Sites
Oiling Your Bike
Mopeds
Bike Safety Loose Parts
Unsafe Substitutes
Toe Clips

Checking Your Bike
Bike Accessories
Being Seen at Night
Vacant Houses and Dumps
Tricycle Safety
Bike Gears and Seat
Extinguishing Campfires
Sports Clothing
Refrigerators
Bike Tires
Tough Sledding
Paint Poisoning
Bike Wheels
Clothing Fires
Swings
Rec Room Safety

"The Popeye & Olive Comedy Show" (1980–1983)

"Private Olive Oyl" cartoons

Mission Improbable
Computer Chaos
Here Today, Goon Tomorrow
Troop Therapy
Goon Native
Alice in Blunderland
Wreck Room

Private Secretaries
Goon Balloon
Tanks a Lot
Rocky Rolls
Infink-try
Basic Training
Jeep Thrills

"Prehistoric Popeye" cartoons

Reptile Ranch
Chilly Con Caveman
Come Back Little Stegosaurus
Neanderthal Nuisance
The First Resort

Vegetable Stew
Snow Fooling
Bronto Beach
Up a Lizard River

"Adventures of Popeye" cartoons

So Who's Watching the Bird Watchers. Olive takes Popeye and Bluto birdwatching, but all three end up in trouble. A good cartoon.

Olive's Devastating Decorators. Popeye and Bluto attempt to redecorate Olive's house, but trouble follows the pair.

Cheap Skate Date. Popeye takes Olive skating, but Bluto rides by to cause a conflict.

The Incredible Shrinking Popeye. Popeye gets sprayed with a shrinking solution and gets smaller and smaller. In the end, Bluto attempts to cook him in a spinach stew. A good entry in the series.

Winner Window Washer. Popeye and Bluto compete to see who cleans Olive's windows the best.

Hot Wash at the Car Wash. Olive takes her new mud splattered car to Popeye's new car wash and Bluto follows her.

The Midnight Ride of Popeye Revere. Last cartoon to date to feature Popeye's nephews as they learn the tale of Popeye Revere and his famous ride. One of the best of its series, this cartoon is always enjoyable.

Popeye Stumps Bluto. Lumber jacks Popeye and Bluto compete for an opening in Olive's tree business.

Olive's Moving Experience. The last regular "Popeye" cartoon is a throwback to the old days. Popeye tries to move Olive's furniture, but Bluto horns in.

Note: The Hanna-Barbera cartoons produced from 1978 to 1983 were extremely popular on CBS Saturday mornings. Right after finishing their network run, they entered TV syndication.

Hanna-Barbera's "Popeye & Son" (1987-88)

Thirteen half-hour shows; two "Popeye & Son" cartoons per episode. Aired on CBS Saturday mornings. EXECUTIVE PRODUCERS: William Hanna, Joseph Barbera and Bruce Palsner; STORY EDITOR: Jeff Segal and Kelly Ward; CREATIVE DESIGN: Iwao Takamoto; ANIMATION DIRECTORS: Frank Andrina and Oliver Callahan; MUSIC AND SOUND EFFECTS: Paul Vitello and Associates.

This was an attempt to update the Popeye mythos by having the sailor married to Olive, with their union producing a blonde-haired, spinach hating son named Junior. While Bluto, Wimpy, the Sea Hag and Eugene the Jeep all appeared, the focus was clearly on Junior and his pals. Fans did not take too kindly to this update and the series only lasted one season. It has aired in syndication, like the previous "Popeye" series, all over the world.

Episodes:

Attack of the Sea Hag
Happy Anniversary (Popeye and Olive
    get married.)
The Sea Monster
Poopdeck Pappy and the Family Tree
Bluto's Wave Pool
Here Today, Goon Tomorrow
Don't Give Up the Picnic
The Lost Treasure of Pirates Cove
Junior's Genie
Mighty Olive at the Bat
Junior Gets a Summer Job

Surf Movie
Redbeard
The Girl from Down Under
Junior's Birthday Roundup
Olive's Dinosaur Dilemma
Dr. Junior and Mr. Hyde
Popeye's Surfin' Adventure
Split Decision
The Case of the Burger Burglar
Orchid You Not (with Eugene the
    Jeep, his wife and children)
Ain't Mythbehavin'

There Goes the Neighborhood
Olive's Day Off (with a cameo appearance by "Granny Popeye")

Prince of a Fellow
Damsel in Distress

"The Popeye Show"

"The Popeye Show" is a half-hour series, airing on the Cartoon Network, which features three "Popeye" films produced by the Fleischer and Famous Studios. Each episode features restored opening and closing sequences to the black and white cartoons, which were never before broadcast on television. Each episode discusses the production of the cartoons, trivia and personnel involved. WRITTEN AND PRODUCED BY: Barry Mills; NARRATED BY: Bill Murray; PRODUCTION STAFF: Woolsey Ackerman, Jerry Beck, Ken Blue, Baco Bryles, John Breston, Matt Maiellaro, Maya McClure, Jack Pendarvis, Tom Race, Vishal Roney, Harold Sellers, Kevin Thomas and Bob Woodhead; SPECIAL THANKS TO: Jerry Beck & Cartoon Research, Leslie Cabarga, Fred Grandinetti and George Feltenstein.

As of February 2003, 45 half-hour episodes of "The Popeye Show" had been produced over the course of three and a half television seasons. One hundred and thirty-five "Popeye" films had been restored to their original theatrical state. The majority of the color cartoons in the Famous Studios series could not be used on this program, as the footage needed for restoration is missing. "The Popeye Show" has proven to do well for the Cartoon Network despite no on-air promotion from the network. Word of mouth, communication via the internet and advertisements placed in periodicals (many by the author) brought well-deserved attention to the series. Producer Barry Mills has done an outstanding job in restoring these classic Popeye cartoons for this informative series.

Season 1

Episode #1: Can You Take It (1934), Me Musical Nephews (1942) and Olive Oyl for President (1948)

Episode #2: Sock-a-Bye Baby (1934), The Jeep (1936) and Fightin' Pals (1940)

Episode #3: Spinach Overture (1935), It's the Natural Thing to Do (1939) and Hill-billing and Cooing (1956)

Episode #4: Goonland (1938), Wotta Nitemare (1939) and Pip-eye-Pup-eye-Poop-eye and Peep-eye (1942)

Episode #5: Cops Is Always Right (1938), Hello, How Am I (1939) and Robin Hoodwinked (1948)

Episode #6: Shiver Me Timbers (1934), Alona on the Sarong Seas (1942) and Insect to Injury (1956)

Episode #7: Man on the Flying Trapeze (1934), I Yam Love Sick (1938) and She Sick Sailors (1944)

Episode #8: A Dream Walking (1934), Organ Grinder's Swing (1937) and Cops Is Tops (1956)

Episode #9: The Hyp-Nut-tist (1935), Child Psykolojiky (1941) and Cartoons Ain't Human (1943)

Episode # 10: I Eats My Spinach (1933), Little Swee'pea (1936) and With Poopdeck Pappy (1940)

Episode # 11: Vim, Vigor and Vitaliky (1936), Happy Birthdaze (1943) and Abusement Park (1947)

Episode #12: Choose Yer Weppins (1935), Mutiny Ain't Nice (1938) and Kickin' the Conga Round (1942)

Episode #13: Never Kick a Woman (1936), Shakespearian Spinach (1940) and Popeye, Ace of Space (1953)

Season 2

Episode #14: What … No Spinach? (1936), Lost and Foundry (1937) and Popeye Presents Eugene the Jeep (1940)

Episode #15: Strong to the Finich (1934), Nurse Mates (1940) and Quiet! Pleeze (1941)

Episode #16: Beware of Barnacle Bill (1934), Wimmin Is a Myskery (1940) and Olive's Boithday Presink (1941)

Episode #17: I Yam What I Yam (1933), Football Toucher Downer (1937) and I'll Never Crow Again (1941)

Episode #18: Hospitaliky (1937), Me Feelins Is Hurt (1940) and The Mighty Navy (1941)

Episode #19: Blow Me Down (1933), Twisker Pitcher (1937) and Nix on Hypnotricks (1941)

Episode #20: Hold the Wire (1936), Ghosks Is the Bunk (1939) and Olive Oyl and Water Don't Mix (1942)

Episode #21: Adventures of Popeye (1935), Stealin' Ain't Honest (1940) and Many Tanks (1942)

Episode #22: Let's You and Him Fight (1934), Onion Pacific (1940) and Baby Wants a Bottleship (1942)

Episode #23: Pleased to Meet-Cha (1935), Let's Celebrake (1938) and A Hull of a Mess (1942)

Episode #24: A Clean Shaven Man (1936), Proteck the Weakerist (1937) and Spinach fer Britain (1943)

Episode #25: Brotherly Love (1936), Popeye Meets William Tell (1940) and Too Weak to Work (1943)

Episode #26: I Wanna Be a Lifeguard (1936), Puttin' on the Act (1940) and Wood-Peckin' (1943)

Season 3

Episode #27: We Aim to Please (1934), Learn Polikeness (1938) and Shape Ahoy (1945)

Episode #28: King of the Mardi Gras (1935), Popeye Meets Rip Van Winkle (1941) and A Haul in One (1956)

Episode #29: Axe Me Another (1934), Never Sock a Baby (1939) and Peep in the Deep (1946)

Episode #30: Morning Noon and Night Club (1937), Flies Ain't Human (1941) and Parlez Vous Woo (1956)

Episode #31: Seasin's Greetinks (1933), Doing Impossikible Stunts (1940) and Wigwam Whoopie (1948)

Episode #32: Dizzy Divers (1935), A Date to Skate (1938) and Assault and Flattery (1956)

Episode #33: Two Alarm Fire (1934), Females Is Fickle (1940) and A Wolf in Sheik's Clothing (1948)

Episode #34: The Dance Contest (1934), Customer's Wanted (1939) and Out to Punch (1956)

Episode #35: For Better or Worser (1935), The House Builder Upper (1938) and Symphony in Spinach (1948)

Episode #36: The Spinach Roadster (1936), Ration fer the Duration (1943) and A Job for a Gob (1955)

Episode #37: Shoein' Hosses (1934), Plumbing Is a Pipe (1938) and Alpine for You (1951)

Episode #38: I Likes Babies and Infinks (1937), Pest Pilot (1941) and Mister and Mistletoe (1955)

Episode #39: Fowl Play (1937), Fleets of Stren'th (1942) and A Balmy Swami (1949)

Season 4

Episode #40: I Never Changes My Altitude (1937), Wimmin Hadn't Oughta Drive (1940) and Marry-Go-Round (1943)

Episode #41: Wild Elephinks (1933), The Hungry Goat (1943) and Tops in the Big Tops (1946)

Episode #42: Paneless Window Washer (1937), Big Chief Ugh-Amugh-Ugh (1938)

Episode #43: Bridge Ahoy (1936), Leave Well Enough Alone (1939) and Pitchin' Woo at the Zoo (1944)

Episode #44: I-Ski Love-Ski You-Ski (1936), Bulldozing the Bull (1938) and Spinach-Packin' Popeye (1944)

Episode #45: You Gotta Be a Football Hero (1935), Olive's Sweepstakes Ticket (1941) and Anvil Chorus Girl (1944)

Episodes in Which Others Ate the Spinach

Perhaps to relieve the monotony of Popeye sucking down spinach at every moment of crisis, scriptwriters soon began to feature plot twists in which other characters ate spinach. Sometimes these spinach-powered characters helped Popeye; sometimes they hurt him; and sometimes they simply generated a lot of chaos. Below is a list of cartoons in which someone besides Popeye consumed the famous vegetable.

Strong to the Finich (1934). To show little children that it is good for them, Popeye feeds spinach to a chicken, cows, a tree and himself.

Never Kick a Woman (1936). After a Mae West–type gym teacher flirts with Popeye and bops Olive Oyl about, Olive takes Popeye's spinach out of his pants pocket and swallows the can's contents. She then turns into a hissing wildcat and overpowers the gym instructor, then punches Popeye about for letting the woman flirt with him.

Hospitaliky (1937). Popeye and Bluto try to get themselves injured to land in the hospital to be close to Nurse Olive. Popeye feeds his spinach to Bluto, who can't control his newfound strength and beats up Popeye, sending him to the hospital.

Proteck the Weakerest (1937). Olive's pooch eats Popeye's spinach to do battle with Bluto's bulldog. This cartoon would be remade two times.

The Twisker Pitcher (1937). Popeye and Bluto are playing baseball, and when Popeye drops his spinach, Bluto eats it to get the upper hand in the game.

Lost and Foundry (1937). Swee'pea gets lost in the factory where Popeye works. Popeye goes after the tyke, but his spinach can is knocked out of his hand. Swee'pea eats the spinach and saves both Olive Oyl and the sailor from being squashed by a giant press.

Let's Celebrake (1938). When Olive's grandmother is fed Popeye's spinach, she becomes a super dancer at the New Year's Eve ball. Great animated dance scenes in this cartoon produced by the Fleischer Studios.

Goonland (1938). Popeye finds his father on Goon Island. After the Goons take Popeye captive, Poopdeck Pappy finds Popeye's spinach can, eats the contents, and aids his son in fighting the Goons.

Flies Ain't Human (1941). A pesky fly is tossed into a spinach can by Popeye. The fly eats the spinach and beats on poor Popeye, who just wanted to take a nap.

Pip-eye-Pup-eye-Poop-eye and Peep-eye (1942). Popeye eats spinach in an effort to show his nephews its benefits ... alas, to no avail. But after Popeye spanks their little bottoms, the lads eat their spinach and pounce on their uncle.

Seein' Red, White 'n' Blue (1943). Popeye feeds Bluto his spinach can and all so that Bluto can help battle a band of Japanese spies.

Too Weak to Work (1943). Popeye feeds spinach to Bluto via a spinach pump to get him working on painting some ships, a job Bluto has put off because he wants to rest.

For Better or Nurse (1945). As in "Hospitaliky" (1937), Bluto is forcefed Popeye's spinach so that he will beat Popeye up, sending him to the hospital to be near Nurse Olive. Trouble is this time she works for an animal hospital.

Spinach Vs. Hamburgers (1948). Olive takes Popeye's nephews to eat at Popeye's eatery, but the boys would rather lunch at Wimpy's Hamburger Heaven. The boys eat their spinach, but only to give them the strength to get Popeye and Olive out of the way; then they head for Wimpy's place.

Barking Dogs Don't Fight (1949). This was a remake of the 1937 cartoon "Proteck the Weakerest," in which Olive's dog eats the spinach to do battle with Bluto's dog.

The Fly's Last Flight (1949). While Popeye tries to nap, a fly bothers the sailor. Popeye makes the mistake of flinging the insect into a can of spinach. The fly eats the spinach and pounds on poor Popeye. A remake of "Flies Ain't Human" (1941).

Baby Wants Spinach (1950). Swee'pea eats Popeye's spinach when the lad wanders into the zoo with Popeye in pursuit.

Farmer and the Belle (1950). Popeye feeds some of his spinach to a chicken, who lays eggs up to the ceiling.

Double-Cross Country Race (1951). Popeye feeds spinach to his car (which has been given poison water) to start up its motor.

Pilgrim Popeye (1951). Popeye gives his spinach to a turkey to build up the bird's muscles. The turkey then eats the spinach to save Popeye from Indians.

Popeye's Pappy (1952). Popeye finds his Pappy on an island. The island people decide to make a stew out of Popeye, so Pappy eats spinach in order to rescue his son.

Lunch with a Punch (1952). Popeye's nephews eat the spinach so they can beat up ol' Bluto, who has grabbed Popeye without his spinach.

Popalong Popeye (1952). Popeye's nephews eat spinach to save Popeye from a horse that has gone wild.

Shuteye Popeye (1952). A mouse eats spinach and tosses Popeye into his small mousehole when the sailor's snoring keeps the mouse up all night long.

Fireman's Brawl (1953). Olive eats Popeye's spinach to save firemen Popeye and Bluto, who are attempting to put out the fire at Olive's house.

Gopher Spinach (1954). Popeye has a gopher in his spinach garden, and the little fellow eats one of the spinach plants so he can save Popeye from a bull with a bad temper.

Beaus Will Be Beaus (1955). Bluto and Popeye have promised Olive that they will stop fighting, but Popeye feeds Bluto his spinach so the bully will break his promise.

Hillbilling and Coo-ing (1956). Olive eats the spinach when a hillbilly gal steals Popeye the Sailor away from her.

Hoppy Jalopy (1960). To overtake Brutus's race car, Popeye feeds spinach-juice to his rundown jalopy a trick he used in 1951's "Double-Cross Country Race."

Beaver or Not (1960). Two beavers eat Popeye's spinach in order to finish the dam they're making.

Fleas a Crowd (1960). Popeye has a flea circus. When Brutus plants a mechanical dog on stage for the trained fleas to jump on, the insects get worn out by the dog's antics. Popeye feeds the fleas his spinach to pep them up.

Popeye's Junior Headache (1960). Deezil, Olive's nasty niece, eats the spinach (off-screen) in her further attempts to harass Popeye, her babysitter.

I Bin Sculped (1960). Brutus is fed Popeye's spinach so he will beat Popeye up, making Popeye the chosen model for Olive's "pooped masterpiece."

Popeye's Pep-Up Emporium (1960). Olive eats the spinach to save herself when Popeye's too busy with Brutus.

Popeye and the Giant (1960). Popeye feeds an oversized Wimpy "essence of spinach" to shrink him down in this terribly animated cartoon.

I Yam Wot Yamnesia (1960). After a bonk on the head, Swee'pea thinks he's Popeye so when we see Swee'pea eating spinach, it's actually Popeye (?).

Popeye's Fix-It Shop (1960). Olive eats the spinach to stop Popeye and Brutus from feuding.

Me Quest for Poopdeck Pappy (1960). Pappy eats Popeye's spinach to save his son from "The Monster of the Sea."

Baby Contest (1960). Swee'pea eats Popeye's spinach to save Popeye from being beat up by bully Brutus.

Gem Jam (1960). Olive eats the spinach to beat up the Sea Hag because Popeye's sailor's code won't allow him to hit a woman.

Love Birds (1960). Popeye gives a bird a little spinach to give it enough courage to stand up to its mate.

County Fair (1961). Brutus and Popeye compete in a spinach-eating contest, which is followed by a "test to prove its strength." In this cartoon we learn that Popeye's spinach is different from everyday spinach. Brutus eats most of Popeye's because, as he puts it, "You didn't think I'd play fair with that runt and take a chance against his spinach."

Hamburgers Aweigh (1961). Popeye feeds spinach to Olive so she can once again take care of the Sea Hag. (See "Gem Jam," 1960.) Popeye, meanwhile, punches out the hag's vulture.

Popeye's Double Trouble (1961). The Sea Hag pretends she's Olive Oyl, which leads to a showdown between the real Olive and the old witch. After Olive eats Popeye's spinach, she gives the hag the "solar sock."

The Cure (1961). Wimpy eats the spinach to bop the Sea Hag's Goon, who is tormenting him as he struggles with his promise to give up hamburgers.

A Poil for Olive Oyl (1961). Popeye goes in search of pearls under the ocean for Olive's birthday present. The Sea Hag wants Popeye to leave her pearl bed, so Olive eats the spinach, dives into the ocean, and flattens the hag.

Giddy Gold (1961). Olive eats the spinach when a siren hypnotizes Popeye.

Popeye Thumb (1961). Swee'pea searches in Popeye's shirt for his can of spinach, causing Popeye to laugh. The lad eats the spinach in order to show some kids he can play baseball.

Popeye's Self-Defense (1978). Bluto tries to give Popeye self-defense lessons, but Olive eats Popeye's spinach and sends them both for a ride on a spinning fan.

Olive Goes Dallas (1978). Olive eats spinach so she can win a cheerleading contest.

Abject Flying Object (1979). A space creature eats spinach to stop Bluto, who wants to capture him.

Pappy Fails in Love (1978). Poopdeck Pappy eats spinach in order to court a rich woman aboard a cruise ship and to stop Bluto from horning in.

I Wouldn't Take That Mare to the Fair on a Dare (1979). Swee'pea feeds spinach to an old horse so it will be able to beat Bluto's horse in a race.

Bad Company (1978). Popeye's nephews feed spinach to a pig that Bluto has roped.

A Goon Gone Gooney (1978). Olive eats the spinach to battle a bunch of Goons who have taken Popeye captive.

Popeye and the Pest (1978). Popeye does battle with a pesty "skeeter" who has eaten his spinach and disrupted his fishing trip.

Ship Ahoy (1978). Popeye and his nephews eat spinach to stop Bluto from ramming them in his boat.

Shark Treatment (1978). Pappy eats Popeye's spinach to stop a shark from causing further havoc.

Steeple Chase at Ups and Downs (1978). Popeye and his race horse eat spinach to win a race after Bluto has cheated.

Ballet Hooey (1978). Olive eats Popeye's spinach to stop both Popeye and Bluto from ruining her ballet dance.

Popeye's Poodle Problem (1978). Olive's poodle, Frenchie, eats spinach with Popeye, and together they take on Bluto and his dog.

Popeye & Son Series (1987-1988). Popeye's son, "Junior," ate the spinach in many of the *Popeye & Son* cartoons as he was the main character in these cartoons. In other cartoons, Poopdeck Pappy ate the spinach, as Popeye of course did. When "Junior" ate the spinach, he got Popeye-style arms.

On occasion, Popeye and his fondness for spinach have managed to pop up in animated cartoon series produced by the Warner Bros. Cartoon Studio. Warner Bros. produced the popular "Looney Tunes" and "Merrie Melodies" animated cartoons featuring Bugs Bunny, Daffy Duck, Porky Pig, and a whole roster of zany characters. Here is a listing of Warner cartoons making reference to Popeye and his spinach:

Porky's Garden (1937). Porky and his Italian neighbor compete for a $2000 cash prize for the largest home-grown product. In one scene, a little chick and a big chicken wrestle over a huge watermelon. The big chicken pokes the little chick away. The crying little chicken calls the big one a "big ox." The little chick eats a spinach leaf and turns into a pint-sized Popeye, complete with squinty eye and big forearms. The "Popeyed" chick mutters under his breath while approaching the chicken. "That's an insulk. Why, he can't do that to me. I'll lay him among the swee'peas the big lug!" The chick then bops the chicken and eats the remainder of the watermelon.

The Major Lied Till Dawn (1938). A very English major tells a tale full of hunting stories. In one scene, all the jungle animals gang up on the major, who pulls out a can of spinach: "I say, if it's good enough for that sailor man … it's good enough for me." The major consumes the spinach and fights off the animals.

Scrap Happy Daffy (1943). After a battle with a scrap metal–eating Nazi goat, Daffy asks the audience for a can of spinach to help him out.

Two other Warner cartoons alluded to Popeye without mentioning his spinach, though his super-strength was certainly part of the joke:

Porky's Hero Agency (1937). The Gorgon is a woman who is turning people into stone statues. In one scene, Porky Pig injects the Venus de Milo with a "life-restoring" needle, bringing the statue to life. Then Porky gives the statue Popeye forearms as a little of the Popeye theme plays in the background.

Porky's Poor Fish (1940). A pussycat attempts to eat a fish in Porky's Pet Fish Shoppe. The cat, however, is no match for a mussel that sprouts Popeye forearms and trounces the feline.

Popeye and Animals

One of the recurring themes in the Popeye animated cartoons is the sailor's adventures with animals. Some animals would embrace the sailor, while others would beat the tar out of him (usually because he was in the wrong place at the wrong time). Here is a sample listing of cartoons where the animal kingdom played a part in Popeye's adventures ... for better or for worse:

Wild Elephinks (1933). Popeye and Olive land on an island filled with jungle animals. They cause problems for the pair until Popeye beats the majority of them into fur coats for Olive Oyl.

Be Kind to Aminals (1935). Bluto is carrying all his fruits and veggies on the back of one overloaded horse. Bluto whips the animal to move faster until Popeye climbs on the horse and takes the lashings meant for the animal, crying out, "Rather me than a dumb animal." By cartoon's finish, Bluto is pulling the heavy load and the horse is whipping him. Segar often showed Popeye's kindness to animals in the comic strip of the 1930s, and this trait carried over into the early animated cartoons.

Little Swee'pea (1936). Popeye takes Swee'pea to the zoo, where the lad gets involved with the caged animals. Popeye gets the wind knocked out of him attempting to save Swee'pea from the animals' clutches.

Organ Grinder's Swing (1937). Popeye fights Bluto, who wants Wimpy the organ grinder, along with his monkey, to leave. The monkey saves the day when he feeds Popeye his spinach to battle Bluto.

I Never Changes My Altitude (1937). Popeye is knocked out of his airplane, but when he feeds his spinach to a passing bird, the bird speeds Popeye back into the fray.

Proteck the Weakerest (1937). Olive asks Popeye to walk her "sissy" dog. Bluto and his bulldog start a battle with the pair. Both Popeye and the dog eat their spinach and take on the bullies. By cartoon's finish, Popeye doesn't think Olive's pooch is a sissy anymore.

Fowl Play (1937). Popeye gives Olive a pet parrot to remind her of him when he's away at sea. Bluto causes problems when he lets the bird out of his cage.

Bulldozing the Bull (1938). Popeye ends up fighting a bull in the arena but doesn't want to kill the beast even though he keeps being thrown a sword. After a spinach-fighting battle, the bull wants to become buddies. Another "be kind to animals" theme, and nicely done.

Females Is Fickle (1940). Olive's goldfish gets thrown in the ocean, and Popeye dives in after it. After Popeye saves Olive's fish, she decides to let it stay in the ocean. Popeye, angered, dumps Olive in the ocean along with the goldfish.

Flies Ain't Human (1941). The first in the series to feature an animal beating up on Popeye. Popeye wants to take a nap, but a fly has other ideas. After eating spinach, the fly beats up the sailor.

I'll Never Crow Again (1941). Olive has crows in her garden and asks Popeye to get rid of them, but he fails. Finally, Popeye dresses up Olive as a scarecrow and plants her in the garden, which scares the birds away.

The Hungry Goat (1943). Another cartoon in which an animal gets the best of Popeye, in this case a ship-eating goat, who bops Popeye about and wins in the end. This cartoon was an attempt by Famous Studios to capture the frantic sense of the Warner Bros. animated cartoons, which really didn't suit Popeye too well.

Woodpeckin' (1943). Popeye goes head-to-head with a woodpecker who's angry that Popeye wants his tree for a mast for his ship. The two reach a compromise by cartoon's finish.

Her Honor the Mare (1943). The first color Popeye cartoon for the short-subject series featured Popeye's nephews taking home a horse for a house pet.

Pitchin' Woo at the Zoo (1944). Bluto the zookeeper and his animals cause Popeye problems.

Klondike Casanova (1946). Popeye does battle with Bluto's bears when he tries to save Olive Oyl.

Rodeo Romeo (1946). Bluto the rodeo star uses a bull's anger to torment Popeye.

Safari So Good (1947). Popeye and Olive are both on safari and run across Bluto the ape-man and his band of wild animals. A monkey saves the day when he feeds Popeye his spinach.

Snow Place Like Home (1948). A seal falls in love with Popeye after the sailor falls in a barrel of black tar and comes out looking like a male seal.

Barking Dogs Don't Fight (1949). Olive asks Popeye to take her dog for a walk, but they run into Bluto and his bulldog. A remake of the 1937 Fleischer cartoon "Proteck the Weakerest."

The Fly's Last Flight (1949). Popeye has a run-in with a spinach-fed fly who battles the sailor. A remake of 1941's "Flies Ain't Human."

Baby Wants Spinach (1950). Popeye takes "Cousin Swee'pea" to the zoo, where the sailor man gets knocked around trying to prevent Swee'pea from getting hurt. A remake of 1936's "Lil' Swee'pea."

Pilgrim Popeye (1951). Popeye tells his nephews a story about his days as a pilgrim to help save a turkey from becoming Thanksgiving dinner.

Toreadorable (1953). Bluto the bullfighter throws the bull around to get rid of Popeye.

Gopher Spinach (1954). A gopher is eating the spinach in Popeye's garden. The sailor wants to get rid of the pest and corners him with a shotgun. Popeye doesn't have the heart to pull the trigger, and the gopher returns the favor by saving Popeye from a bull.

Insect to Injury (1956). Termites destroy Popeye's house, but Popeye eats his spinach and defeats the insects by making his house out of steel.

Foola-Foola Bird (1960). Popeye and Olive go in search of the Foola-Foola Bird, with Brutus close behind the pair.

Sheepich Sheepherder (1960). Poopdeck Pappy's sheep are being stolen by Brutus.

Dog-Gone Dog Catcher (1960). Popeye dresses up as a dog to rescue Olive's captured French poodle, Zsa Zsa.

Beaver or Not (1960). Two beavers wreck Popeye's outing in the country.

Canine Caprice (1960). Popeye gets involved with Roger, the talking dog.

Roger (1960). Olive and Popeye get mixed up in more antics of Roger, the talking dog.

Fleas a Crowd (1960). Popeye does an act with his trained fleas, which Brutus wants to wreck.

Bird Watcher Popeye (1960). Olive wants Popeye to take up bird watching.

Popeye's Pet Store (1960). Brutus steals all of Popeye's customers' pets.

The Blubbering Whaler (1960). Popeye helps a whale stop Brutus from harpooning his fish-friends.

Tiger Burger (1960). Wimpy and Popeye go hunting and meet a nasty old tiger.

Popeye and the Polite Dragon (1960). Popeye takes in a polite dragon and cares for it as it grows up.

Camel-Ears (1960). Popeye and Brutus encounter Olive as a princess in the desert. They also run into horrible animation.

The Square Egg (1960). Popeye gets involved with his hen's square egg and Brutus the egg-napper!

Jingle Jangle Jungle (1960). Popeye, Olive, and Brutus go hunting in the jungle.

Mobey Hick (1960). Popeye goes after Mobey Hick, whom the Sea Hag says is a danger to children. She's lying. Of course the hag wants a treasure the whale swallowed.

Dog Catcher Popeye (1960). Brutus the dog catcher is after a pup who has fallen for Popeye.

Love Birds (1960). Popeye and Olive get involved with two warring love birds.

Who's Kidding Zoo (1961). Popeye and Brutus compete for a job of assistant zookeeper at Olive's zoo. An elephant saves the day when he feeds Popeye his spinach.

The Whiffle Bird's Revenge (1961). The Whiffle Bird casts a spell on Wimpy when the moocher tries to eat the bird. The Whiffle Bird was a creation of Segar and appeared in the story in which Popeye made his comic strip debut in 1929.

I Wouldn't Take That Mare to the Fair on a Dare (1979). Swee'pea wants an elderly horse to compete for first prize in a contest.

The Great Speckled Whale (1978). Bluto goes whale-hunting.

A Seal with Appeal (1978). Popeye's nephews want to keep a seal as a pet.

Getting Popeye's Goat (1978). Popeye is under orders to babysit a goat who eats everything in sight... including dynamite.

Shark Treatment (1978). Poopdeck Pappy and Popeye go after a mighty shark who is Pappy's old enemy.

Polly Wants Some Spinach (1978). Olive's parrot gets loose, and Popeye and Bluto go after the bird. Popeye learns that the bird returned shortly after the sailor went off to look for it, and that he caught another parrot instead.

On Mule-itary Detail (1978). Popeye and Olive try to return an army mule back to its base, only to discover that the animal is retired and should have been left alone.

Olive's Bugged House Blues (1979). A cricket keeps Olive awake, and since the bug was a present from Popeye, the sailor has to find it.

Popeye's Poodle Problem (1978). Popeye takes Olive's pooch, Frenchie, to a dog show, where Bluto and his dog, Butch, cause trouble.

The Delmonica Diamond (1978). Popeye and Olive become involved with hypnotized animals in this "Treasure Hunt" adventure from Hanna-Barbera's "All New Popeye Hour."

A Horse of a Flying Color (1978). Popeye and Olive try to capture a flying horse before Bluto gets his hands on it.

King of the Rodeo (1979). Part of the "Popeye's Sports Parade" segment from the "All New Popeye Hour." Popeye and Bluto compete in a rodeo with raging bulls.

Popeye's generosity, morals and values have helped endear him to audiences all over the world for the past three-quarters of a century.

APPENDIX A:
SELECTED SCRIPTS FROM THE ANIMATED CARTOONS

"What ... No Spinach?" (Fleischer, 1936)

(*Scene opens in Bluto's diner with Bluto cooking and Wimpy daydreaming about hamburgers as he grinds up beef.*)

WIMPY

(*Singing.*) There's nothing in the world that can compare with a hamburger juicy
   and rare.
A hamburger lives for the pleasure it gives,
it's a thrill on the bill of fare. Such heavenly food deserves the best,
a home and contentness beneath my vest.
There's nothing in the world that's so divine
as a hamburger tender and mine.
(*Bluto sneaks up behind Wimpy.*)
I adore you hamburger mine. (*Bluto hits Wimpy over the head.*)

BLUTO

Oh yeah ... HAAA! Mooching hamburgers again huh! What a guy!
(*Bluto opens his safe to keep the burger away from Wimpy.*)
There's one hamburger he won't get ... that guy will eat all my profits!

WIMPY

Hmmmmm ... hmmmmmm. (*Popeye comes in the diner.*)

POPEYE

(*Singing.*) I'm Popeye the Sailor Man (*toot*) ... I'm Popeye the Sailor Man (*toot*)

271

... hmmmm, it's a lil' weak (*Popeye uses a stove to fuel his pipe*) ... I'm Popeye the Sailor Man (*TOOT! TOOT!*)
What 'cha gut? (*Wimpy presses his lapel and the menu appears on his shirt.*)
Well ... uhhhhh. (*The menu flashes on his shirt.*)

POPEYE

Menu ... I don't want any of that ... hamburgers ... roast duck ... hamburgers ... soup ... hamburgers ... nice selection ya gut here. Roast Duck!

WIMPY

Roast Duck!

POPEYE

Yeah! Roast Duck! What's the matter, ya deef...

WIMPY

One hamburger!

BLUTO

Okay! Comin' right up. I gut a nice secondhand one in here. (*He pulls a burger out of the safe and tosses it to Wimpy.*)

WIMPY

A lil' mustard!

BLUTO

HEY! (*He uses a fork to flip the burger away from Wimpy and over to Popeye.*)

POPEYE

I says Roast Duck ... take this thing back. (*He flips the burger back to Bluto.*)

BLUTO

Roast Duck ... coming up! I gut an old duck in here ... I'd never eat it myself ... give it to that guy! Hah ... I'll give it a lil' bath, put a pair of leggins on it and off she comes! (*He flips it to Wimpy.*)
(*Wimpy takes the Roast Duck and ties strings to the legs.*)

POPEYE

'Bout time ya got over here with that thing, I'm starvin' to death! This is gonna be ducky. Me favorite piece too! (*He tries to grab a leg but Wimpy pulls it off the plate.*)
I wonder where that went to ... huh! Well here's another one! (*Wimpy pulls the other leg away.*) Huhhhh ... that's the funniest duck I ever tried to eat!
(*Wimpy is putting salt on the legs and is about to eat them when Bluto sees what he's up to.*)

BLUTO

HEYYYY! (*Bluto sends a model ship towards Wimpy's head which drops its anchor on the moocher's noggin.*)
Put 'em back ... put 'em back!

WIMPY

Ohhhhh!

POPEYE

(*Still looking for the missing legs, which Wimpy has put back on his plate.*) WOW!!!!

WIMPY

My word, this is becoming serious. (*Wimpy sees a bottle of hot sauce and gets an idea.*) Be some flies around here. (*He waves his hands around Popeye's face and pours hot sauce on his food.*) ... BZZZZZZ ... BZZZZZZ.

POPEYE

Hey stoo-pid who ya wavin' at? I don't see no flies around here ... I think you've been out in the sun too long ... that's what's the matter with you! (*He swallows the duck.*) WWWWOWWWW!!!! (*He breathes fire from the hot sauce.*) I've been per-sioned! Ya not gonna try that stuff out on me! (*Popeye prepares to walk out of the diner.*)

BLUTO

Hey! You can't get away without paying! (*Bluto grabs Popeye and turns him upside down, and Popeye's money falls out of his pockets. Popeye grabs Bluto's feet and they both roll back into the diner.*)

WIMPY

Hah! Now's my chance! (*Wimpy attempts to open Bluto's food safe but he can't.*)

(*Popeye gets thrown up against the wall.*)

BLUTO

Why you little shrimp. (*Bluto begins tossing objects at Popeye.*)

POPEYE

Ouch! Ow! Fine way to treat a customer! Ow! Ouch! (*A can of spinach bounces off Popeye's face and on the way down to the ground gets split in two by an axe, causing its contents to fall into Popeye's mouth.*)

(*Popeye hits Bluto.*)

WIMPY

Hit him with this! (*Wimpy points to the food safe.*)

BLUTO

Well ya finally got an' idea, hit him with it ... why, I'll crown him with it!

POPEYE

Look out, I'm (*The safe falls on Popeye, but he bursts through the safe door.*) comin' through!

(*Wimpy goes in the safe while Popeye and Bluto continue to mix it up.*) (*Popeye punches Bluto into a table-prison.*)

BLUTO

What is it around here?

(*Wimpy walks out of the safe, stuffed with food.*)

WIMPY

Hmmmmm ... hmmmmmm ... I adore you hamburger MINE!!!!

"I'll Never Crow Again" (Fleischer, 1941)

(*Scene opens with Olive Oyl washing dishes and singing, while crows are picking food from her garden.*)

OLIVE

It's a hap-hap-happy day ... tool-lool-lay ... hmmmm ... hmmmm ... it's a hap-hap-happy day. OOP ... hey ... get out of my garden!

CROW

Aw stop yer crowin' ya old buzzard! (*The crows throw food at Olive.*) CAWWWWWW! CAWWWW!

OLIVE

Stop ... don't you dare hit me ... OPPOMMPH! I must call Popeye ... operator ... operator!

(*Scene changes to Popeye clipping his toenails, singing.*)

POPEYE

It's a hap-hap-happy day ... doo-doo-doo. (*His phone rings and he answers it.*) Oh ... hello!

OLIVE

Popeye ... hurry over here right away ... there are a lot of crows in my yard an' they're all eatin' all the vegetables in my garden ... hurry over quick and chase them 'cause they're chasin' me ... make it snappy and hurry up over here... (*While Popeye listens to Olive his ears swell in pain!*)

OLIVE

Hurry Popeye ... hurry!

POPEYE

Okay Olive, I'll be over before ya can say Jack (*His phone clicks.*) (*Popeye arrives at Olive's.*) Robinson!

OLIVE

What are you standing there for ... GO OUT AND CHASE THEM AWAY!!

POPEYE

Aw right ... stop pushin' now!! What's yer hurry, they'll still be there. I'll surround them. (*Popeye attempts to sneak up on the crows and makes a funny face to frighten them off.*) BLLAAAAAAWWW!

CROWS

(*Make a funny face right back at him.*) BLAWWWWWWWW!

(*Popeye picks up a stick and waves it in the direction of the crows.*)

POPEYE

That's yer last swallow ... git back ta Capistrano! (*The crows fly away.*) Well that's that! Okay Olive, I got rid of them.

OLIVE

Popeye, yer wonderful!

POPEYE

That goes fer me too. (*Olive sees the crows are back.*)

OLIVE

Yeah ... didn't chase them away, they're still in my garden ... now get right out there and do something!!

(*Popeye is making a scarecrow with clothes.*)

POPEYE

Do something! Well I'll do something all right ... this will be the scariest scarecrow they ever saw! (*A crow flies to Popeye's scarecrow.*) (*The crow pulls off the scarecrow's clothes.*)

CROW

Mmmmmmm ... nice material. (*The crow tries on the clothes.*)

OLIVE

Oh Popeye ... look!

POPEYE

Dat boid is usin' fowl tactics. (*Popeye sneaks up on the crow, who is smoking a cigar and blows smoke in Popeye's face.*)

POPEYE

COFFFFFFFAAAAAACOFFFBOOOOOAAAAAA!!!!

OLIVE

Tee-hee! Tee-hee!

POPEYE

Wimmen laugh at the funniest things! I'll scare these crows personally! (*Popeye then sticks his arms out like a scarecrow.*)

(*A crow lands on Popeye's arm and tries to catch Popeye with his eye open. The crow then pulls Popeye's hat down over his face.*)

POPEYE

Hey ... what makes it so dark in the light!?!

OLIVE

(*Laughing loudly.*) Tee-hee! Tee-hee! Hee! Hee!

POPEYE

Stop laughin' before I loses me temper!

(*Two crows land on Popeye's arms and start doing a see-saw motion.*)

POPEYE

Hey what's this! What's cookin' ... I'll teach ya ta scare scarecrows ... huh!

(*Two crows get some tomatoes.*)

CROW

My, look at the bad scarecrow!

CROW

Yeah ... I'm afraid! We'd better go! (*They throw their tomatoes at Popeye.*)

POPEYE

Is my face RED ... I'll catch up with them!

CROW

Hey stupid (*looking like a scarecrow*) ... look I'm a scarecrow ... I'm a scarecrow ... CAWWWWWHAWWWW ... HAWWW!

POPEYE

He's a scarecrow ... ggrr ... this is next to the last straw... (*Popeye looks as though he has an idea. He runs into Olive's house and gets a rifle. He fires at the crows but misses them all.*)

OLIVE

Hee ... hee ... hee ... hee!!!

POPEYE

Whaaa ... umph. (*He breaks the rifle in two.*) That's all I can stand! NAR-RRRRLLLL ... NARRRLLLL ... (*Popeye looks like a madman and heads towards the laughing Olive.*)

CROW

Okay boys, the coast is clear!

OLIVE

Hee ... hee ... OH ... he's gone stark mad ... don't you dare come near me ... oh ... don't you touch me. (*Popeye picks her up.*) ... OOOOHHH!!!!!

OLIVE

Put me down! OMMMMHHHH!

(*We then see Popeye clapping his hands, laughing. The crows see something too ... Olive tied to a post like a scarecrow. An ugly scarecrow!*)

CROWS

AWWWWWWWWKKKKKKKK!!!!!!! (*The crows take off.*)

"Spinach-Packin' Popeye"
(Famous, 1944; written by Bill Turner)

(*Scene opens with Popeye lying on a bed after just giving blood.*)

NURSE

You just gave a gallon of blood. You'll have to rest now, Mr. Popeye.

POPEYE

Who me? ARF, ARF, ARF, Sorry but I've got an importink fight on tonight!

(*He starts to spin and dance around the bed like a prizefighter, and the scene changes to the prizefighting ring.*)

ANNOUNCER

In this corner ... Popeye the Sailor!! And his opponent ... Bluto the Bruiser!!

RADIO ANNOUNCER

Here we are at ringside folks and the fight is about to start. (*The fight bell rings and the scene changes to Olive Oyl listening to the fight on the radio. Olive moves around like the fighters in the ring.*)

RADIO ANNOUNCER

There's the bell folks ... they move out to the center of the ring ... they circle each other slowly and cautiously ... slowly and cautiously ... each man knows the other packs a blockbuster in each fist ... and there's a left ... a right ... a left ... a right ... a left and he's DOWN! Here's the count, two, four, six, eight, ten and he's OOOOOUUUUT!

OLIVE

Yipppeee! (*She hugs the radio.*)

RADIO ANNOUNCER

What an upset ladies and gentlemen ... Popeye the Sailor knocked out!

OLIVE

HUUUUHHHHHHHH!

RADIO ANNOUNCER

I said Popeye the Sailor was knocked out!!

OLIVE

That weakling Popeye. (*She puts her foot through the radio, causing a plant to fall on her head. Popeye walks in the front door with a BLACK EYE!*)

POPEYE

Hello Olive ... how's me lil' sweet patootie tonight ... huh!

OLIVE

Don't you sweet patootie me ... you ... you ... Palooka ... lost your strength ... you're washed up ... you're a WAS-BEEN and I'm through with you. (*Olive goes behind a screen and changes into an army uniform.*) ... I like strong men. (*She flips to the front a picture of Bluto in an army uniform.*)

POPEYE

But listen, Olive, I've licked a hundred guys better than him already. (*Olive pushes Popeye as she heads out the door.*) Here, look at the feats of strength I did in me picture Sindbad the Sailor! (*Popeye shoves out his diary and sticks it under Olive's nose.*)

(*Scene changes to Popeye, Sindbad, and Olive Oyl.*) (*Sindbad has grabbed Popeye.*)

SINDBAD

Well ... let's see how great you are! (*Sindbad punches Popeye into the claws of his giant bird.*)

POPEYE

OOHHH ... Hey what's this ... let me down, ya big overgrown canary ... what are you doin', taking me for a ride or something ... huh ... I'm not goin' yer way ... Hey!

OLIVE

Popeye, my Popeye ... come back to me!

SINDBAD

Ho! Ho! Ho! Ho!

(*Suddenly there is a tremendous battle and Popeye comes spinning back—holding Sindbad's bird on a platter, cooked and ready to be eaten.*)

POPEYE

ARF, ARF, ARF, there ya are ... with gravy!

SINDBAD

NO! NO! NO!

(*Scene changes back to Popeye and Olive.*)

OLIVE

Oh dear ... how boring!

POPEYE

Wait a minute Olive ... I'll show ya how I licked the forty thieves in me picture Ali Baba!

(*Scene changes to Popeye suspended over a pool of sharks.*)

POPEYE

Hey what is this ... a wishing well or something ... I wish I was out of this place ... that's what I wish ... Ohhhh ... (*A shark tries to take a bite out of Popeye.*) ... oooohhh ... a lil' flounder. (*Another shark jumps at him.*) ... a lil' snapper ... ooohhh! Hey yer liables ta hoit ya teeth on me! Somebody's gonna be sorry for this. (*Popeye then slugs one of the sharks.*) ... that'll hold you for a while.

(*Popeye then pulls out a can of spinach.*) Open-Sez-Me! (*The can opens slowly. Popeye eats the spinach, and tanks form in his muscles. He then uses the rope he's tied to and spins back into Ali Baba's men. A battle rages as Popeye spins, rolls, jumps into Ali Baba's clothes and finally punches Ali Baba into a treasure chest, locking him up!*)

(*The scene changes back to Popeye and Olive.*)

POPEYE

There ya are ... is that proof enough of me amazing strength?

OLIVE

You may have been strong then, but you're just a weakling now. Good-bye! (*She tosses Popeye onto her couch as he bobs up and down on the sofa.*)

(*Scene changes back to a doctor's office, where a nurse is waking Popeye up.*)

NURSE

All right, Mr. Popeye, you may get up now!

POPEYE

Where am I? Ohhh … ohhh … Olive … me lil' sweetie … Ohhhh … Ohhhh!
(*Popeye dashes out of the doctor's office and heads for Olive's house.*) Olive … Oh
Olive!!

OLIVE

Oh hello Popeye!

(*Popeye then lifts up Olive's house.*)

POPEYE

Olive, don't you think I'm a strong man? (*He shakes the house.*)

OLIVE

Ohhhh! Ohhhh! (*Olive falls out a window but lands in Popeye's arms.*) Popeye
… yer just about the strongest man in the whole wide world!

POPEYE

That's all I wanted ta hear … 'cause I'm Popeye the Sailor Man (*Toot! Toot!*)

"If I Were President"—sung by Olive Oyl (Mae Questel) in "Olive Oyl for President" (Famous, 1948)

If I were President,
If I were President.

There'd be at least ten months of June,
For folks to spend their honeymoon.
And every blooming flower
Would have the sweetest scent,
If I were President!

If I were President,
If I were President.

Silk worms in every house would grow,
And they would all be on the go
In case there was a stocking accident,
If I were President!

There would be lamp posts like you've never seen,
And streets would all be spotless clean!

If I were President,
If I were President.

I'd have a cure that would work right
For those who couldn't sleep at night.
The time they stayed awake would be well spent!
If I were President!

If I were President,
If I were President.

The dogs whose habits all are strange
Would undergo a brand new change,
And all the ice-cream cones would cost a cent,
If I were President!

If I were President,
If I were President.

Each bus would have a smoother run,
With lots of seats for every one.
Apartments once again would be for rent,
If I were President!

There would be no wrangling anymore,
For drumsticks that fell short before.

If I were President,
If I were President.

I'd pick up feminine morale
And get a man for every gal.
More holidays would get my strong consent,
If I were President!

"There's No Space Like Home" (King Features, 1960; produced by Gene Deitch and William Snyder)

(*Scene opens with Popeye reading a newspaper.*)

POPEYE

Spaceship sighted over town ... wow ... this gives me a swell idea for Olive's costume party tonight ... huh ... I'll calls the costume shop and dress up like a spaceman ... ARF, ARF, ARF, ARF!

(*Scene changes to Brutus looking in a mirror.*)

BRUTUS

There ... I make a handsome sheik if I do say so myself. I wonder what that little runt Popeye is going to wear at Olive's party!

(*Back at Popeye's house, where he's putting on his space helmet.*)

POPEYE

ARF, ARF, ARF. Olive will never recognize me in this outfit. (*Brutus is peeping in his window.*)

BRUTUS

So the lil' runt is goin' as a spaceman, eh? HEE … HEE … HEE … that gives me a swell idea. (*He rushes to a pay phone and calls the police.*) Police, police … I just saw a spaceman on Elm Street … yeah, the street Popeye lives on. (*Soon sirens approach Elm Street.*)

BRUTUS

HAH … HAH … HAH. That lil' runt will never get to Olive's party now!

(*The police catch up with Popeye and catch him in a bag.*)

POPEYE

Hey … what's goin' on around here … lets me outa dis blastid bag!

POLICEMAN #1

Stand back men … he may have a space gun!

POLICEMAN #2

He may be radioactive!

POLICEMAN #3

Take that spaceman to headquarters. We'll examine him there. He sounds almost human!

(*Brutus is walking to Olive's house.*)

BRUTUS

This will be a swell party … I'll have Olive all to myself … HUH! (*He sees a real spaceman … but thinks it's Popeye.*) Curses … I thought sure the police would pick Popeye up … I still don't want him at that party. (*He kicks the spaceman in the air.*) Yuck, yuck … I almost put him in orbit. (*Brutus then throws the spaceman in a trash can.*) So long chump … I'll see ya at Olive's party!

SPACEMAN

Help! Help! Help! I've been attacked by an earthman!

(*Two spacemen fly out of their ship, grab Brutus's cape and drag him back to their ship.*)

BRUTUS

Hey, cut it out. Who are you? Ohhh … ohhh!

(*Meanwhile at the police station, Popeye is behind bars.*)

POLICEMAN

What planet are you from? What are you doin' here?

POPEYE

I yam what I yam and that's all what I yam. I'm an earthman. Whats am I under arrest for?

POLICEMAN

Now, now, take it easy ... you're not under arrest ... we just want to examine you, spaceman.

POPEYE

Nots under arrest huh ... then I don'ts have ta stay here if I don't wants ta. (*He pulls out a can of spinach.*) I'll takes a lil' spinach appetizer. (*Popeye bursts through the prison wall.*) An' away I go! So long fellas ... I'll see ya on Mars! ARF, ARF, ARF!

POLICEMAN

Wow ... what strength!

(*Scene changes to Brutus in a spaceship high above the earth.*)

SPACEMAN

So ... you earthmen attack us, eh? We declare WAR!

BRUTUS

You guys are KOOKS ... I'm gettin' outa here and goin' to a party. (*Brutus jumps into space, but turns his cape into a parachute only to get zapped in the rear by the spaceship's ray gun.*) OWWWWWWW—OUCH!

(*Back at Olive's house.*)

OLIVE

Oh Popeye, what a cute costume ... what made you so late, spaceman?

POPEYE

Oh my gorsh ... it's a long story, cowgirl. I ... (*Brutus rushes past them.*)

BRUTUS

Help! help ... I'm being chased by spacemen!

OLIVE

HA! HA! HA! What an entrance! C'mon, Popeye, let's join the party.

POPEYE

Why that corny ham. (*Two spacemen land near Popeye.*) Hey, Olive, ya guts some more guests. C'mon in, fellas. Hey ... hey ... takes it easy, that's part of me costume. (*One spaceman pulls off Popeye's space helmet and smashes him over the head with it.*) What's goin' on around here? (*The other spaceman shoves the door on Popeye. Brutus is hiding behind the sofa.*)

OLIVE

That was a good gag, Brutus, but come out now! (*The spacemen dump the punch bowl on Olive's head.*)

OLIVE

GGGGGGGUUULLLLL ... spacemen ... GLLLLLLL!

(*The spacemen attack Brutus from behind by shoving Olive's mail box into his back, slamming him against the wall near the fallen Popeye. Brutus slips his hand under Popeye's shirt and pulls out a can of spinach.*)

BRUTUS

This looks like a job for Popeye ... here, chum. (*He feeds Popeye the can of spinach. Popeye turns into a rocket and blasts off to get the spacemen.*) That-a-boy, chum ... they went that-a-way!

(*The spacemen are chasing after a screaming Olive, but Popeye stops them in their tracks and punches them back into their spaceship. Popeye picks up the spaceship and throws it into space.*)

OLIVE

Well, boys, you can unmask and we'll enjoy the party!

BRUTUS

We're not wearin' masks!

POPEYE

We gut black eyes!

OLIVE

HA! HA! HA! OOOOOHA!

POPEYE AND BRUTUS

HAW! HAW! HA! HAW!

Barbecue for Two" (King Features, 1960; produced by Jack Kinney; written by Dick Kinney and Al Bertino)

Note: This was the first Popeye cartoon produced by Jack Kinney. It is interesting to note that this cartoon featured Popeye's bearded rival but he was not called Bluto *or* Brutus. He was referred to as "Neighbor." Popeye and Olive's character designs in this film were based on the comic strip/Fleischer versions, making this the only King Features TV cartoon to present them in this manner.

(*Film opens with Popeye preparing a barbecue for Olive Oyl.*)

POPEYE

Barbecue ... da ... diddly ... doo ... doo ... fer me ... an me sweetie ... barbecue for two ... for who? ... me sweetie an' me ... that's who! Skeed ... da ... da ... doo ... oo ... Oh ... no flowers fer me sweetie! I'll just borrows some from me good neighbor. (*He reaches his hand over the fence and yanks some flowers from his neighbor's garden.*)

NEIGHBOR

My favorite pet-petunias! Why I'll... (*He slams his fist down on Popeye, who begins bending like an accordion.*)

NEIGHBOR

MMMMM ... a barbecue ... I love barbecues!

POPEYE

I loves barbecues too. (*Popeye blows into his captain's hat, turning it into a chef's hat.*) But you ain't invited! It's just fer me an' me sweetie!

NEIGHBOR

(*Thinking to himself.*) I'm gettin' an invite to this shinding if it's the last thing I...

POPEYE

One side buster ... beat it! (*Popeye pours the charcoals onto the grill, then he pours on the gas.*)

NEIGHBOR

Can I give you a match?

POPEYE

Natch! Be my guest! (*Neighbor throws a match on the grill, which explodes in his face.*)

NEIGHBOR

Hamburgers ... Ohhh ... yummy ... yummy!

POPEYE

Ya, but no yummy fer you, dummy!

NEIGHBOR

MMMMMM ... MMMMMM... (*The aroma of the cooking hamburgers travels across town to the nose of Wimpy.*)

NEIGHBOR

What's that? A plane, a train? a rocket? It's a … it's a … it's a…

POPEYE

It's Wimpy!

SWEE'PEA

(*Looking from his crib out the window.*) Goody … Goody!

WIMPY

I'll have two … medium rare.

POPEYE

Listen … this barbecue is jus' fer me sweetie an' me! Out! Out! Out! Out! Lout! (*Swee'pea crawls towards Popeye's feet.*)

SWEE'PEA

Swee'pea … swing? (*He points to the swing-set.*)

WIMPY

A little service please … a little. (*Wimpy and the Neighbor are sitting at a table pounding with forks and knives.*) (*Popeye charges at them.*)

POPEYE

This is it! (*Popeye scoops them all up in his arms and heads for the gate to toss them out.*)

OLIVE

Ohhhhh! a party … I love big parties! (*Popeye drops his human load with a loud thud.*)

OLIVE

Ohhh … what a handsome brute … too!

POPEYE

OOOhhhh!

NEIGHBOR

Allow me!

SWEE'PEA

AHHHHHHHH! (*The lad is crying because the swing isn't moving.*)

WIMPY

Garson! (*Popeye pushes the swing and brings Wimpy two burgers.*)

NEIGHBOR

(*Preparing Olive some coffee.*) And how many lumps, my sweet lady?

OLIVE

Ohhhh ... two. (*Her two toes burst through her big shoe.*)

NEIGHBOR

Sweets for the sweet, my sweet! One ... two!

POPEYE

An' how many lumps do you want?

NEIGHBOR

Just one!

POPEYE

Okay ... one lump ... comin' up! (*Popeye punches him over the fence.*)

POPEYE

Now for the overture. (*He pulls out an accordion.*) Music always gets 'em!
(*The neighbor stretches the accordion while Popeye is holding it next to Olive's head
... he lets it snap back, and it slams into Olive Oyl!*)

NEIGHBOR

(*Pointing to Popeye.*) He did it!

POPEYE

But ... but ... but ... but...

OLIVE

Popeye, you are no gentleman, and if there's nothin' I like the least ... no gentleman is the most ... an' besides I don't like this corny music! (*She kicks the
accordion.*) I like modern music ... like rock an' roll!

NEIGHBOR

Rock an' roll?

(*Swee'pea is crying again and Wimpy wants more burgers.*)

WIMPY

Garson!

(*Neighbor now is singing and playing a guitar for Olive.*)

NEIGHBOR

Don't drop no mustard on my clean white shirt baby!
Don't drop no mustard on my clean white shirt baby!

(*Swee'pea is bawling again and Wimpy wants more burgers.*)

OLIVE

Popeye ... take care of your guests!

(Popeye pushes Swee'pea's swing and brings Wimpy two more burgers. Popeye keeps charging the Neighbor, who keeps kicking him away. He kicks Popeye onto the hot grill. Popeye zooms into the path of the Neighbor's guitar. With a mighty blow, the Neighbor bashes Popeye into the house, where a can of frozen spinach lands on his pipe. He thaws it out and eats it. Wimpy and Swee'pea take one look at the fierce look on Popeye's face and depart quickly.)

POPEYE

Junior... *(Popeye beckons for the neighbor to come towards him.)*

NEIGHBOR

Junior! Don't call me a sissy name like that! My name is... *(The Neighbor charges towards Popeye sounding like a steam engine.)*

GRRRRROOOOOOOWWWWWLLLLLLL! *(Popeye merely stands there twirling his fist and then lands one single blow on the Neighbor's chin which sends him flying off the planet and onto the other side of the world. Olive skids towards Popeye as the earth leans forward due to Popeye's blow.)*

OLIVE

Oh Popeye ... Save me!

POPEYE

Alone ... at last!

OLIVE

But Popeye ... I ain't et yet!

(Popeye is seen at the grill, cooking dozens of burgers and tossing them at Olive.)

OLIVE

I jus' love barbecues for two ... crowds...

POPEYE

Ohhhhhh!

"Kiddie Kapers" (King Features, 1961; produced by Paramount; written by Joseph Gottlieb)

(Scene opens with Popeye and Olive passing some store windows.)

POPEYE

That's right, Olive, I promises ta buys ya anything ya wants for your birthday!

OLIVE

Oh Popeye ... would you buy me one of those? (*She's looking at a wedding dress.*)

POPEYE

Why ... ya gettin' married or something? ARF, ARF, ARF!

OLIVE

No, I'm not getting married, especially not to you! We've been going together for so long you're ... you're ... you're an old man!

POPEYE

Old man! Me? That's re-dick-ulos! (*A Boy Scout comes along to help Popeye across the street.*)

BOY SCOUT

Can I help you across the street, sir?

POPEYE

WHAT!?!? (*The Boy Scout runs off in the direction of Brutus.*)

BOY SCOUT

What's with him? (*Talking to Brutus.*) He didn't want to be helped across the street and you said he... (*Brutus claps his hand over the boy's mouth.*)

BRUTUS

Never mind sonny ... let's say it's yer good deed for the day!

POPEYE

The nerve of that kid!

OLIVE

I'm going to look for somebody who's young and handsome!

BRUTUS

Young and handsome, eh! I've got an idea!

(*The scene changes to the Sea Hag's house.*)

BRUTUS

Sea Haggy, ya gotta help me! I wanna get young and handsome!

SEA HAG

You? Young and handsome ... that's a pretty tall order ... hee ... hee!

BRUTUS

Never mind the wisecracks, you're no prize winner yerself!

SEA HAG

I'll have to give you my extra strong formula!

BRUTUS

You think it will work?

SEA HAG

Watch this! (*She lets a chicken drink some youth potion, which causes it to turn back into an egg.*) VWA-LA!

BRUTUS

Terrific! Gimme that!

SEA HAG

You must be careful not to take more than one drop! (*Brutus takes a drop and turns into a handsome young man. He looks in a mirror.*)

BRUTUS

Hey ... not bad!

SEA HAG

Why Brutus ... you handsome devil! Sit down, let's talk for a little while!

BRUTUS

Some other time, Sea Haggy ... I've got a date with a doll!

(*The scene changes to Popeye and Olive sitting on Olive's porch.*)

BRUTUS

Buenos-de-as Seniorita!

OLIVE

Ah ... uh ... hi!

BRUTUS

I would be delighted to know your name, gorgeous!

OLIVE

Why it's Olive Oyl I'm sure!

BRUTUS

I am Don Juan!

OLIVE

Don Juan?!

POPEYE

Yeah ... when you've Don Juan ... you've done 'em all! ARF, ARF!

OLIVE

Won't you please sit down, Mr. Don Juan?

BRUTUS

It would give me great pleasure.

POPEYE

I could think of something that would give me greater pleasure!

BRUTUS

Your beauty speaks to me with the voice of sweet eternity!

OLIVE

Oh, more! more!

POPEYE

Speakin' of voices, haven't I heard yours somewhere?

BRUTUS

No! Ya ... uh ... I mean ... I don't think we've ever met before!

POPEYE

Ah ... I gut it now ... it's Brutus' voice. C'mon, take off that mask. (*Popeye pokes at Brutus' face.*)

OLIVE

Popeye ... have you gone mad?

POPEYE

It's him, Olive ... it's Brutus!

OLIVE

Popeye, how can you be so silly? Brutus is ugly ... but Don Juan here ... OOOOHHHHH ... he's handsome!

BRUTUS

Thank you, my dear! (*Brutus bends over, and Popeye sees the bottle of youth potion in his pocket.*)

POPEYE

Hey, what's this? Youth potion ... the more ya takes the younger ya gets! Caution: uses only 1 drop! So that's it, huh! If one drop cans do that fer Brutus, imagine what a big swig will do fer me ... huh! (*Popeye takes a swig of the potion, which turns him into a baby.*)

OLIVE

What happened?

POPEYE

Whaaaa ... mommy!

BRUTUS

Quiet!

POPEYE

Waaaaa ... aaaaaa!

BRUTUS

Okay, I have a cure for that. (*He picks up Popeye and begins to spank him.*)

OLIVE

Popeye was right! You are Brutus! (*Olive runs to get Popeye a can of spinach.*)

BRUTUS

(*Still spanking Popeye.*) This is a chance I've been waitin' for fer years!

(*Olive feeds Popeye a teaspoon of spinach. Popeye then bounces Brutus in the air and when he lands, starts spanking him. He then punches him across town.*)

OLIVE

Oh Popeye ... no matter how old you are, you're still my hero. I don't want anything to keep us apart anymore. (*Olive takes a swig of the youth potion and turns herself into a baby.*)

POPEYE AND OLIVE

(*Playing patty-cake.*) Vaaaa-haaaa-gggoooo-ggoooooo-goooo!

"Baby Phase" (King Features, 1960; produced by Gerald Ray; written by Henry Lee)

(*Scene opens with the mailman bringing a magazine to Swee'pea.*) (*The mailbox opens and Swee'pea is inside.*)

MAILMAN

Hello, Swee'pea.

SWEE'PEA

Hello ... uh!

MAILMAN

Here's what you've been waiting for.

SWEE'PEA

Whhhooo ... goody goo ... goody goo!

MAILMAN

You're welcome. 'Bye now!

SWEE'PEA

Bye, bye, bye bye, boy ... boy ... oh boy... (*Swee'pea crawls away with his maga-zine, which is titled, "How to Juggle" by Dexter Dexterity.*) (*Swee'pea crawls into the house and pops up on the roof, juggling various objects. One, an iron, falls from his hand and hits Popeye on the head. Popeye has been sleeping on a hammock.*)

POPEYE

OHH! Yoo-hoo ... Swee'pea, ya dropped ya ... hey Swee'pea!

(*Swee'pea slips and falls off the roof.*)

POPEYE

Oh my gorsh ... easy now... (*The objects Swee'pea was juggling hit Popeye before he catches the lad.*) OOmmph! Ouch! Ooh! Naughty, naughty ... little boys shouldn't play on roofs! Yer liables ta gets hoit! Now you play in the house where it's nice and safety! (*He then dumps Swee'pea in the house.*) Well back to me mowing! Well ... AHHHHHHHH. (*Popeye takes a big yawn and climbs back into his hammock. Suddenly he's hit on the head again.*)

POPEYE

Oh no! Not again!

SWEE'PEA

Goo-goo-goodie-gggggggg!

(*Popeye rushes up to the roof and grabs Swee'pea and puts him in his crib.*)

POPEYE

I warned ya Swee'pea ... an' now, for being a naughty boy, Popeye's gonna half ta punish ya. I'm puttin' ya ta bed without any lunch!

SWEE'PEA

NNNNN ... AHHHHHH!

POPEYE

I'm sorry, but ya made yer bed and now ya has ta cry in it! (*Popeye goes back to his hammock and looks at all the junk Swee'pea dropped which is on the ground.*)

POPEYE

Look at this mess ... I wonders... (*He picks up the magazine Swee'pea was read-ing.*) Well ... so that's what got him started ... huh! How could Swee'pea git interested in this sort of thing? Hmmm ... world's famous jugglers ... huh! The greatest of them all was the great Leon ... AHHHHHH (*He yawns.*) juggled 62 balls and a goldfish at once ... AHHHHH ... ZZZZZZ ... ZZZZ (*He falls asleep with the book on his face. The scene changes to a circus with a sign reading, "Swee'pea, the World's Greatest Juggler."*)

POPEYE

Swee'pea, oh my gorsh ... he runned away and joined the circus 'cause I was so mean! Yoo-hoo, Swee'pea, yoo-hoo!

RINGMASTER

Ladies and gentlemen, it's my pleasure to present for you the world's greatest juggler ... Swee'pea! (*Swee'pea is juggling in a lion's cage.*)

POPEYE

Oh my gorsh ... he might get cat-nipped!

RINGMASTER

Hey! Where you think you're goin'?

POPEYE

I gotta get that little boy out of there! What would happen if them lions ate him up?

RINGMASTER

It is simple... (*In a thick Italian accent.*) we get another juggler!

POPEYE

Yeah, but I can'ts get another Swee'pea! Stand aside! (*Popeye bursts into the lion's cage and tosses the animals out.*)

POPEYE

Please forgive me, Swee'pea ... I'm takin' ya home where you belong!

RINGMASTER

That's what you think! He belongs to me. (*He shoves a contract under Popeye's nose.*)

POPEYE

Mmmummble ... mmummble ... holy smokes! Swee'pea! You signed a ninety-nine year contract!

SWEE'PEA

Oh ... googy ... goody ... goo ... goo ... gAA!

RINGMASTER

C'mon, kid, you gut a really tough act comin' up now. (*He carries off Swee'pea, who is juggling.*) Cums-a-now, the biggest thing in the show! Up in the air, 5,000 feet in the air ... he's the world's greatest juggler ... Swee'pea!

POPEYE

Well blow me down!

RINGMASTER

Swee'pea is a-gonna dive off that platform, juggle in the air all the way down and land in this here wet cloth!

POPEYE

Don't do it, Swee'pea! (*Popeye runs after Swee'pea. Swee'pea dives off the platform ... juggling!*)

POPEYE

Oh my gorsh, he'll get killed! (*Popeye dives off the platform after him.*) Me spinach ... it's our only chance! (*Popeye pulls out his spinach can, but loses his grip on it.*) Whoops ... oh no! Swee'pea ... Swee'pea!

(*The scene changes and we see Popeye fall out of his hammock.*)

POPEYE

Where am I? What happin'? Swee'pea ... sheeeshhh ... just a bad dream ... serves me right treatin' Swee'pea that way! (*Popeye runs in the house to see Swee'pea in his crib, still juggling.*)

POPEYE

Swee'pea! Eat yer spinach, Swee'pea ... this is the way to become the world's greatest juggler!

SWEE'PEA

(*Now juggling spinach cans.*) HA-A! Goodie ... goodie ... g-g-g-WOW!

POPEYE

He'll juggle his spinach and fight to the finish, says Popeye the Sailor Man. (*Toot! Toot!*)

"Voo Doo to You, Too" (King Features, 1960; produced by Paramount; written by Seymour Kneitel)

(*Scene opens with the Sea Hag and her vulture coming ashore.*)

SEA HAG

Hee, hee, hee, hee... Well, here we be ashore again, dear vulture, after our long sea voyage, and there's a house that looks ship-shape for our shore lodgings. (*They enter Olive Oyl's house.*)

OLIVE

OH! The wicked Sea Hag! Who gave you permission to barge into my house?

SEA HAG

I take what I want!

OLIVE

Then take yourself right out of here before I call the police!

SEA HAG

AH ... HA ... that's mutiny talk! Grrr ... I'll fix you to obey my orders! Zoola-Kazu-Zoola-Kaza ... you are now my zombie slave! (*Olive goes into a trance.*)

OLIVE

What are your orders, master?

SEA HAG

We want vittles! Bring us plenty of grub!

(*Popeye takes a peek in Olive's window.*)

SEA HAG

More grub and drinks! Here on the double, my zombie slave ... and make our beds, too!

POPEYE

Shiver me timbers, the Sea Hag's made Olive into a zombie! (*Popeye jumps into Olive's room where she's making the Sea Hag's bed.*) Snaps outa it, Olive ... c'mon, snaps outa it!!!

SEA HAG

I'll fix that swab for buttin' in to me affairs ... this wax candle I'll shape into a wax doll of Popeye ... hee, hee, hee, and with a hair to make the voo-doo spell right ... I tie the arms to the side ... real tight! (*Suddenly Popeye's arms are pressed against the sides of his body.*)

POPEYE

Oh my gorsh ... I can'ts move me arms!

SEA HAG

Popeye, as long as this doll is tied with me magic voo-doo hair, you'll never be able to move your arms! Now, into the sea chest it goes! And now, me faithful vulture ... take it out and lose it! This key will always be with me. (*The hag swallows the chest's key.*) Now, zombie slave … heave that swab overboard! (*Olive shoves Popeye out the door.*)

POPEYE

But Olive, wakes up … it's me … your fe-on-sca, Popeye! (*We see Popeye walking by himself, looking helpless.*) I'll have to get somebody to help me find that sea chest with the doll in it to break this voo-doo spell!

(*Eugene the Jeep appears.*)

EUGENE

JEEP, JEEP!

POPEYE

Eugene the magical Jeep! Eugene, I'm in trouble and…

EUGENE

JEEP, JEEP!

POPEYE

Uh oh … ya knows about it … well then, can ya helps me?

EUGENE

JEEP, JEEP!

POPEYE

Oh my gorsh … he knows what I want without me asking him … huh!

EUGENE

JEEP, JEEP!

POPEYE

Okay Eugene, shoves off an' I'll follows ya! (*The two look for the sea chest.*)

EUGENE

JEEP, JEEP!

POPEYE

Hey … waits fer me, Eugene! Ahoy, there's the sea chest! But the Sea Hag's got the key!

(*Eugene turns his tail into a key that opens the chest.*)

POPEYE

Well blow me down!

(*Eugene takes the doll out of the chest.*)

POPEYE

Now unties the hair, Eugene!

(*The Jeep tries, but it won't untie.*)

POPEYE

Uh oh ... it's a magical hair and ya can'ts unties it!

(*Eugene then walks through Popeye's pants and fumbles about in his shirt.*)

POPEYE

Hey Eugene ... what'cha doing ... ARF, ARF, ARF ... Oh that tickles ... oh!

(*Eugene then reappears holding a can of spinach.*)

POPEYE

Yip-eeee!! Me spinach!

(*Eugene then feeds Popeye the spinach, but nothing happens.*)

POPEYE

Gorsh! I still can'ts move me arms! That voo-doo spell is stronger than the spinach!

(*Eugene then feeds the spinach to the Popeye doll.*)

POPEYE

Feedin' spinach to a doll ... why that's silly!

(*The doll swallows the spinach and breaks the hair tied around its arms.*)

POPEYE

Me arms are as good as new! Thanks Eugene!

EUGENE

JEEP, JEEP!

(*Back to Olive's house, where she's fanning the Sea Hag.*)

SEA HAG

Faster, you zombie, it's hot in here!

(*Popeye smashes through the door.*)

SEA HAG

Popeye!

POPEYE

Avast, Sea Hag, the jig is up!

SEA HAG

Take care of him, my trusty vulture!

VULTURE

Caw, caw. (*The vulture and Popeye mix it up until the bird smashes through the roof carrying the Sea Hag, who's hanging onto the creature's legs.*)

SEA HAG

Faster, faster ... go, go, go!

POPEYE

Olive ... wakes up ... snaps outa it. (*Popeye snaps Olive out of her trance.*)

OLIVE

Oh! I must have fallen asleep! (*She looks around at the house, which is in a shambles.*) Popeye, look at the mess you made!

POPEYE

But, but ... Olive, I didn't make any.

OLIVE

Here! (*She hands him a broom.*) Clean it all up!

POPEYE

Gorsh...
    It may sound amusin'
    but wimmen are confusin'
    ta Popeye the Sailor Man (*Toot! Toot!*)

"The Bathing Beasts" (King Features, 1960; produced by Paramount; written by Irving Dressler)

(*Scene opens with Olive in the front seat of her new car.*)

OLIVE

OOOOHHHH ... I can't wait to try out my new car! Would you boys like to ride with me?

POPEYE AND BRUTUS

Why sure Olive!

BRUTUS

Back seat drivers must sit in the back, shorty! (*Brutus tosses Popeye in the back seat.*) Ha! Ha! Ha! Okay, Olive, give her the gas and let's go!

POPEYE

Waits a minute Olive ... I think yer front tires is soft! Lets me fix 'em for ya!

BRUTUS

That's a man's job and I'll take care of it! (*He gets out of the car.*) Olive, ya front
tires ain't soft at all! (*By now Popeye is in the front seat of the car.*)

POPEYE

Only yer head is soft, Brutus! ARF! ARF! ARF ... Blupppp! (*Brutus grabs Popeye and the two tangle. Each keeps jumping in the front seat, only to get grabbed
and tossed in the back by the other.*)

BRUTUS

Oaky-Doke!

POPEYE

Jus' steps on the gas...

BRUTUS

Don't press down too far...

POPEYE

I'm all set...

BRUTUS

To try ya new car... (*Brutus and Popeye are really going at it as Olive looks at a
billboard.*)

OLIVE

Boys, look!

POPEYE AND BRUTUS

(*Reading.*) Men ... enter now ... Mr. America Contest!

OLIVE

All righty ... the one who wins the contest will ride in the front seat with me!

POPEYE AND BRUTUS

That's a good idea, Olive!

(*Scene changes to the contest area where Wimpy is the judge and announcer.*)

WIMPY

Ladies and gentlemen ... the first event is the bathing suit contest, and the first
contestant is Mr. Brutus. (*Brutus strides across the stage in his bathing suit.*)

OLIVE

Hoooo-ray for Brutus!

WIMPY

The next contestant is Mr. Popeye! (*Popeye walks out on stage, but Brutus grabs a loose thread on his bathing suit and pulls it. As Popeye walks along, his suit begins to come off.*)

OLIVE

Popeye! Your suit! (*Popeye jumps into a barrel.*)

POPEYE

Oh my gorsh ... this is em-bara-skin!

WIMPY

The next event is the acting contest!

(*Popeye is dressed as a Frenchman.*)

POPEYE

Ohhhh Maun Sherie ... I have the burning desire to kiss yer lips ... you have lighted a fire in my heart! (*Brutus lights a fire under Popeye.*) YOWWWWW!!!

POPEYE

(*Brutus is holding a skull.*)

BRUTUS

Friends, countrymen and Romans ... lend me your ears ... alas, poor Yorick ... I knew him well. (*Popeye slips chattering false teeth in the skull's head.*) YOWWWWW!!!

POPEYE

ARF, ARF, ARF!

WIMPY

And now for the musical talent test!

BRUTUS

Look, ladies and gentlemen ... no hands!

OLIVE

Ohhh! No hands! (*Brutus is playing the harmonica which is shoved in his mouth.*) Hoooray for Brutus!

POPEYE

Great work, maestro! (*Popeye whacks Brutus on the back and he swallows the harmonica.*)

POPEYE

Look, ladies an' gents ... no instruments!

OLIVE

Ohhhh! No instruments! (*Popeye raps out a song on his bald head.*)

OLIVE

YAAAAAA! YAAA! (*She claps loudly.*)

WIMPY

And now and the last and most difficult category ... feats of strength! (*Popeye and Brutus are preparing to lift barbells.*)

BRUTUS

This sleeping pill will mean shut-eye for Popeye. (*He gives Popeye a glass of the drugged water.*) Here pal, I thought you'd might want a nice cool glass of water to brace yerself!

POPEYE

Gee, thanks, Brutus! (*Popeye drinks the drugged water.*) I guess I misjudged Brutus ... he's a real ... YAWWWN ... swell ... YAWWWWNNN ... pal ... I can'ts understands it ... all I wants ta do is sleep ... hhhhhhhh!

BRUTUS

One side, weakling! (*He pushes away the sleeping Popeye, causing the sailor's spinach can to roll out onto the floor, next to Popeye's mouth.*)

OLIVE

Hoooo-ray for Brutus! (*Brutus lifts the barbell and slams it down on the spinach can, causing the contents to fly into Popeye's mouth.*)

BRUTUS

This oughta clinch the contest! (*He lifts the barbell higher.*) HUH! (*Popeye is holding up Brutus and the barbell.*)

WIMPY

First prize goes to Popeye!

(*Scene changes to Popeye and Olive in Olive's car.*)

POPEYE

Ya can drives now, Olive!

OLIVE

OOOOHHHHH ... I don't know if I can, Popeye. I never tried before. (*Upon hearing that, Popeye takes off.*)

OLIVE

Coward!

(*Popeye is hiding in a tree.*)

POPEYE

I'd rather be alive
Than with a woman learnin' ta drive!
Says Popeye the Sailor Man (*Toot! Toot!*)

"Popeye's Double Trouble" (King Features, 1961; produced by Paramount; written by Joseph Gottlieb)

(*Scene opens with Popeye on a park bench.*)

POPEYE

Oh my gorsh ... I gotta think of someplace ta goes on me date with Olive tonight!

NEWSBOY

Here ya are ... get yer entry blanks ... sign up for the big event ... here ya are, mister! Read all about it!

POPEYE

Ohhh ... dance contest tonight ... loving cup to the winners ... now that's an idea fer me date with Olive Oyl! Hmmm ... I wonders if they still dances the bunny-hug ... ARF, ARF, ARF!

(*The Sea Hag and her vulture are in the bushes watching Popeye.*)

SEA HAG

BAHHHH ... there's that Popeye the Sailor again ... who's always gettin' in me way!

POPEYE

Maybe me and Olive can win the loving cup if we're lucky!

SEA HAG

So he's looking to be lucky, eh? Hee, hee, hee! Fetch me that bad luck coin, my faithful vulture! Now to have some fun with that meddling sailor! (*She tosses the coin at Popeye's feet.*)

POPEYE

Huh! What's that! Sees a coin and picks it up and all the day you'll have good luck ... hmmmmm, I wonders if that's true?

SEA HAG

Hee, hee! Now his troubles begin!

POPEYE

I wishes I had a car and chauffeur ta takes Olive to the dance. (*A car and chauffeur drive up.*) Well, blow me down!

CHAUFFEUR

Your car is ready, sir!

SEA HAG

BAH! (*To her vulture.*) You stupid bundle of feathers! You gave me the wrong coin! He has my good luck coin and it has three wishes that go with it ... and he's used up one already! Oohhhhh ... we must get it back before he has a chance to use the other two!

POPEYE

To the residence of Ms. Olive Oyl, my good man!

SEA HAG

Hurry, you bungling fool! We'll have to get to Olive's house before Popeye! (*The Hag and her vulture are flying to Olive's house.*)

(*Scene changes to Olive's house, where the Sea Hag has bound and gagged Popeye's girlfriend.*)

OLIVE

GGGGGMMMMMGGGGG!

SEA HAG

This will keep you outa the way while I go to the dance with your boyfriend. And now to transform myself to look like YOU! (*The Sea Hag waves her hand over herself and becomes Olive Oyl.*) Ah ... there he is now. Watch her, my trusty vulture, and see that she stays tied up!

OLIVE

MGGGGGGG!

POPEYE

Olive, I'm in luck! I has a big car and chauffeur ta takes ya to the dance tonight!

(*The Sea Hag attempts to imitate Olive's voice.*)

SEA HAG

Oh, Popeye ... what a wonderful surprise!

POPEYE

Huh ... what's the matter with yer voice, Olive?

SEA HAG

Koff ... koff ... must be the cold I've got, Popeye!

POPEYE

Hmmmmm ... I can swears that ya sounds jus' like the ol' Sea Hag!

(*The scene changes to the dance.*)

ANNOUNCER

Ladies and gentlemen ... get your partners for the big dance contest!

SEA HAG

Now to shake that good luck coin out of him before he has a chance to use the other two wishes!

(*The dance music starts.*)

POPEYE

Does ya remembers how ta dance the bunny-hug, Olive?

SEA HAG

Oh c'mon, Popeye ... I'll show you the latest! It's called the space-bounce ... and this is the blast off! (*She spins Popeye into a frenzy.*)

POPEYE

OOOOOHHHHH ... I think I sees the moon already! (*He smashes into a wall.*) An' the stars too!

SEA HAG

MMMMFFF! That didn't get the coin out ... GRRRR ... I'll have to get a lil' rougher!

POPEYE

OOOOOhhhhhh ... takes me to yer leader!

(*Back at Olive's house.*)

OLIVE

Rock-a-bye vulture on the tree top ... when the rope breaks ... the vulture will drop... (*The bird falls asleep and Olive breaks free of her ropes.*) At last! I thought I'd never get loose! And now to get to the dance and find out what the Sea Hag is up to!

(*Back to the dance.*)

OLIVE

Huh! The nerve of that Sea Hag! Dancing with my Popeye!

SEA HAG

Arrrgggghhh ... that coin must be welded to him! (*She's banging Popeye on the floor and spins him into Olive Oyl.*)

POPEYE

Whhhhhooooppps! Oh my gorsh, I must be seeing double! Which one is the real Olive Oyl?

SEA HAG

She's a fake!

OLIVE

Oh Popeye, she's an impostor!

POPEYE

Ohhh ... I wishes I knew which one was tellin' the truth!

(*The Sea Hag changes back to herself.*)

SEA HAG

BAHHHH! That's his second wish!

POPEYE

So! Yer really the Sea Hag!

(*The Sea Hag grabs Popeye by his legs and begins pounding him face first into the floor.*)

SEA HAG

I've gut to get that coin before he makes that third wish!

POPEYE

Ohhhh ... I can'ts hit a female woo-men ... I wishes there was a way ta makes her stop. (*All the pounding has shaken loose Popeye's spinach can, which rolls over to Olive.*)

SEA HAG

HA! HA! That's the third wish and nothing can help you now! (*She belts Popeye.*)

OLIVE

Oh boy! I'll take care of that sailor-snatcher. (*She eats Popeye's spinach and goes into some kind of dance/spin and bops the Sea Hag.*)

ANNOUNCER

And the winner of the most original dance, "The Solar Sock," is Ms. Olive Oyl!

OLIVE

Ohhhhhhh!

POPEYE

Arf, Arf, Arf!

"Winner Window Washer" (Hanna-Barbera, 1980)

(Popeye is reading the help-wanted section of the newspaper.)

POPEYE

I needs woik ... now let's me see ... help wanted, mattress tester ... huh ... sounds like a soft job ... I'll have ta sleeps on that one, arf, arf, arf! Well looks at that, help wanted ... Olive Oyl's Window Washers, Inc. Oh boy! I'll looks in on this!

(Suddenly Bluto rises up below Popeye's feet.)

BLUTO

Outa my way shrimp! This job's fer me!

POPEYE

Comes back here! Where'd he go? Let me down!

BLUTO

Goin' down ... basement, bargain and trash! Hurry, hurry, hurry! Stick around, squirt, and watch me gets ahead in the world!

POPEYE

That Bluto can be a real pain in the neck! As a window washer he'll be one big "pane" all over! *(Popeye goes after Bluto.)*

(At Olive Oyl's Window Washers, Inc., Bluto tries to get the job.)

BLUTO

If ya want yer windows washed by a pro, you're lookin' at him.

OLIVE

Oh?

POPEYE

Looks again, Bluto! I saw the sign foist!

OLIVE

Boys, boys! Stop fighting or nobody gets the job!

BLUTO

Anything you say, doll! (*Bluto lets go of the sign he and Popeye were fighting over, sending Popeye flying into Olive's broom closet.*) I always said he was a bucket brain!

POPEYE

Yeah, but I ain't washed up yet!

OLIVE

That's enough! I suppose the only way to settle this is to step outside!

BLUTO

That's fine with me!

POPEYE

There's nothing fine about you!

BLUTO

Yeah? Well watch yer step ... ready, squirt?

POPEYE

I'm rights behind ya, blubbo!

(*Outside the building the trio stare at Olive's tall, tall building and the windows that need to be washed.*)

OLIVE

Bluto will take this side of the building, Popeye will take the other side.

POPEYE

Well blow me down! That's a lot of windows ... but who's counting?

OLIVE

The first one to finish cleaning the windows on his side wins the job.

POPEYE

That's me!

BLUTO

Not if I can help it!

OLIVE

Oh, what a nice spirit of competition.

(*Later.*)

OLIVE

I'd better check up on the boys' progress ... Bluto? Well, how does he expect to get the job if he's not even here?

BLUTO

I'll get the drop on Popeye now! (*Bluto pulls the safety belt Popeye is on and tosses him into Olive, who is looking for Bluto.*)

OLIVE

Oh my! (*The safety belt stretches with both Popeye and Olive in it. The belt springs back and knocks Bluto into a part of the building.*)

OLIVE

Bluto's ruining my building!

POPEYE

Well ... looks at it this way, Olive, it's one less window ta washes.

BLUTO

Popeye looks a little washed out ... this paint will add some color! (*Bluto tosses a bucket of green paint near Popeye and the sailor dips his scrub brush in it by mistake.*)

POPEYE

Huh! This water is so polluted it's turning the windows green!

OLIVE

Popeye, have you seen Bluto? (*Olive opens up a window, causing the bucket of green paint to go flying through the air and land on Bluto's head.*)

BLUTO

Hee, hee, hee ... Hey!

OLIVE

Oh, there he is! You must be doin' a good job, Popeye! Bluto's green with envy!

POPEYE

Arf! Arf! Arf!

(*Popeye is climbing the building with suction cups.*)

POPEYE

If ya wants to get the job done right ... ya gots to stick to it!

OLIVE

Oh, Popeye, one more thing. (*She slams the window pane into Popeye who gets stuck to the wall.*) Popeye? Oh, that Popeye moves so fast I can't keep track of him.

POPEYE

If I moved a little faster ... I'd be a lil' fatter!

BLUTO

It's never too "oily" ta gives that drip the slip! (*Bluto pours oil on the surface Popeye's climbing on.*)

POPEYE

Hey, waits a minute ... whhoooooooo! (*But Popeye manages to bounce off Bluto.*) Thanks for the head start, Bluto!

BLUTO

SNNNARGGHHH!!!! Why you... (*Bluto then snags Popeye's rope and spins the sailor into a knot, tied to a pole.*)

POPEYE

Well blow me down ... caughts like a puppet on a string!

BLUTO

While Popeye's all wrapped up in his work, I can get started on my side. (*He pulls open a fire hydrant and the water splashes on Olive's windows.*) Just a twist of the wrist and presto ... instant window washing!

OLIVE

He's not there. I wonder what Bluto's up to. (*The water from the hydrant scoops up Olive, and she finds herself clinging to the water tower on top of her building.*) Help! Popeye! Anybody! Get me down!

POPEYE

Oh my gorsh! Olive is in trouble! I knows I have a can of spinach here somewheres! (*Popeye pulls out a can of spinach, but drops it. The can gets caught in an awning, shoots up by Popeye, and lands in a window, which closes on it ... causing the spinach to pop out and fall into the sailor's mouth. Popeye then saves Olive.*)

OLIVE

Popeye, you saved me!

POPEYE

But Bluto's almost finished cleaning his windows!

BLUTO

Just a couple more floors and I'll win that job!

POPEYE

Stands back, Olive, and watches me do some fancy window washing! (*Popeye zooms to the water tower and breaks open the sides of it, causing the water to pour on Popeye's side of the building.*) I'll patches up this tank later. Hangs on, Olive!

OLIVE

Oh, Popeye, you cleaned all my windows! You're hired!

POPEYE

Thanks, Olive ... or should I say, "tanks."

BLUTO

I say I was robbed! That's not fair ... I was rained out!

OLIVE

The contest is over! (*Bluto kicks a fire hydrant and the water pops from the top, sending him upward.*)

BLUTO

Hey! Turn it off! HELLLPPP!

OLIVE

Looks like Bluto got sent to the showers!

POPEYE

It's about time he cleaned up his act!
If yer windows are "doity"
I'll make them look "perty"
Says Popeye the Sailor Man (*Toot! Toot!*)

    Many of the "Popeye" cartoons featured little songs which enhanced the plots of the cartoons. Here is a selection of tunes from the 'toons!

Popeye and Bluto sing this song at the opening of "The Two-Alarm Fire" (Fleischer, 1934)

BLUTO

Rare and tear and yell and shout,
if there's a fire around the bout,
rare and tear and yell and shout,
company B...will put it out!
HAW! HAW! HAW!

POPEYE:

Ebity bibity abbity snare,
when there's a fire just tell me where,
no matter what day I'm always there....
bibity, bibity, what do I care.

Popeye sings this song at the opening of "The Spinach Roadster" (Fleischer, 1936)

POPEYE

When I'm at the wheel of my automobile,
I feel just like a king (toot!)
She ain't much ta see but she's okay with me...
she's got that certain swing! (toot!)
We take the bumps together
as easy as anythingggggg!
When I'm at the wheel of my automobile,
I feel just like a king (toot! toot!)

Olive sings "Why Am I So Beautiful" from "Morning, Noon and Nightclub" (Fleischer, 1937)

OLIVE

Why..y..y..y..y am I so beautiful,
Why do all the fellers fall for me?
Why..y..y..y..y am I so beautiful
Why do all the women envy me?
Can it be my grace or my form de-vogue
Can it be my face
or these pretty feet of mine? Wow!
Why..y..y..y am I so beautiful?
Why oh why oh me oh me oh-whooooooo!

Bluto, portraying Abu-Hassen, sings this song at the opening of "Popeye the Sailor Meets Ali Baba's Forty Thieves" (Fleischer, 1937)

BLUTO

You better lock up your doors today
cause Abu-Hassen is on his way...
Go in hiding
When I go riding
Just me and my forty thieves!

Having just eaten his spinach, Popeye is ready to battle the forty thieves. From "Popeye the Sailor Meets Ali Baba's Forty Thieves" (1937), the second of the three two-reel color specials produced by The Fleischer Studios.

Your wives and children ignore me too...
I'll steal them from you before I'm through!
I'm out gunning
So start in running
from me and my forty thieves
Abu-Hassen

THIEVES: ABU-HASSEN

My gang's the roughest
but I'm the toughest
and that's no lie!
Abu Hassen

THIEVES: ABU-HASSEN

You've got to hand it
to this bad bandit
cause I'm a terrible guy!

(though the title of the cartoon states, "Ali Baba," Bluto calls himself Abu-

Hassen, and I'm assuming that's how you would spell the name! I always thought "Ali-Bluto" would have been more fitting.)

Popeye and Bluto sing this song at the opening of "We're on Our Way to Rio" (Famous Studios, 1944)

POPEYE & BLUTO

I'm on my way to Rio

POPEYE

To love and laughter and soft guitars

BLUTO

It's always gay in Rio

POPEYE

With lovely ladies 'neath the stars

POPEYE & BLUTO

Each neighbor should try to be good

BLUTO

And I'll be good so have no fear...

POPEYE & BLUTO

Tell all the girls in Rio...

POPEYE

That Popeye...

BLUTO

And Bluto

POPEYE & BLUTO

Are here!

Olive sings this song in "The Man Who Hated Laughter" (Hal Seeger/Jack Zander, 1972)

OLIVE

Don't I look dreamy in my new bikini!
Don't I look dreamy in my new bikini!

Olive is excited to learn that she and Popeye will be going on an ocean cruise from "The Man Who Hated Laughter," the one-hour special that aired as part of "The ABC Saturday Superstar Movie."

Won't ya come and see me in my new bikini...
uh-huh!
Ohhhhhh!
I've been a-waiting oh so long
to shake my hips
and to sing this song,
Ohhhhhh!
Don't I look dreamy in my new bikini...
uh-huh!
Ohhhhhh!
I've been a-waiting oh so long
to shake my hips and to sing this song
Don't I look dreamy in my new bikini!

Appendix B:
The International
Popeye Fanclub

Despite all of Popeye's success as an animated cartoon superstar, an official fan club to honor the character wasn't established until 1989, the six-tieth anniversary year of Segar's famous creation. Here is the story of the formation of the club, by club co-founder Michael Brooks:

Fifteen years ago, my wife (then my fiancée) and I were browsing through a local department store. As we proceeded to investigate bargain bins, I spotted a long, metallic tube emerging from the masses of discounted items. Intrigued, I picked up the tube and found it contained a poster of Popeye the Sailor Man throwing a punch. I commented to my wife that Popeye was my all-time favorite cartoon character as a child. I started to lay the poster down, but my wife said, "It's only three dollars. Why don't you get it?" I said, "May as well, because you never see Popeye things nowadays." That com-ment was made 15 years and 2,400 pieces ago. We were hooked. We would pick up a piece here and there, all the while wondering if there were other Popeye collectors out there. As we gradually amassed the pieces that built up our collection, we continued to speculate about the possibilities of other "Pop-eye Nuts."

Sometime around 1982 or 1983, we placed an ad in a magazine called *The Toy Collector,* stating we were looking for Popeye items. Our ad was answered quickly by a fellow named Jerome Walker from Chicago. Walker told us that he, too, was a longtime Popeye collector, and that he was primarily on the lookout for old tin Popeye toys (the expensive stuff). We were amazed. There was actually another person on the planet that had a hobby like ours.

Come and Enjoy the
15th Annual
POPEYE'S
PICNIC

©K.F.S.

September 9-10-11
1994
at Chester, Illinois
..."Home of Popeye"

Supplement to the Randolph County Herald Tribune
September 8, 1994

A newspaper advertisement announcing the date of the 15th annual "Popeye's Picnic" celebration which was held in 1994. Pictured are Bud Sagendorf's renditions of Popeye, Olive Oyl, Wimpy and Brutus.

A few years later, Walker told us of another fellow that was "really into Popeye." His name was Fred Grandinetti, and he lived right outside of Boston in the small hamlet of Watertown. We contacted Grandinetti, and another friendship began. Then Grandinetti and I began to wonder if still more people shared our addiction to Popeye. But how could we find out?

Then it hit us. There must be a Popeye fan club; after all, the character was the star of the longest running animated cartoon series. We contacted King Features Syndicate to find out how we could join the club. King Features told us there was no such organization. We were downhearted and disappointed. Then another idea emerged. We would ask KFS if we could start our own fan club for Popeye. After establishing guidelines and rules to follow (one being to stay nonprofit), we were granted permission to proceed. We were thrilled, to say the least. Now we were going to test the waters. We already knew that Chester, Illinois, was the hometown of Popeye's creator, Elzie Segar. We also knew that Crystal City, Texas, was billed as the spinach capital of the world. And we knew that both places had erected statues to Popeye. So it seemed logical to launch our club by placing ads in the local newspapers of these places. "The International Popeye Fanclub" was on its way ... or so we thought!

We waited and waited. There was no response. Those sacks of mail that we expected weren't rolling in. We were disappointed, but definitely not beaten. After all, we had made it this far. We even had our first issue of the newsletter together. Clearly, now was the time to reach for a can of spinach!

We placed several ads in other sources, and bingo, the fan club was off and running. A shaky start, but nevertheless, we were finally a real entity. This was late 1989.

Grandinetti and I had decided from the start that a newsletter would be an important part of our club's work. He and I came up with material and I acted as editor, carefully shaping the material into a quarterly newsletter. My wife, Debbie, was recruited as our first public relations person.

By the end of our first year we had over 60 members and had added a second PR person, Laurie Randall of Danbury, Connecticut. During our first year we decided to venture to Chester, Illinois, during their annual Popeye festival (which honors Segar and his creation). We met Laurie and Dave Randall; Tom, Kande, Patrick and Mariette Gordinier of Rochester, New York; and several other attending club members. The townspeople were great. We became friends with Ernie and Lorraine Schuchert and Willard and Elvera Rathert. Schuchert is a descendant of Bill "Wimpy" Schuchert. We also met Segar's nephew, Louis. The whole visit was so great that we decided Chester was going to be the fan

Make checks payable to the Fanclub
Mail to:
Fanclub Dinner 2000, 1001 State, Chester, IL, 62233

Dinner is still $7.50 per person RSVP. This is non-refundable, and reservations MUST be made in advance, so we will know ahead of time exactly how many meals to prepare. Please fill in this form and return it to us post haste. Thank you for your cooperation.

PICNIC 2000

©KFS

This year the Saturday night dinner has been moved from the American Legion Hall to the Moose Club facility. The festivities will still begin at 5:30pm on September 9th and a meal will be served. We are hoping that the acoustics in this new meeting place will surpass the previous hall. If all goes well, the Moose Club will be the permanent location of future Fanclub dinners.

-- fill this in, clip it and send payment to the shop -

RSVP Form for POPEYE DINNER 2000

Name of Party:

_____

Number of people in Party:

( )

Total Amount: $7.50 times people
$_____.___
©KFS

Flyer sent to members of "The International Popeye Fanclub" informing them of the dinner that was held as part of the "Popeye's Picnic" celebration in 2000. Club members from all over the world get to meet at the dinner and the picnic's many events.

club's once-a-year gathering place. And so it has become. Robin Bert and family and Bob and Dorothy Garris are the proprietors of "Robin's Nest" in Chester. This has become our headquarters away from home. Visitors to Popeye's hometown can join the fan club as they shop.

We returned the second year. Both co-founders (Fred and I) were there. We had booths at the picnic grounds and in the flea market/museum. The museum housed many Popeye collectibles from the 1930s to present day ... what a sight to behold! Tom Gordinier designed a float so we were able to be in Chester's annual "Popeye Parade," and we topped it all off with our first official fan club dinner Saturday night. Around 70 people attended the dinner, and we added new members to the ranks that evening. There were stronger bonds between us than Popeye that night; respect, kindness, and friendship were there too. New members Pauline and Tom Shaw came all the way from Canada to be with us.

For over twenty years, Chester, Illinois, has honored E.C. Segar and his "Thimble Theatre" characters with the "Popeye's Picnic" celebration.

We returned in 1992 for another gathering and the bond between the members had increased, as had the membership. Everyone seemed to agree that the 1992 gathering was even better than the last.

Over the years, the annual Popeye's Picnic continues to attract new fans of the sailor. We began a tradition, which continues to this day, screening 16mm "Popeye" cartoons outside for everyone to enjoy. We have had several guests who have been associated with the sailor's career visit the picnic celebration. They have included: local television personality "Cousin Cliff Holman," long associated with Popeye in Alabama starting in 1958 and Fleischer Studios animator, Gordon Sheehan, in 1993. Many people were grateful for the opportunity to meet Mr. Sheehan, who had worked on the Fleischer Popeye films prior to his passing in 1996 at age 86. George Wildman, Popeye comic book illustrator, attended in 1994. Representatives from Universal Studios, promoting Popeye's addition to their theme park, also attended that year. Jon McClenahan, who worked on the production of the sailor's animated adventures for the "All New Popeye Hour," attended in 1995. Rocky Fiegel, E.C. Segar's inspiration for Popeye, was honored with a memorial tribute in 1996. Hy Eisman, who draws the "Popeye" Sunday strip, was the guest for the 1997 celebration. Each year, an original Popeye story is performed by attendees, "The Birthday Surprise," "Myskery in Segar Park" and "Wimpy the Mechanical Moocher" being some of the examples.

In 1994, Debbie and I, along with Laurie and Dave Randall, decided to move to Chester, IL. We opened a shop called "Spinach Can Collectibles"— the only Popeye store in the country. It is a store of collections. Popeye is the main interest, but we have also featured Betty Boop, *Star Trek*, Tweety Bird, old quilt books, antiques and household merchandise.

We have developed a line of merchandise featuring "Chester, Illinois ... Home of Popeye." These have included, license plates, tote bags, magnets, key chains, postcards and shirts. We do a large amount of business through mail order and have become a popular tourist attraction. In the store, we have housed many Popeye collectibles, which are on display.

Popeye and Olive take a break during the 2001 "Popeye's Picnic" celebration.

The television show, "Neat Stuff," produced by The Learning Channel, taped a segment of their program during the 1996 "Popeye's Picnic" celebration. As of 2002, "The International Popeye Fanclub" celebrated the publication of its 50th news magazine and its 14th anniversary.

For information, please write to:

Fanclub
101 State Street, Chester, IL 62233

CARTOON TITLE INDEX

Numbers in **boldface** refer to pages with illustrations

323

NAME INDEX

Numbers in **boldface** refer to pages with illustrations

330